Blake's Nostos

SUNY Series in Western Esoteric Traditions
David Applebaum, Editor

Blake's Nostos:
Fragmentation and Nondualism
in
The Four Zoas

Kathryn Freeman

State University of New York Press

Sections of chapters 1 and 3 are reprinted with permission from "Narrative Fragmentation and Undifferentiated Consciousness in Blake's *The Four Zoas*," *European Romantic Review* 5, no. 2 (winter 1995): 178–92.

The cover illustration and figures 4–8 are reproduced from Blake's *The Four Zoas* manuscript with permission from the British Library.

Published by
State University of New York Press

For information, address the State University of New York Press, State University Plaza, Albany, NY 12246

Production by Bernadine Dawes • Marketing by Fran Keneston

Library of Congress Cataloging-in-Publication Data

Freeman, Kathryn S., 1958–
    Blake's nostos : fragmentation and nondualism in The four zoas / Kathryn S. Freeman.
        p. cm. — (SUNY series in western esoteric traditions)
    Includes bibliographical references (p. 187) and index.
    ISBN 0-7914-3297-1 (hc : acid-free). — ISBN 0-7914-3298-X (pb. : acid-free)
    1. Blake, William, 1757–1827. Four zoas. 2. Epic poetry. English—History and criticism. 3. Prophecies in literature. I. Title. II. Series.
    PR4144.F683F74   1997
    821.'7—dc20   96-42241
                                                                       CIP

To the vision of my parents,

Ann Cassel Freeman and Joseph Freeman

Contents

Illustrations

Acknowledgments

Many sources of insight and support have contributed to this book. The late Michael G. Cooke was instrumental in my earliest ventures into studying *The Four Zoas,* first through his graduate seminar and then as my dissertation director. I thank the University of Miami for generous grants that gave me summers to complete research and revisions. For guidance during the publication process, I am grateful to members of the University of Miami Department of English, with special thanks to John Paul Russo for sharing his expertise in the eighteenth-century sublime as well as for his editorial assistance. I am indebted to both Frederick Burwick, editor of *European Romantic Review,* for publishing an earlier version of sections of chapters 1 and 3, and to William Eastman of SUNY Press for his interest in the project and for this opportunity. I am grateful to the Rosenwald Collection of the Library of Congress for providing prints from their original copy of Blake's *Songs of Innocence and of Experience* as well as to the British Library for permission to use prints of *The Four Zoas* housed in their Manuscript Collection. Finally, my deepest gratitude goes to my family for their unwavering patience and encouragement through the many stages of this project.

A Note on Abbreviations

In addition to the abbreviation *MHH,* standing for *The Marriage of Heaven and Hell,* two abbreviations—"E" and "K"—are used in the text for citations of works by Blake. "E" stands for *The Complete Poetry and Prose of William Blake,* ed. David Erdman (New York: Doubleday, 1982). "K" stands for *Blake: Complete Writings,* ed. Geoffrey Keynes (New York: Oxford University Press, 1970). The Keynes edition is chosen over the Erdman edition primarily when I discuss Blake's early drafts of the two versions of Night the Seventh. Keynes's edition presents the two versions of Night the Seventh separately, whereas Erdman places the [b] version between the two "halves" of the [a] version to form a single Night the Seventh.

For either edition cited, the abbreviation is followed by the page number, Blake's plate number or manuscript page number, and the line number. All other references in the text and notes use *The Chicago Manual of Style*'s author-date system, which is keyed to the bibliography.

CHAPTER I

Blake's Mythos:
Nondual Vision in a Dualistic World

THE HIERARCHICAL SCHEME OF ENLIGHTENMENT EPISTEMOLOGY, which crowns reason as the mind's highest faculty, topples in the disorienting mythos that evolves out of Blake's struggle to redefine the relationship between consciousness and the phenomenal world. Divorcing reason from intuitive vision, the deistic Enlightenment appears in many guises in Blake's work, including the Spectre in *Jerusalem*:

> . . . I am God O Sons of Men! I am your Rational Power!
> Am I not Bacon & Newton & Locke who teach Humility to Man!
> Who teach Doubt & Experiment & my two Wings Voltaire: Rousseau.
> (E. 203, 54:16–18)

Blake does not stand alone in this revolt; many philosophers and poets of his time attempted to rescue what the materialist philosophers deemed the lower faculties of sensation, emotion, and imagination.[1] By contrast to his contemporaries, however, Blake does not merely invert the order of mental faculties. Instead, he represents them as fragments of a subsuming consciousness.

Enlightenment thought draws on the mind's identification with time, space, and logic. For Blake, these constructs are the modifications of consciousness that create the illusion of a physical universe separate from the self. The materialist tendency to contract consciousness thus spawns dualism, the separation of self and other, ultimately emptying consciousness of all vitality. The mind limited to its own modifications is the essence of what Blake portrays as the fallen state.

Blake perpetually describes the mind limited to sense perception in relation to unmodified, or undifferentiated, consciousness. In Blake's earliest engraved work, "All Religions are One," the nondual state appears as the Poetic Genius, which, Blake writes, "is the true Man. and . . . the body or outward form of Man is derived from the Poetic Genius" (E. 1). For the Poetic Genius, there is no essential difference between body and soul. Although this potential for nondual vision is the birthright of every human being, consciousness loses contact with the Poetic Genius, fragmenting into warring psychic forces. In this way, nondualism gives way to dualism.

Blake extends this principle of the fragmentation of individual consciousness to the fragmentation of humanity into nations and religions: "The Religions of all Nations are derived from each Nations different reception of the Poetic Genius which is every where call'd the Spirit of Prophecy." The fragmentation of humanity into groups living by conflicting codes is merely the result of different interpretations of this spirit. As consciousness split into inner and outer realms, "[A] system was formed" that abstracted "the mental deities from their objects." Thus, Blake concludes, "men forgot that All deities reside in the human breast" (*MHH*. E. 38, pl. 11).

By taking away the easy surface logic associated with duality, as he does in "the Voice of the Devil," Blake disorients the Enlightenment mind: "Man has no Body distinct from his Soul for that calld Body is a portion of Soul discernd by the five Senses. the chief inlets of Soul in this age" (*MHH*. E. 34, pl.4). The emphatic message is that one cannot separate body and soul: both are aspects of a single consciousness. The design of *The Marriage of Heaven and Hell's* title page provides visual evidence of Blake's nonduality: "The words 'HEAVEN & HELL' are placed below ground level, as if to say that heaven is really part of hell" (Ferber 1991, 91). Blake does more than invert conventional duality; he calls the notion of duality itself into question. In this way, Blake challenges the premise of Enlightenment thought.

While fallenness is the result of the separation of the human and divine, Blake also celebrates the potential for redemption through the capacity of consciousness to reintegrate itself. "What is Above is Within, for every-thing in Eternity is translucent," Blake writes in *Jerusalem*. He describes the reinternalization of divinity arising when traditional dualities are overcome: "The Circumference still expands going forward to Eternity. / And the Center has Eternal States!" (E. 225, pl. 71, 6–8). In this equipoise, which Blake sometimes calls Eden, one sees time and space as constructs subsumed by the eternal.

Blake's description of the fallen state of experience as being contracted or bound and the redeemed or innocent as being expanded or unbound helps to show that the relationship between the two states is not a duality itself. The fallen state, a contraction of undifferentiated, expanded consciousness, is therefore subsumed by the redeemed rather than being antithetical to it. This view differs from the common critical strategy that maintains the concept of duality inherent in rationalistic thinking, in spite of attempting to contrast Blake's universe with the quantitatively organized universe of eighteenth-century rationalism. Antithetical concepts are merely replaced rather than reflect Blake's challenge to the fundamental principle of dualism. As John Beer writes, "The opposites of this universe were human extremes: the 'contracting' of a man in the moment of pathos on the one hand, his 'expansion' in the moment of sublimity on the other" (1969, 6).[2] This doubleness, however, never appears as oppositional in Blake's mythos.

Writing to Thomas Butts on 2 October 1800, for example, Blake describes the relationship between the contracted and expanded states in his first Vision of Light. At the epiphanic moment, Blake says, "My eyes did Expand / Into regions of air." Significantly, Blake does not say that the senses must be overcome as such: the eyes do not shut, which would contract consciousness, but rather "Expand." The Poetic Genius dissolves the subject-object distinction imposed by perception limited to the senses. In this moment of revelation, his eyes

> Continue expanding
> The heavens commanding
> Till the Jewels of Light
> Heavenly Men beaming bright
> Appeard as One Man

(E. 713)

Blake contrasts this expanded state with experience, in which "We like infants descend / In our Shadows on Earth." Blake overcomes Enlightenment Deism, in which the duality of good and evil depends upon the opposition of senses and spirit, by describing the fall into experience as contraction and innocence as perpetually available through expansion of the senses.

Characterizing innocence as energetic and intellectual, Blake distinguishes it from the nondifferentiation of naïveté. In a penciled note on the *Four Zoas* manuscript Blake writes, "Unorganizd Innocence, An Impossibility / Innocence dwells with wisdom, but never with Ignorance" (E. 838, VIIb, 93).[3] This note appears in Night the Seventh, the poem's spiritual and textual crisis: it is here that the fallen and redeemed face each other most directly in the poem, making it the watershed moment in the poem's turn to apocalyptic vision. The note, which appears at the moment of crisis in the poem, points to the integral relationship between redemption in the Prophecies and innocence in the *Songs*. Innocence must be distinguished from naïveté for the same reason that the epic *nostos* of Night the Ninth— the return home of consciousness to its expanded state—must be distinguished from the nostalgia of the characters in their fallen state for an irretrievable past.[4]

Nostalgia masquerades as wisdom for many of Blake's figures, from the old folk of "The Ecchoing Green" to Enion's lament that ends Night the Second of *The Four Zoas*. Yet this is one end of the spectrum of distorted responses to the perceived loss of innocence among the figures trapped in dualism. At the other end is insanity, which, as we know from "Mad Song," is a state that projects a material universe and then imprisons the self in it:

> Lo! to the vault
>   Of paved heaven,
> With sorrow fraught
>   My notes are driven

(E. 415)

Blake's apocalypse, by contrast, is a state that expands the universe, destroying not people, nature, time, or history, but the illusion of their otherness. The representation of such an unhesitating dissolution of boundary lines distinguishes Blake from the poets of the high romantic sublime, who tentatively probe nonduality but ultimately retreat to the familiar ground of their separate existence.

Apocalypse in Blake's mythos can defy madness because it is inextricably linked to organized innocence, the awareness of absolute and unconditional nothingness in the midst of the drama held to be solid reality and around which the limited self is oriented. The magnitude of Blakean innocence calls to mind the words of a modern mystic for whom, it is said, the only difference between the Buddhist void and the existential abyss is fear.

Because Blake's concern with the representation of innocence is related to his struggle with the representation of redemption in *The Four Zoas*, it is helpful to trace the emergence of the fallen and redeemed states of the Prophecies out of the relationship between the states of innocence and experience in the *Songs*.[5] A common assumption in Blake scholarship has been that a dialectic underlies the "contrary" nature of the relationship of Innocence and Experience.[6] This reading is often taken further in conjunction with yet another common premise, namely, that Blake represents a "higher" and a "lower" innocence.[7] Actually Blake never represents the states as linear or even cyclical. Pointing instead to a more complex interplay between innocence and experience, Stephen Cox challenges the traditional hierarchy:

> [J]ust where, if anywhere, does the contrast or comparison of contraries lead? If it is meant to lead the reader to a state of "higher innocence," as has often been claimed, then the reader is justified in asking what ideas are distinctive of that state. It is far from clear that those ideas are developed. (1992, 107)

One answer to Cox's question is that the characteristic of experience to differentiate and separate runs counter to the pull of innocence, in whose atemporality boundary lines dissolve in the intersubjectivity between self and other, and the human and divine. Innocence perpetually eludes the endeavors of the mind of experience, whose tendency is to feel loss, to create separation, and to fragment. Making qualitative distinctions between

the self and the phenomenal world, experience creates and exists in dualistic worlds of time and space. It externalizes divinity, which it thereafter
flees from or yearns after. Innocence, rather than appearing antithetical to
experience, recognizes all phenomena to be endowed with a pervasive consciousness. Thus, in the 1800 letter to Butts, every object Blake beholds is
saturated with the intelligence and spirit of a single consciousness.

Language—spoken, written, and sung—is central to piecing out the
relation between duality and nonduality in Blake. Many of Blake's speakers, including singers, engravers, poets, and storytellers, are themselves caught
in the duality inherent in the formulation "every Word calls for a reply,"
which assumes a separation between self and others (Lacan 1968, 9). Returning to the letter to Butts, the "fall" inherent in the phrase "We like
infants descend" suggests that differentiation, a contracted state, involves
loss. For Blake, though, language can either exist in and perpetuate a contracted state or it can embrace in its purest form the expanded or nondual
state toward which the prophetic poet aspires.[8]

This potential of language to reflect the state of the speaker appears
throughout the *Songs*, whose variety of vocalizations reflects the diverse
states of the speakers. Verbal echoes in *Innocence* can be seen as manifesta-
tions of a dissolved duality.[9] In "The Ecchoing Green," nature echoes back
the children's carefree cries, suggesting a pure communion between subject
and object. This echoing contrasts Old John and the other "old folk," who
also echo the children but, trapped in the illusion of time, do so in an
imperfect and distorted way. Although they laugh away care, they "unsay"
that happy return by experiencing it as nostalgia:

> Such such were the joys.
> When we all girls & boys,
> In our youth-time were seen,
> On the Ecchoing Green.
>
> (E. 8, lines17–20)

The repetition of "such" reflects the hollowness of nostalgia, suggesting
that the speaker reinforces the sense of loss by verbalizing it. As the old folk
turn the echoing green to the darkening green through their contracting
senses, they transform the subject-object relation from pure communion to
absorption or tainting:

Till the little ones weary
No more can be merry
The sun does descend,
And our sports have an end:
.   .   .   .
And sport no more seen,
On the darkening Green.

(E. 8, lines 21–30)

"Echoing," or the pure repetition that represents nondifferentiation, is replaced by "darkening," with its association of separation, loss, fear, and
death.

By contrast to the old folks' nostalgic voice of experience, the decep-
tively simple poem "The Laughing Song" exemplifies the perfect unity represented by repetition:

When the green woods laugh, with the voice of joy
And the dimpling stream runs laughing by,
When the air does laugh with our merry wit,
And the green hill laughs with the noise of it.

(E. 11, lines 1–4)

The vocalization, laughter, is not language as such, but rather the human
counterpart to the sounds of nature. Nature is not just personified with
"dimpling stream" and laughing meadows, but forms a perfect
intersubjectivity with laughing humanity. This state of equipoise between
subject and object is organized innocence. Blake gives a visual reminder
that organized innocence does not necessarily belong to childhood. Though
one might assume the figures of this poem to be children, Blake depicts
them as adults in the design (figure 1).

The most famous instance of a pure communion between inner and
outer worlds in the *Songs* is "The Lamb." The speaker repeats the question
and answer in an echoing motif that contrasts Old John's in "The Ecchoing
Green." In "The Lamb," the literal echo suggests that the vales, as with the
Green, echo back the child's simple truth: "Dost thou know who . . . /
Gave thee such a tender voice . . . , / Making all the vales rejoice!" (E. 8,
lines 2–8). Deepening this effect is the linguistic echo found in the child
naming the Lamb's maker:

Fig. 1. "Laughing Song" (courtesy of the Library of Congress)

He is called by thy name,
For he calls himself a Lamb.
. . . I a child & thou a lamb,
We are called by his name.

(E. 9, lines 13–18)

Harmony exists not only between speaker and object, but also among speaker, object, and Creator.

Huizinga's "essential oneness" of "sacred play" provides a key characteristic of the organized innocence of such poems as "The Lamb" and "The Laughing Song":

> When a certain form of religion accepts a sacred identity between two things of a different order, say a human being and an animal, this relationship is not adequately expressed by calling it a "symbolic correspondence" as *we* conceive this. The identity, the essential oneness of the two goes far deeper than the correspondence between a substance and its symbolic image. It is a mystic unity. The one has *become* the other. . . . The concept of play merges quite naturally with that of holiness. (1950, 25)

This mystical unity of sacred play can be applied to the child's "conversation" with the lamb. For G. J. Finch, noting the child's nondual state in "The Lamb," the subject "is not really the lamb but the child. . . . He sees the lamb as another self. There is nothing egotistic *about* this. . . . The child's experience is holistic, the logical boundaries between self and other do not exist" (1991, 197). It is essential, therefore, that the dissolution of ego not be regarded reductively as a state of naïveté but as an expanded state of organized innocence.

By contrast to the child in "The Lamb," the speaker of "The Tyger" appropriately experiences quite the contrary of "sacred play." In his "earnestness," to use Huizinga's term, he enacts a disjunction among self, object, and Creator. Whereas in "The Lamb," the lamb, speaker, and Creator are all one, the Tyger here appears as a threatening other, and the Creator an even more alienating divinity. The speaker's questions do not echo in affirmation but intensify in self-perpetuating anxiety, leading to total alienation:

When the stars threw down their spears
And water'd heaven with their tears:

Did he smile his work to see?
Did he who made the Lamb make thee?[10]

(E. 25, lines 17–20)

The poem parodies "The Lamb." The speaker, both creator and created, has cast out these aspects of himself, thus projecting them as other and threatening to his own identity. Steven Shaviro writes that "the speaker of 'The Tyger' imagines terrifying powers and ascribes them to God conceived as absolute Other" (1982, 247). Yet retaining the notion of a Blakean system, Shaviro extends this observation to include both poet and reader in the "sterility" of the speaker's epistemology: "[T]he poet or reader, in reclaiming those powers for the human, necessarily arrogates to an idealized image of humanity the unapproachable prestige of that Otherness as well." Shaviro's indictment of "humanistic claims for the Imagination" here needs to be examined in the context of the fuller scope of the *Songs*: Blake's insistence on the human divine as an attainment of speaker and audience points to a disjunction rather than a conflation of speaker, poet and audience in the poem.[11]

While "The Lamb" portrays nonduality from the perspective of the child's simplicity, the "Introduction" to *Innocence* confronts the dilemma that besets the adult who must form a bridge between the realms of innocence and experience. The Piper's role is thus prophetic, for he must convey the vision of the divine to humanity. But, as is the case with the Piper's biblical precursors, "prophecy is never complete in itself; it is a burden, a tension, a call, the waging of a battle, never a victory, never a consummation" (Heschel 1962, 2:141). The dilemma for Blake is that the prophet must convey his message through language, which easily obstructs vision in its mediation. As opposed to the child of "The Lamb," the Piper's challenge is to maintain vision while commuting between the realms of innocence and experience. The "Introduction" thus opens with the paradox of the Piper being directed by the visionary child to pipe a song about a lamb, to sing—to vocalize it—and finally to write it, at which point the child disappears:

Piper sit thee down and write
In a book that all may read—
So he vanish'd from my sight.
And I pluck'd a hollow reed.

And I made a rural pen,
And I stain'd the water clear,
And I wrote my happy songs
Every child may joy to hear

                                                              (E. 7, lines 13–20)

The Piper recognizes the causality inherent in this sequence: as soon as he begins to write, the visionary child who has directed him to pipe, sing, and write disappears. "Apart from, and often against, his own will the prophet must take over and fulfill his task," observes Abraham Heschel; "he must both apprehend and preach inspired truth. Thus he knows a twofold necessity—that of accepting and experiencing and that of announcing and preaching" (1962, 2:225). For Blake, the challenge of organized innocence is to maintain the connection to vision and, for the prophetic poet, to communicate it in the world of experience.

Stanza by stanza, the child's command that the Piper teach the song of innocence to all people is increasingly problematized by language itself. From vocalizing to writing, the narrator's intuitive apprehension of divinity is further and further mediated, reducing it to mental constructs. The Piper's challenge is to convey what Coleridge calls the secondary imagination, which "dissolves, diffuses, dissipates, in order to re-create," an achievement akin to Blake's organized innocence (1983, 304). By concluding the Introduction with the act of writing, Blake indicates that the poet conveys the vision of organized innocence in a highly paradoxical medium. How does one know that, when piped, the song is about a lamb? The visionary child apparently knows without language. But for "all" to understand, words are necessary, even beyond singing the song, which may be without language.

Though most likely alluding to Blake's art of illumination, the phrase "I stain'd the water clear" remains paradoxical: either its primary meaning is that the Piper stained the water that had been clear, thus darkening or tainting the message of the visionary child; or, he made the message clear by staining it. But either way he must communicate the message to others. What is essential and transparent in the state of innocence must be made accessible to those in experience—all readers, that is, since they must communicate through language.

Language, of course, reflects different aspects of consciousness. Thus, the syntax of the "Introduction" to *Innocence* is of the simplest grammar. The ideas are often connected by parataxis: "And I pluck'd . . . / And I

made . . . / And I stain'd . . . / And I wrote." This accretion reflects freedom
from the discursive complexity of more intricate mental constructions, such
as the Bard's hypotaxis in the "Introduction" to *Experience*. By contrast to
the elusively intuitive communication of the visionary child in the "Introduction" to *Innocence,* the Bard in the "Introduction" to *Experience* announces his prophetic power in terms of "The Holy Word." One soon
learns, however, that prophetic language in the Bard's fallen world is
grounded in time, in contrast to the atemporality of the Piper's apprehension of the visionary child:

> Hear the voice of the Bard!
> Who present, past and Future sees
> Whose ears have heard,
> The Holy Word,
> That walk'd among the ancient trees.
>
> (E. 18, lines 1–5)

The Bard casts the pure embodiment of a language that is spirit, "The Holy
Word," into time-oriented incarnation. From this perspective, the Bard
seems less a Blakean persona, as is often assumed, than a Deist: the prophetic role is bound by its emphasis on the physical world.[12] The Bard
urges the lapsed soul "Turn away no more. . . . The starry floor / The watry
floor / Is giv'n thee till the break of day" (lines 16–20).[13] His evangelical
urgency that the limits of this universe are only available till the break of
day contrasts with the Piper who seeks to remain in the eternal by conveying the intuitive message of the visionary child.

   The crucial irony underlying the "Introduction" to *Experience* is that,
while the Bard cries out for renewal, he himself creates the contracted world.
The Bard calls the lapsed soul "That might controll, / The starry pole; /
And fallen fallen light renew!" (lines 8–10). The repetition associates forward movement in time with movement downward. The verb "renew"
heightens the irony, since what is being renewed is actually light of ever
diminishing intensity. Repetition here thus contrasts with *Songs of Innocence*, where echoing is associated with a dissolution of spatial and temporal duality.

   Intensifying his separation from the Earth he addresses, the Bard follows the "fallen fallen light renew" with another repetition: "O Earth O
Earth return!" This deepening divide between Bard and Earth contrasts the

Piper's attempt to dissolve difference.[14] The Bard's projection of a limited world is related to the fearful universe the narrator of "The Tyger" projects; as opposed to the sharp irony of "The Tyger," however, the Bard's tone suggests empathy for the plight of those, including the Bard himself, trapped in the material world of their own creation.

The frontispiece designs to *Innocence* and *Experience* respectively represent the distinction between the human divine and the externalization of divinity (figures 2a and 2b). The Bard of *Experience* grasps the arms of the child who had been flying freely above the Piper of *Innocence*. The Bard transforms the visionary child into "the covering cherub," a figure that represents externalized divinity and reappears in *The Marriage of Heaven and Hell* as well as the Prophecies.[15] Far from being an agent of salvation or divine protection, the covering cherub is an outward projection that insidiously prevents the human from recognizing his or her own divinity. The design accompanying the "Introduction" to *Experience* suggests that by transforming the visionary child into a covering cherub, the Bard literally embraces duality. In so doing, the Bard violates the dictum for entering eternity, according to Blake's epigrammatic poem by that name:

> He who binds himself to a joy
> Does the winged life destroy
> But he who kisses the joy as it flies
> Lives in eternity's sunrise.

> (E. 470)

The paradoxical psychology here, as well as that described by the frontispiece designs, is that letting go of an apparent object leads to bliss, while clinging to the objectified bliss destroys it.[16]

The sinister nature of the covering cherub as externalized divinity is best shown by "The Angel" of *The Songs of Experience*. The Angel's mission is to repress the "hearts delight" of the speaker; having succeeded, the Angel has left her, only to return in the hope of renewing his former repression:

> Soon my Angel came again;
> I was arm'd, he came in vain:
> For the time of youth was fled
> And grey hairs were on my head.

> (E. 24, lines 13–16)

Fig. 2a. Frontispiece to *Songs of Innocence* (courtesy of the Library of Congress)

Fig. 2b. Frontispiece to *Songs of Experience* (courtesy of the Library of Congress)

For this speaker, regret is directly related to the fear of otherness. This sense of separation links such figures of experience as the old folk in "The Ecchoing Green" and the narrator of "The Tyger," whose self-created separation and fear are reflected in increasingly anxious rhetorical questions.

Blake addresses the problem of naming most subtly in "Infant Joy," a song of innocence:

> I have no name
> I am but two days old.—
> What shall I call thee?
> I happy am
> Joy is my name,—
> Sweet joy befall thee!

                                                          (E. 16, lines 1–6)

Repeating at the end of the second stanza the last line of this first stanza— "Sweet joy befall thee"—calls attention to the curious word "befall," which lends an ominous tinge to the apparent benediction. The very act of naming, it implies, begins the fall into the realm of experience. The paradox that naming joy brings about its fall, or contraction, is reminiscent of the stain that results when the Piper writes down the song of the visionary child.

The design accompanying "Infant Joy" reinforces the undercurrent of threat: a full open blossom at the top of the page contains the mother holding the infant. A winged figure stands before them, with hands open toward the child, perhaps a type of covering cherub. On the left below is a closed, drooping blossom, suggesting the fallen state the blossom is entering (figure 3). The design suggests a fall into life, similar to the fall into life Blake describes in his 1800 letter to Butts with the phrase "We like infants descend / In our Shadows on Earth."

One of Blake's earliest narratives that relates innocence to apocalypse and redemption appears in a pair of poems in *Experience* entitled "The Little Girl Lost" and "The Little Girl Found."[17] The narrator, an engraver, is a more complex persona as artist-prophet than either the Piper or the Bard:

> In futurity
> I prophetic see,

Fig. 3. "Infant Joy" (courtesy of the Library of Congress)

That the earth from sleep,
(Grave the sentence deep)

Shall arise and seek
For her maker meek:
And the desart wild
Become a garden mild.

                                        (E. 20, lines 1–8)

The verb "grave" denotes an imperative directed to himself, an engraver whose prophetic power to behold the apocalypse is linked to his craft. The pun on the word suggests that the prophetic engraver raises language from the dead.[18]

The poem's structure is one of the most complex of the *Songs*, forecasting the more fully developed myth of *The Four Zoas* in which organized innocence is achieved in, through, and out of experience. Because the story of Lyca follows the introduction by the engraver, the association of the engraver with the renewal of the earth is linked to Lyca's journey, which brings about the renewal of her parents' innocence. Lyca can be seen as a prototype for Vala in *The Four Zoas*. Both figures are associated with nature and sexuality, and are also responsible for renewing the innocence of those around them. Vala's often overlooked transformation in Night the Ninth reveals that she is not simply a symbol of nature, but reflects the projection of human consciousness onto nature. In the fallen world, Vala is accused of seducing Albion; he has cast his vision outward, forgetting that there is no difference between himself and the phenomenal world, and so Vala is blamed for having become objectified. By Night the Ninth, however, Vala leads the other Zoic fragments into what Blake calls the "sinless" state: she recognizes that all she beholds is part of the Self, and that she, in turn, is the divine embodied in the human. Because Lyca's homecoming renews her parents' innocence, Lyca looks ahead to Vala's restoration of organized innocence.

    Just as Lyca is prototypical of Vala, the engraver, who has access to organized innocence, looks ahead to Los in *The Four Zoas*. It is impossible for Los to build Golgonooza, the City of Art, until he can paradoxically free himself from time. Golgonooza cannot be built in Night the Seventh, since it is not until the apocalypse, when the separation of subject and object is overcome, that Los and Urthona are rejoined and can create, or re-create.

━▼.▶━

The subject of *The Four Zoas* is the fall of consciousness from whole-ness into fragmentation and its reintegration at the apocalypse in Night the Ninth. The fallen state is not a moral lapse but rather the limited mind's tendency to contract through conceptualizing, fictionalizing, and image making. Such an apocalypse is potential in every moment rather than oc-curring at the end of time. Because the fallen and redeemed states coexist, Blake's greatest challenge is to represent as nonlinear the relationship be-tween the first eight Nights and the apocalypse of Night the Ninth, in which the precarious equipoise of fragmented consciousness emerges.

The superimposition of apparently incompatible impulses helps create Blake's powerfully individual voice and mythos. The poem's teleology mir-rors its central paradox that history moves toward nondual vision, a state outside of time. This does not give rise to a voice of frustration or anxiety on Blake's part as one might expect. "Blake's work," Finch states, "is rela-tively free from the personal anxieties, insecurities and soul searching of the poets of his own time—Wordsworth, Coleridge or Keats; anxieties due in part to the felt pressure of an externally conceived reality bearing down inexorably on the poetic imagination" (1991, 193).

Because the emphasis of this study is Blake's means of representing the attainment of nondual vision in the midst of the duality of waking life, it is structured according to the central elements of Blake's mythos that con-tribute toward the interplay of the nondual and dual states. The book avoids the linear procedure that has impeded previous analyses of *The Four Zoas*. Wilkie and Johnson (1978) were the first to devote a book to the poem. They acknowledge its difficulties, but because their approach is introduc-tory they reduce the complexities of the text to try to make it more acces-sible. Thus, their study proceeds Night by Night, assuming a linearity in this structure and summarizing rather than challenging prior critical inter-pretations.

In *Narrative Unbound* (1987), Donald Ault probes Blake's revolt against linearity. Ault thus contributes the first full-length poststructural study of the poem, arguing that Blake's procedure is antinarrative. Like Ault's work, several recent studies have reevaluated the concept of Blake's "system," a notion that had led formalists to the dismissal of *The Four Zoas* as "unfinished"; Frye, for instance, famously had described it as an "abortive masterpiece" (1947, 269). Harold Bloom underscores this rejection with the statement that Blake "gave up *The Four Zoas* because it explained, too well and in too many ways, how the world had reached the darkness of his own times, but explained hardly at all what that darkness was, and how it was to be enlightened" (1963, 311). Blake defies the expectations this approach imposes, describing rather than explaining the relationship between such darkness and light. Shaviro refutes the projection of Blake as a systematizer, noting that Los's statement in *Jerusalem*, "I must Create a System, or be enslav'd by another Mans" (E. 153, 10:20–21), is not necessarily Blake's point of view (1982, 229), as Frye and many others had assumed; in other words, Los is not necessarily a stand-in for Blake.

Though poststructuralism has thus significantly redefined the incompleteness of *The Four Zoas* as compositional strategy rather than formal weakness, the poem's vision of wholeness has gotten lost in the reaction against formalism. The present book maintains that wholeness, vital to Blake, is not outside of or prior to human perception, but is rather the achievement of nondual vision.

Ault, working from this poststructural methodology, contributes insights into the workings of the fallen world, yet he reduces any appearance of wholeness in the poem to an ironic representation of Newtonian physics:

> By incorporating "redemptive" references into the poem in the way he did, Blake either failed to graft an authentic external redemptive scheme onto the fluid perceptual narrative field of *The Four Zoas*, or succeeded in exposing the falsity of and the imaginative danger inherent in presenting a true redemption in completed narrative form on the surface of the text. In either case, the external redemptive scheme is found wanting, and Blake plays off this profound frustration against our desire to see the enormous complexity and confusion of Night VIII resolved in the narrative events of Night IX. Whatever Blake's intentions were in grafting references to "redemptive" forces onto earlier Nights, the cumulative effect of such revisions is to undermine the unambiguous authority of such forces to act as powers that can redeem or save the characters, the narrative world, or the reader. (1987, 243)

Ault equates wholeness with the New Critical emphasis on formal completeness or Newtonian unity. According to Molly Rothenberg, Ault characterizes "the worldview that gives ontological priority to external objects, rejecting the possibility that 'the way something is perceived constitutes its being or reality,' as corresponding to the 'Single vision' that Blake despises" (1993, 113). The "redemptive scheme" Ault describes, however, is emphatically not external in Blake's mythos, in which redemption is the recognition of the human divine, the dissolution of boundaries between external and internal. The problem lies in confusing Blake with the characters who, in their fallen state, project divinity outward. This tendency of fallen consciousness to externalize divinity stands in dramatic contrast with the reintegration of the human divine in Night the Ninth. Because he follows Wilkie and Johnson with a Night by Night account, Ault does not acknowledge the interplay between Night the Ninth and the preceding Nights, thus limiting the exploration of Blake's antinarrative principle.[19]

The most recent books on *The Four Zoas*—George Rosso's *Blake's Prophetic Workshop* (1993) and Andrew Lincoln's *Spiritual History* (1995)—differ from Ault in their emphasis on cultural context and cohesiveness as opposed to fragmentation and disorder. In Rosso's case, this challenge is through a search for a coherent social and intellectual history, while Lincoln, more dismissive than Rosso of the poststructural approach, seeks to uncover the poem's textual history.

Lincoln's book is a valuable contribution to scholarship on the poem, providing a detailed analysis of the layers of the poem's composition. Structuring his study according to these stages, Lincoln offers fascinating suggestions about the progress of Blake's myth, speculating on reasons for changes in the manuscript. The present study stands closer to Rosso than either Lincoln or Ault, since it emphasizes the importance of the dynamic between fragmentation and wholeness rather than choosing one over the other.

In spite of the diversity among critical readings of *The Four Zoas,* there has been a common inability to account for Night the Ninth and its relationship to the preceding Nights, because these studies disregard the vital orientation of Blake's apocalypse in Night the Ninth. This study argues that the powerful though tenuously held vision of nonduality in Night the Ninth provides a touchstone for the rest of the poem and that the organized innocence of Night the Ninth is fully cognizant of the fragmented world of the first eight Nights.[20]

To overcome the problem of finding a means to address Blake's non-linear revision of traditional narrative, the structure of the present book revolves around the centrality of Night the Ninth's apocalypse. Such a structure allows a study of the centrality of the apocalypse, in linear and epistemological terms, alongside the fallen Nights that precede it in the poem. The following chapters are devoted to the elements of Blake's mythos, including its principles of causality, narrative, figuration and teleology, all having both dual and nondual, or fallen and redeemed, versions. The disjointed narratives and narrative interruptions of the first eight Nights, for instance, are replaced in Night the Ninth by a sequence of epiphanies that depend one upon the other and, in turn, radically revise the narrative problems of the previous Nights. Fallenness manifests as well through image forming. The vortex appears throughout the fallen Nights, describing the chaotic movement toward a fearful empty center. In Night the Ninth, a redemptive, vortical movement unbinds the dualistic mind. As a quest to an imageless center, the epic itself is vortical; it describes a paradoxical journey in which labyrinth is goal, and circumference and center are the same. At the heart of the paradox lies the question of how one can speak of redeemed forms when the goal toward which consciousness strives is to recognize that, as Shelley writes in *Prometheus Unbound*, "the deep truth is imageless" (1977, 175, line 116). The pivotal moment of this crisis of representing the imageless is Night the Seventh, whose two versions are contemporaneous paths representing at once the extreme of the fallen state and the greatest promise of redemption.

Nowhere does Blake represent the flux of differentiation and non-differentiation more dramatically than *The Four Zoas*. Although Blake describes these states in the engraved Prophecies,[21] it is only in *The Four Zoas* that Blake challenges traditional narrative method and figuration. It has been commonplace in Blake scholarship to regard *Jerusalem* as the culmination of Blake's achievement.[22] Even poststructural studies critical of the formalist systematizing of Blake's corpus privilege the engraved Prophecies. Stephen Cox's 1992 study sees *Jerusalem* as a corrective of *The Four Zoas;* he argues, for instance, that Luvah is too limited in Night the Ninth to be fully identified with Jesus, a point this study counters.[23] In the engraved Prophecies, however, Blake did not have the freedom to pursue experimentation with matters of narrative method and symbolism that he did in the *Zoas* manuscript; consequently, the engraved Prophecies use more traditional narrative and apocalyptic symbolism. The radical revision of such traditional forms as epic, dream vision, and quest romance are the means by which the poem superimposes the states of duality and nonduality. Blake represents this interplay between the limited mind and undifferentiated consciousness dynamically: in the epic structure of *The Four Zoas* consciousness is the wandering hero that undergoes many ordeals—delusions that correspond to its multiple ruptures—in its quest for reintegration. These ordeals manifest on all levels, including the psychological, theological, and sociopolitical.

The fact that previous treatments of the poem have been linear in structure reflects the reliance of Blake studies on fundamentally dualistic Western systems of thought whose scaffolding ultimately constricts their analysis. Because of the lack of a paradigm in Western models to describe undifferentiated consciousness as an attainment rather than a regression, several critical problems have become ingrained even among conflicting readings of Blake's poetry.

The most significant result of framing critical approaches to Blake with theoretical models limited in their epistemological scope has been the reduction of Blake's densely woven mythos to a single, and often rather thin, layer.[24] Western models that are used to describe Blake's mythos have in common the precept that wholeness is either the result of a primitive state of undifferentiated consciousness, as in psychoanalytic theory, or, as in deconstructive readings, that it is an illusion Blake rejects as the fabrication of Enlightenment propaganda. In fact, however, Blake's organized innocence is an undifferentiated consciousness achieved with the full recognition of differentiation. This is disregarded by most criticism in the interest of fitting Blake's mythos into a constricting theoretical framework or dismissed as a regression to nostalgia.

Much poststructural criticism argues unequivocally against the existence of a Blakean apocalypse. Leopold Damrosch, one of the most influential poststructural readers of Blake's mythos, states that "[r]ather than rhapsodizing about Blake's apocalyptic breakthrough as if it were easily attained, we might dwell instead on the bitter honesty with which he has dramatized the pre-apocalyptic condition, which may be the only condition we can ever know" (1980, 371). Such statements as this and the notion, according to another reading, of the "dark threat of non-differentiation" in Blake's poetry suggest that fear underlies most Western concepts of nondifferentiation (Rothenberg 1993, 2). The central irony of the poststructural claim that Blake stops short of the apocalypse is that the critical approach itself stops short of Blake's representation of apocalypse. In *The Four Zoas*, nondifferentiation is the key to apocalyptic transformation in which the realization that there is no Other brings with it freedom from fear.[25]

Focusing on Blake's dualism, Damrosch follows Morton Paley's claim that "Blake was a monist who found his mythology entrapping him in a dualistic position" (Paley 1973, 123). Damrosch's position, that Blake creates a "troubled dualism—his dualistic monism," leads to the conclusion that Blake ultimately surrenders to orthodoxy (1980, 175).[26] Though Paley, Damrosch, and those who have followed them rightly recognize the conflict between these powerful dynamics, Blake's mythos is far from imprisoned or even compromised by dualism.[27]

Though in its attempt to demystify Blakean apocalypse much poststructuralist criticism has disregarded the nondual element of Blake's mythos, recent scholarship has begun to restore the visionary to the critical discussion. Several scholars have taken into account that the twin impulses of the visionary and the worldly coexist, even in conflict, in Blake's work. It has been proven possible to take a poststructural approach, in fact, without compromising the fuller perspective of wholeness in Blake's mythos. Blake's organizing principle, according to George Rosso, is to "pit the prophetic and rationalist versions of Creation on a collision course" (1993, 63). This recognition that the poem itself opens up the conflict between the two forces is an important shift from Damrosch's conclusion that Blake abandons nondual vision in a capitulation to orthodoxy. More viable than such an exclusively deconstructive approach is Lorraine Clark's observation that Blake is both deconstructive and antideconstructive: "Battle with the Spectre . . . leads, in *Milton* as in *The Four Zoas*, to the redemption of reason not to its casting-off" (1991, 77). Blake can be seen as either deconstructive or antideconstructive, depending on whether he is conveying the fallen characters' anxiety about what they regard to be instability or whether he is conveying the redeemed state that is liberated from the mind's constructs at the apocalypse. It is indisputable that in Blake any surface text is unstable. W. J. T. Mitchell points out that Blake is of less interest to deconstruction than the other romantic writers because "there is no solid

surface there to be disrupted" (1986, 91). The key is that the characters'
anxiety about this instability should not be confused with Blake's willful
disorientation of traditional narrative structure.

Clark thus helps solve the problem raised by Shaviro who, though recognizing the double perspective of differentiation and nondifferentiation,
seems to confuse their relationship. Blake's "doctrine of contraries," Shaviro
states,

> is differential and anti-discursive in terms of its polemical content, but
> universalizing, conceptual and systematic in terms of its form. It becomes
> necessary simultaneously to read Blake's text both in terms of its System,
> or conceptual unity, *and* in terms of its anti-conceptual differentiality, or
> ironic perspectivism and dramatic contextualizations. (1982, 232)

Because he does not show how Blake reconciles system and "anti-concep-
tual differentiality," Shaviro appears to retain the systematizing that he seeks
to eschew.[28]

These observations suggest that, though poststructuralism has been
useful in allowing the poem to assert its own logic as a corrective to formalist demands for coherence, by applying deconstructive methodology too
absolutely the poem's internal logic is compromised. For Peter Otto, "there
are cogent thematic and contextual reasons to entertain the possibility at
least that when Blake finally stopped working on the manuscript he believed that the form taken by the work was the only one that the subject
matter could assume" (1987a, 144). Such an acknowledgment allows for a
logic peculiar to the work itself to emerge, surely a more viable approach
than imposing a logic from outside the poem, especially a logic clearly at
odds with the text itself.

Otto's observation gives important insight into coping with the problematic state of the *Four Zoas* manuscript, a dimension peculiar to this text
that further vexes the problem of wholeness and fragmentation. Readers
often attempt to retrace the poem's textual history in order to extract an
authorial voice. They often apply their speculations about the relationship
between early and later versions to hypothesize about which version Blake
would have chosen.[29]

Eluding completion both by its author and the subsequent hands that
attempt a finishing order, however, *The Four Zoas* manifests exuberance not

only in its unbounded experimentation with form and meaning but also in its textual state of suspended animation, leaving interpretation that depends on textual completion in a stalemate. Magno and Erdman, attempting to reconstruct the scenario of Blake's composition of the poem over time, assume his desire for its completion and therefore marketability:

> Blake evidently would have finished the whole work (and replaced the proofs with drawings) if he had found a customer. Failing that, he kept the leaves at hand, working over the text year after year, with increasing doubt that a perfected volume would ever be called for. The first revisions he made were done with care. He would erase words or lines and inscribe the revisions in as neat an engraver's hand as could be managed on the rough surface of erased paper. As he continued to revise, he subsided to a plain, workaday handwriting. . . . As time passed with no customer in sight, Blake made revisions with less and less attention to any finished appearance: a final draft of the manuscript would have had to be a fresh labor; this manuscript subsided into the category of preparatory sketches. At this stage of the game the drawings of bodies, for example, could be tried out in various positions, given more arms or legs than a Hindoo deity. (1987, 13–14)

This reading rests on the hypothesis that the poem must be incomplete because the author's motive for working on it depended on a paying reader. Vincent De Luca's alternative approach to the state of the manuscript, however, seems truer to Blake's project:

> Revision and interpolation are rarely neutral elements in the Blakean text, rarely data of bibliographical interest only. They are part of its system of signification, like the pictorial designs. . . . [M]ost of Blake's revisions are indeed re-*visions*; they register the eruption of new or deeper conceptions of a subject already rendered, and the fact of the re-seeing may form as much an element of what Blake wishes to impart as the conception seen anew. (1991, 114–15)

For a work to be free to pursue its own conditions, it must be free of enslavement to the demands of patronage. What Magno and Erdman's imaginary scenario calls to mind is the necessary reconciliation readers of *The Four Zoas* manuscript and its facsimiles must find between the "workaday" and the freedom from work. Blake's frontispiece, "Rest before Labor" suggests that the act of "keeping" the poem, as one keeps a journal, is not the conventional *otium* of a pastoral dream world but rather, as Blake's first illustration shows, the sleeper tossing with dreams (figure 4). The authorial "voice" of the dreamer suggests, further, that the poem's play is a radical departure from the engraved works, which cannot take the risks in structural terms that *The Four Zoas* does. It grants itself the freedom to pursue its central paradox: even as the human condition is locked in contraries, the apocalypse that liberates the mind from duality is at the center of every moment.[30]

Through his study of Blake's revisions, John Pierce has contributed insights about Blake's developing mythos, particularly regarding the roles of Tharmas and the Spectre of Urthona. The development of Tharmas and the Spectre, according to Pierce, is Blake's means of moving farther away from narrative causality. Pierce rightly points to the elegiac nature of the fallen world of Night the Third through Night the Seventh [a], concluding that "Blake seems to have realized, even during the composition of *Vala*, that those who caused the fall, Orc and Urizen, could not repair the damage" (1989, 499). Yet as Otto suggests, when the manuscript is studied as Blake left it, the nostalgia of these early Nights can be seen from the wholeness of Night the Ninth, the epic nostos. This return of consciousness to a state of wholeness alters the perspective of the elegiac, since a return actually takes place. In this way, the palimpsest-like state of the manuscript can be seen to reflect the poem's struggle to represent the relationship between time and eternity.[31]

The question of what role Blake's visual design plays in interpreting the manuscript has become a central concern of recent studies. In particular, Blake's use of his proof sheets for the illustrations of Young's *Night Thoughts* has fascinating implications for the debate over Blake's relationship with Christian orthodoxy. De Luca states that one cannot dismiss Blake's use as

> nothing more than an exhaustion of his supply of blank paper. . . . Critics have long suggested that in *Vala* Blake was attempting to vie with and supersede Young's *Night Thoughts*. Nothing illustrates the attempt with more striking visual force than the inscription of Blake's original poetry in a space designed to hold the lines of Young—a space, moreover, that breaks into the forms of the surrounding designs, which are the product of an earlier Blake half in contractual bondage to the conceptions of a dead poet and half his own man. . . . A whole history of displacements,

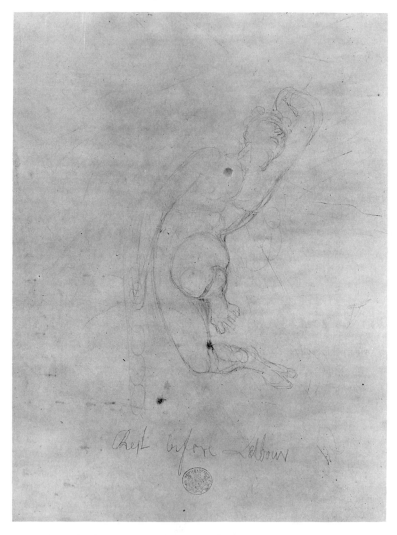

Fig. 4. Night the First. Pencil Drawing from *The Four Zoas*. MS. 39764, folio lv, reprinted with permission from the British Museum, London.

then, is encoded in the material substrate, the new paper supply, and this code is subtly employed to direct our reading of the poet's latest thematic intentions. (1991, 121–22)[32]

Grant Scott's observations on Blake's use of the *Night Thoughts* proofs suggest its inextricable link to the relation of word and image in *The Four Zoas*. Scott describes the text panel

> as a kind of square womb . . . out of which these naked foetal figures are being born, or against which they are struggling and writhing. . . . It is hard to resist seeing these images as self-portraits, renderings of Blake's own beholdenness to Young's text, or as concise visual allegories of the whole project itself, bodies born out of words. (1994, n.p.)

The agonistic relationship with Young through the designs is testimony to Blake's struggle against tradition.

The common assumption of Blake's surrender to orthodoxy is the most dire misreading of Blake's mythos, especially in *The Four Zoas*. Night the Ninth reveals that healing can only take place when externalized divinity, the deus ex machina created by the fallen characters, is reintegrated in the form of the collective epiphany of Albion, Zoas, and Emanations who no longer regard the outer world as separate from them. Just as consciousness creates its own fragmentation in the poem, healing is integral to consciousness. Psychoanalytic approaches to *The Four Zoas* often disregard the reintegration of fragmented vision in Night the Ninth. Paul Youngquist identifies the critical moment in Night the Second that gives rise to duality: "Albion's ocular turn outward is the epistemological equivalent of a retreat inward. He no longer sees 'reality' sustained by vision, but only himself and his 'Sons,' his own consciousness, that is, and its factions" (1989, 106). Though this analysis accurately describes the fallen world, its claim that Albion does not recuperate from the turn outward is challenged by Albion's epiphany in Night the Ninth. There is far more to Blake's myth, therefore, than a representation of schizophrenia (111). Such a thesis leads to the distorted conclusion that healing can only be offered by a deus ex machina: "Blake makes these changes in order to work a kind of conversion upon his own poetry, healing the psychic dissociation it dramatizes with a vision descending from above" (132). The externalizing of divinity, however, is the kind of solution Blake portrays as the projection of the fallen state.[33]

For this reason the providential element in the poem, a source of critical bafflement throughout the history of Blake scholarship, needs to be
reexamined from the perspective of Night the Ninth. Many critics claim
that Blake imports an external divinity to save humanity when his own
"system" fails. Adopting Damrosch's claim that Blake must resort to a deus
ex machina to heal the fragmented world, P. M. S. Dawson describes the
poem as moving "in the direction of Christian (more specifically Protestant)
orthodoxy" (1987, 142). Rather than falling into the trap of equating Blake
with the narrator or, for that matter, the characters in their fallen state, it is
crucial to allow for the poem's interplay of fallen and redeemed perspectives.

Phenomenology has been helpful in emphasizing the subjectivity of
what is for Blake fallen perception, precisely because it describes the way
inner states are projected outward onto the physical world. The strongest
element of Ault's reading of the fallen Nights of *The Four Zoas* is his appro-
priation of the phenomenological method. For Ault, Urizen projects his
fear onto what he perceives as Luvah in Night the Fifth; this demonstrates
that he, Urizen, does not realize that "the pulsation emanates from his own
trembling fear" (1987, 203). However, as is the case with the psychoanalytical
approach, phenomenology is only useful insofar as it describes the fallen
tendencies of the first eight Nights. At the apocalypse of Night the Ninth
the boundary between self and other is dissolved. The revelation that dualism has been an act of projection is made through nondual awareness, a
recuperation. Phenomenology cannot explain the phenomenon in which
nondual consciousness no longer projects the will of a subject onto a differ-
entiated other.

A promising alternative to these partial approaches has been the recent
trend to explore the sociopolitical and visionary forces as vital to each other
for Blake. These cultural, historical approaches acknowledge the inextricable links between Blake's social concerns and his lifelong commitment to
his vision. In diverse ways, these studies suggest that Blake's involvement in
the world and his mysticism must be explored as aspects of his complex
epistemology. Arguing against Damrosch's claim that Blake was fundamentally orthodox, Brian Aubrey points out that the presence of both dual and
nondual moments is not a matter of inconsistency, as Damrosch would
have it, but rather the paradoxical nature of "mystical consciousness":

> [These paradoxes] are inescapable elements of the mystical conscious-
> ness, which is able to function in two apparently contradictory modes,

able for example to perceive all the diversity of the phenomenal world as
an expression of a unity which underlies and pervades it, and also able to
accommodate the idea of a large Self which contains and completes, but
does not annul, all individual selves. (1986, 3)

Aubrey thus points to Blake's inclusion of dualism within the scope of
nondual vision rather than treating these forces as polarities.

The reintroduction of the mystical element in Blake, with the hindsight of poststructuralism, has revived Foster Damon's original observation
that "Blake is even in accord with Eastern mysticism; Urthona is Dharma;
Urizen, Karma; while both Tharmas and Luvah are included in Maya" (1947,
145). Frye's observation that "Blake was among the first of European ideal-
ists to link his own tradition of thought with the *Bhagavadgita*" (1947,
173) also warrants review, suggesting that Blake was interested in superimposing two ostensibly incompatible traditions. The recent criticism takes
a significant step beyond noting local influences, however. E. P. Thompson
details Blake's involvement in "breakaway sects" that believed that "Christ
was in all men" (Aubrey 1986, 7).

Blake's nonduality is therefore not derived exclusively from the mysticism of a single source such as Boehme, as is often conjectured. Thompson
emphasizes that "Behmenist scholarship was a polite and retiring occupa-
tion" and that Blake's antinomianism came from breakaway Protestant sects
such as Baptists and Methodists (1993, 47). Tempering Damrosch's emphasis on the influence of Western mystics, Thompson's argument suggests
that Blake came in contact with many systems of thought and adopted
some for a time, but ultimately refused to embrace any single one at the
expense of others.[34]

This is likewise the case with Blake's exposure to Eastern texts. Although there is scant evidence that Blake had direct exposure to such works,
it is probable, though as yet unconfirmed, that Blake read Sir Charles
Wilkins's translation of the *Bhagavad Gita*, the most influential text of Eastern nondual philosophy.[35] In his descriptive catalog Blake lists a now-lost
portrait of Wilkins translating the *Gita*: "The subject is, Mr. Wilkin, translating the Geeta; an ideal design, suggested by the first publication of that
part of the Hindoo Scriptures, translated by Mr. Wilkin" (E. 548). Blake
links the Poetic Genius to the east, as Ezekiel tells the narrator of *The Marriage
of Heaven and Hell*: "The philosophy of the east taught the first principles
of human perception. . . . [W]e of Israel taught that the Poetic Genius (as

you now call it) was the first principle and all the others merely derivative" (E. 39, pl.12). From Blake's association of the Poetic Genius with Eastern thought, one can infer that Blake's attraction to Eastern philosophy was its nondualism.

Although these references suggest a direct influence of Eastern thought on Blake, it is not presented here as the source of Blake's nondual vision. As Jung notes, "It seems to me beyond question that these Eastern symbols originated in dreams and visions, and were not invented" (1953, 92). The present use of the Eastern analogue is therefore not meant to discount the rich tradition of Western mystical writers, including Plotinus, Boehme, and Spinoza. As Raymond Schwab notes, "[T]he accumulation of coincidences among the intellectual fashions which promoted Boehme, Schelling, and the Upanishads simultaneously is striking" (197). Eastern nondualism, however, is a more accurate analogue for Blake's mythos both because of its freedom from the Western orientation of space and time in describing the relationship between the dual and nondual and because of its depiction of consciousness as inclusive of the physical world. Introducing the Eastern analogue, therefore, is not meant to provide a panacea for the ills of previous critical approaches, nor is it meant to exclude the innumerable insights that Western models have already provided in analyzing the dualistic world in Blake's myth. Rather, Eastern nondual philosophy provides a means of representing the undifferentiated element in Blake's mythos that has eluded exclusively Western methodologies. C. S. Singh comments on the *Vedas* that "[i]t is not a multitude of gods that the subject is encountering but the soleness (wholeness) of *Brahman*. . . . The duality of subject and object is fused each in the other" (1988, 26). Nondualism is the crucial factor that reorients all the others in Blake's myth.

Eastern nondualism thus provides an analogue to describe the expansion beyond the limited ego, crucial to Blakean innocence but unexplored by exclusively dualistic models. For Eastern philosophy, undifferentiated consciousness is a state of achievement and ecstasy. It thus helps convey with greater accuracy the relationship between the contracted and expanded states of consciousness, a significant and overlooked dimension of Blake's mythos. Contrary to the orientation of Western psychology, for which nondifferentiation is a primitive or naive state that precedes differentiation, Blake represents undifferentiated consciousness as an ever present state that is nevertheless difficult to achieve in a world of differentiation. The nondualism of Kashmir Shaivism, an ancient Indian philosophy, describes consciousness in terms of the flux of differentiation and nondifferentiation:

> The self-referential capacity of consciousness is united with all things. From within its very self, this capacity of consciousness differentiates the other, and from the other it actualizes itself again. It then unifies both of them, the self and the other, and having unified them, it submerges them both back into itself. (Abhinavagupta 1938–43, quoted in Müller Ortega 1989, 96)

The nondual state both subsumes and interacts with the limited state of duality. The pulsation between the two states this relationship describes suggests the nonlinear interplay of the fallen and redeemed in *The Four Zoas*.

The Four Zoas thus does more than reverse the positions of reason and intuition in its revolt against Enlightenment thought. According to the poem, consciousness limited to the passive reception of outer phenomena never exists separately from its expanded state, which recognizes that those phenomena are no different from itself. Though the nondual relationship between subject and object is a tenuous attainment, as Blake shows in various ways, it is potential at the heart of the direst moments of fragmentation, separation, and fear. The goal is the dynamic balance of the mind's dualistic tendencies to divide body and soul, self and other, and the human and divine with the nondual state that heals these divisions. In epic terms, the achievement of nondual vision at the apocalypse of Night the Ninth is the nostos, the return home of consciousness to wholeness.

CHAPTER II

"Pangs of an Eternal Birth":
The Four Zoas and the Problem of Origin

WITHIN ALBION'S SLEEPING FRAME in *The Four Zoas* the figures that compose him undergo various incarnations and deaths, sleeps and awakenings, and obfuscations and revelations. These figures, each contributing to and perpetuating the fallen state, participate as well in the movement toward redemption in Night the Ninth. Urizen, with renewed wonder, marvels at this emergence: "How is it we have walkd thro fires & yet are not consumd" (E. 407, 138:39).

How this is possible, as Urizen asks, is obliquely addressed in the final words of the poem: "End of the Dream" seems an arbitrary closure after the poem's accumulation of endings and new beginnings. Margoliouth, in his 1956 edition of *Vala*, notes,

> The words "a Dream of Nine Nights" were at one time put on, and then deleted from, the title-page. At the end of Night IX Blake scrawled "End of the Dream." Young's Nights were nights of meditation. If Blake's Nights were intended as anything but a pointless imitation of Young, what were they? (1956, xvi)

Contrary to Margoliouth's answer that the dream is "the Eternal Man's," the phrase "End of the Dream" suggests that the poem itself is a dream containing that of Albion, who has long since awoken. As Wilkie and

35

Johnson note, Blake decided not to introduce the poem as a dream: "Although Blake cancelled his original subtitle, 'A DREAM in Nine Nights,' the phrase is descriptive of the cosmic, but more especially the personal, nightmare universe of the poem. . . . We need not insist on the dream-form as crucial in itself" (1973, 203). Blake's leaving the end frame, however, is an important detail regarding the relationship of the sleep of Albion to the authorial voice. To grant that the outermost narrative of the poem is a dream is to allow the poem freedom from the waking rules of time and space. The teleology or "end" of Blake's dream narrative is the movement not toward a final goal in time, but toward eternity. *The Four Zoas* represents the paradox of movement in time toward a goal outside of time by superimposing glimpses of eternity onto moments in the fallen state. These moments of revelation are the unbinding of the human mind from its dualistic separation from the phenomenal world.

What is it that wakes up from the dream of a dualistic world, of history as the vortical chaos of warring contraries? Blake's combining and redefinition of quest romance and dream vision suggest a possible hero-as-dreamer who encompasses the range of the poem. This dreamer creates the universes and characters—and their assertions about God, the fall, and each other—yet remains formless and silent behind the continuously fluctuating forms, fictions, and cosmic structures that it dreams. The hero can be called consciousness itself, which subsumes the mind and its faculties.

According to Blake's use of the archetypal elements of quest romance, consciousness as a whole must move through the intricate changes of perception that constitute its fallen or contracted state before it can pass through the apocalypse to reach divinity at the center. Such a sleeper spins out the dream of a human mind and human history, emerging as the dream passes through the apocalypse, the archetypal ring of fire that surrounds the sacred center. This limitless frame and center, eluding image and concept, literalizes the paradox of God as a circle whose center is everywhere and circumference nowhere.[1]

Consciousness itself, then, creates and experiences the fallen and redeemed states. Blake transforms the biblical duality of the fallen and redeemed into a nondual relation between the two states because, in the poem, the fallen mind is composed of and by dreaming consciousness. The poem embraces both states, which are ultimately inextricable from each other. While Morton Paley reads early signals of regeneration as "grafting," he concludes that they "simply do not work; the regeneration theme does not grow out of *Vala* but is superimposed on it, as Blake himself must eventually have realized" (1970, 161). The contemporaneousness is not mere grafting, however, but rather the retrospectively shown relation of fallenness and redemption. On closer inspection, this superimposition can be seen as the method by which Blake challenges traditional linearity.

Characters in the poem are quick to blame each other for the fallen state, but what they cannot see in these fallen moments is the totality of which they and their actions are only a part. Through a series of epiphanies in Night the Ninth, the literal veil of their own fallen understanding is dropped in an equally literal unbinding of consciousness. Nelson Hilton's concept of Blake's "literal imagination" is helpful in understanding Blake's figuration:

> Literal . . . does not mean actual, straightforward, or reduced: to see or hear a word in or through its literal expression is not to see some single meaning, any more than meeting a friend is to see the letters of his or her name. Seeing and hearing the word is meeting it alive in its force-field of sound, etymology, graphic shape, contemporary applications, and varied associations. (1983, 7)

The very energy of Blake's figures stands in contrast to the deadened effect of Urizenic allegory, which deprives images of the vitality that results from their inseparability from that which they represent. Gadamer's observation that "[i]t is only because what is symbolized is present itself that it can be present in the symbol" underscores this notion of the literal imagination (1993, 154).

In this way, chains binding the figures and the world itself in the contracted state burst link by link as Los, Urizen, Albion, Tharmas, and Vala each have a dramatic revelation in which his or her own limitation and how it has contributed to and perpetuated the fallen state become clear. Albion's epiphany not only depends on the unbinding of the other figures' fallen tendencies but is clearly subject to the mind's inevitable tendency to turn revelation into concept or image. In this way, Albion, who seems until the final moment to be the outermost dreamer, or circumference of the dream vision, is subject to the script created by the dreamer suggested at the end of the poem. Kathleen Raine notes that the "determining national archetype [of the 'matter of Britain'] is that of the Sleeping King. It is not, it seems, the pursuit of forbidden knowledge but the tendency . . . to fall asleep that besets the English. Perhaps Faust will one day be saved; and one day the sleeper of the ancient British kingdom will awaken" (1986, 689). This pattern of mythical narcolepsy touches on an important source of Blake's epic. It suggests an affinity with the Song of Solomon and such medieval dream visions as *Piers Plowman* in which, as the dreamer Will goes deeper beyond the discursive faculties, his heart awakens. Though Langland is more systematic than Blake in shedding discursive faculties as he penetrates to God at the heart, the element of the sleeping persona is crucial in exploring the way the poem works with the voices it assumes, externalizes and discards at the apocalypse. For Blake, the "heart," or that which awakens, is a vexed issue, since he inverts the relation of dreamer and dreamed. As opposed to medieval dream visions, in which prophetic vision is experienced when the limited self sleeps, for Blake the life of the mind—in both a personal lifetime and human history—is a drama enacted by a subsuming consciousness.

The mind, which tends to contract through conceptualizing, fictionalizing and image making, is redeemed through the perspective of Night the Ninth, in which consciousness expands beyond these limitations. Husserl's discussion of the relation of ego to its experiences helps convey the relationship Blake creates between the limited self and undifferentiated consciousness. In this relationship, Husserl explains,

> is included much that is real . . . and intentional. The phrase "It lives them" does not mean that it holds them and whatever is in them "in its glance," and that it apprehends them after the manner of immanent experience . . . ,or any other immanent intuition or presentation. It is ideally possible for every experience not included in the glance to be "brought under it"; a reflective act of the Ego is directed towards it, and it now becomes an object *for* the Ego. (1962, 197)

Blake's treatment of causality, by contrast, complicates the role of ego.[2] As opposed to the phenomenological view, Blake has the limited self subsumed by consciousness in its movement beyond duality.

The revelations of Night the Ninth have in common a celebration of the visible world; all that had seemed separate from and threatening to the figures as limited selves is seen as the same Self they comprise. This is why the apocalypse does not destroy the phenomenal world as such, but rather dissolves the dualistic sense of its otherness. Such a revelation is key to the way Blake's figuration works. At the apocalypse, the subject and phenomenal world, as well as its representation, are reunited. Even such figures as the Daughters of Beulah, acting as "covering cherubs," are no less projections of a single consciousness. These seemingly protective agents, projected as nonhuman, exhibit the same shortsightedness of the human figures and, more problematically, the Council of God.

During Albion's sleep, the unbound Self, or undifferentiated consciousness, contracts into waking life as the human mind knows it. Yet the unbound Self remains both witness to and creator of its fragmentation. In the fallen state, the figures who turn from one concept or figure to another in search of causes outside their limited selves in space and time comprise the fragmented mind. Night the Ninth reveals that freedom lies beyond describing one's relation to another in terms of contraries. It is therefore beyond virtue as well as vice, since virtue only exists as the antithesis of vice. For Blake to represent human history, the expanse of the cosmos, and the projections of an externalized divinity as the creation of a single dream is not to renounce them but to suggest a human divine that eludes limiting concepts that separate the human and the divine.

With this sense of an authorial voice as a creator-consciousness, one can approach the problems of the manuscript with more flexibility. There are two levels of play in the poem: the poet's play, which is manifested in the fluid nature of the manuscript, as well as the cosmic play of the creator-consciousness, the poem's subject. The studies of play by Huizinga and Gadamer help explain the poem's freedom from dualism. Gadamer states that "play fulfills its purpose only if the player loses himself in play. . . . The players are not the subject of play; instead play merely reaches presentation (Darstellung) through the players" (1993, 102–3). This aptly describes the essential and overlooked quality of play in *The Four Zoas*, for not only does it represent a subsuming nondualism that orients the dualism of the fallen world, but its teleology is contingent on the dissolution of agency by a single subject. Gadamer suggests this as well: "The movement of playing has no goal that brings it to an end; rather, it renews itself in constant repetition. The movement backward and forward is obviously so central to the definition of play that it makes no difference who or what performs this movement" (103). This definition of play illuminates the poem's characteristic defiance of linearity in its peculiar brand of repetition, namely, the inter-play of fallen and redeemed tendencies.[3]

According to Blake's myth in *The Four Zoas*, there was never a time when there was no dream. Structurally, the poem's play takes liberties with the causal relation of fallenness and redemption. The greatest structural riddle of the poem is the relation between the affirmation of Night the Ninth and the chaos that precedes it, a question that has led to linear or dialectical descriptions of the poem's movement and also to the criticism that Blake later inserted the Council of God passages as a deus ex machina to solve these complications and assert his theological orthodoxy. Behind the search for such cause-and-effect relations is the ingrained assumption that a strong measure of a poem's success is the cohesiveness of its structure in temporal terms. Yet at the heart of Blake's poem is the principle that although waking life, personal and historical, is dominated by fallen con-sciousness, it has an atemporal relation to redemption that recognizes di-vine vision within the human, hence within the fallen.

The structure of the poem defies the study of causality that depends on temporal orientation.[4] The relation of fallen and redeemed moments in the poem is comprised of various forms of anticipation and echo, the dramatic manifestation of the redeemed within the fallen. In the largest sense, Night the First through Night the Eighth gain meaning through the revelation of Night the Ninth, which in turn is achieved through the experience of the first eight Nights. The presence of an innocence assumed to be temporally prior to the experience of the fall further complicates this interplay of prolepsis and metalepsis. To speak of causality in the poem, one must dis-tinguish between the poem itself as Blake's myth and the mythmaking among the figures within the poem prior to Night the Ninth. Fictions that shape the dream make up the bulk of the poem, but none stands as the absolute around which the others are oriented.

Separating the authorial voice from the voices of splintered conscious-ness, the dramatis personae, is one of the poem's most difficult problems. Such a voice can be gleaned through two patterns of movement: that which binds, a series of fallen gestures that constitute literal links of the chain, and that which liberates, a sequence of epiphanies that bursts the contracted mind free from fear and secrecy, the tendencies associated with the illusion of duality. Because Blake does not create a moral dualism of the fallen and redeemed, gestures of fallenness do not merely parody gestures of redemption. Instead, they are patterns that suggest each other, creating a complex dialogue of imagery and rhetoric between the fallen world of Night the First through Night the Eighth and the apocalyptic vision of Night the Ninth.

Acknowledging this interplay avoids the danger of describing redemption in finalistic terms. The paradox at the heart of Blake's myth is that movement to the center entails discarding images and concepts. Gadamer's definition of the symbol is akin to Blake's visionary representation, realized in Night the Ninth:

> A symbol not only points to something; it represents it by taking its place. But to take the place of something means to make something present that is not present. Thus in representing, the symbol takes the place of something: that is, it makes something immediately present. Only because it thus presents the presence of what it represents is the symbol itself treated with the reverence due to the symbolized. (1993, 154)

Blake endows his figures with "presence" and energy, making the goal of imagelessness a striking paradox. The most dramatic instance of Blake's paradoxical figuration, in which the symbol makes something present that is not present, is Albion's recognition that Jerusalem, the poem's figure of intuitive vision, is his link to divinity: "Behold Jerusalem in whose bosom the Lamb of God / Is seen" (E. 391, 122:1). She is never absent but perceived so from the opening of the poem, when Tharmas claims to have hidden her, until this moment in Night the Ninth. One senses that Albion now understands that she is an embodiment of the imageless divine; the infinite movement toward the center thus redeems the vortical chaos of fallen consciousness.

Significantly, Urizen, in Night the Ninth, hears and shares Albion's revelation that Jerusalem is within him and "within" her is the Lamb of God. At the opening of Night the Second, it is Urizen to whom Albion turns when he loses the divine vision: "Albion calld Urizen & said. Behold these sickning Spheres. . . . / Take thou possession! take this Scepter . . ." Urizen at this point in Night the Second establishes his part in the fallen world: "No more Exulting for he saw Eternal Death beneath / Pale he beheld futurity" (E. 313, 23:14–15). It follows that in Night the Ninth, Albion appears to need Urizen's own understanding of the moment in order to overcome his own deathly sleep. Urizen has just discovered that "futurity is in this moment" (E. 390, 121:22). His hindsight of the horrors of apocalypse is the first step in the move from self-fulfilling prophecy to divine vision:

> . . . O that I had never drank the wine nor eat the bread
> Of dark mortality nor cast my view into futurity nor turnd
> My back darkning the present clouding with a cloud. . . .
> Thro Chaos seeking for delight & in spaces remote
> Seeking the Eternal which is always present to the wise
> Seeking for pleasure which unsought falls round the infants path.
>   (E. 390, 121:3–11)

Urizen recognizes that futurity is a state of mind: to cast one's view into futurity is not only to forecast the future but to move from one point in time to the next in an act of self-fulfilling prophecy. The act of self-protection thus becomes the danger itself, namely, beholding destiny as externally wrought and eternal in its meting of retribution. The realization of this particular irony of fallenness leads to the larger comprehension of the union of the human and the divine in eternity. The nondual vision in Night the Ninth has a dynamic relationship with earlier fallen moments such as the crucial opening of Night the Second in which Albion becomes a dualist, turning his eyes outward.

Through the tangle of paradox, seeking the unsought, Urizen transcends his obsessive flight from mortality. The process of "unreasoning," defying logical consistency, parallels and redeems the chaotic panic of "unreasoning" in the fallen world. Through the redemption of "unreasoning," Urizen attains a comprehension of divinity. As Hazard Adams observes, the fallen Urizen is

> locked in the circle of spatial dimensions. He thinks that his world is
> infinite and unbounded whereas it is really finite and circular. He sees
> everything inside out. He thinks he stands on the egg called the world,
> but actually he revolves inside it. He looks to the stars for guidance when
> he should look into himself. (1955, 292)

This is seen when, having set aside his fear of the illusion of futurity in Night the Ninth, Urizen can respond to Albion not in his former mode of "determined decree," but rather in the expression of true wonder—a nonrhetorical, nonironic question: "Where shall we take our stand to view the infinite & unbounded" (E. 391, 122:24). He has made the crucial turn from fending off mortality with finite and bound systematizing to wondering how one takes a mortal stance in owning eternal vision: "Or where are human feet for Lo our eyes are in the heavens" (122:25). Eliade notes on the symbolism of the center:

> There is not only an intimate interconnection between the universal life and the salvation of man; but . . . *it is enough only to raise the question of salvation*, to pose the central problem; that is *the* problem—for the life of the cosmos to be for ever renewed. For . . . death is often only the result of our indifference to immortality. (1969, 56)

Questioning is also key to Blake's notion of salvation, but how one even asks the question is still more at issue for Blake.

Finding one's stance in eternity depends on orienting oneself causally, which, as Urizen shows at this point in Night the Ninth, is not a matter of describing the relation of historical acts in time, and so casting into futurity, but finding the equipoise between vision and fallen consciousness. As De Luca notes,

> In the midst of [the] forward momentum, there are repeated moves to catapult imagination back into the past. This is seen particularly in the characters' obsessive quest for origins, their attempts to recover the events of the fall, of the time before the fall, and even of earlier falls in shadowier times before that. (1991, 116)

This observation leads to the question of how Blake would have the reader distinguish between a wrong understanding of causality, such as this, and true origin. Blake's distinction between memory and vision in *A Vision of the Last Judgment* suggests that origin must be sought through vision rather than through the fallen faculty of memory, retrospect that is time-bound:

> The Last Judgment is not Fable or Allegory but Vision Fable or Allegory are a totally distinct & inferior kind of Poetry. . . . Really & Unchangeably. Fable or Allegory is Formd by the Daughters of Memory. Imagination is Surrounded by the daughters of Inspiration who in the aggregate are calld Jerusalem. (E. 554)

Urizen elaborates his awe at being free from mortality in Night the Ninth with the image of liberating the light of vision trapped in the circadean measurings of his own fallen labor: "What chain encompassed in what Lock is the river of light confind / That issued forth in the morning by measure & the evening by carefulness" (E. 391, 122:22–23).

No sooner does he ask this than the apocalypse begins in a literalizing of his metaphor, the reversal of time in an eternal birth:

> He ceasd for rivn link from link the bursting Universe explodes
> All things reversd flew from their centers. . . .
> In pangs of an Eternal birth
>
> (E. 392, 122:16–30)

The apocalypse points the seeker of causality to the source of myth. Yet the source of myth is one of the poem's greatest puzzles. Cassirer argues that myth "begins with the intuition of purposive action—for all the forces of nature are for myth nothing other than expressions of a demonic or divine will" (1955, 49). This has implications for the limited perception of Beulah as well as for the redeemed vision of Night the Ninth. When divine will is internalized, one can regard the source as the center, whereas in the chaos of the fallen world, it is externalized through the simultaneous labors of the Daughters of Beulah and Urizen.

Blake complicates spatial orientation in his narrative to achieve the effect of bafflement that comes with the opening of time into eternity and with the fallen presumption that orientation has external referents. Salvation is found in the mutual epiphanies of Albion and Urizen through the practically simultaneous question by Urizen and recognition by Albion.

In Night the Ninth, therefore, Albion beholds divinity at the center. This center or "bosom," containing the Lamb of God, is Blake's version of the archetypal temple, traditionally achieved after a linear quest through a labyrinth. Blake portrays the paradoxical revision of quest spatially and temporally: His radical revision of the labyrinth and temple in the archetypal quest is his means of representing the coeternal relation of fallenness and redemption. The poem opposes the image of fallen motion, the vortex, whose chaos surrounds an infinitely empty center, to this infinitely central vision that, when achieved, holds all the elements of human consciousness in equipoise.

For Blake, the irony underlying the notion of quest is that the temple is always present at the center of the labyrinth; in fact, the labyrinth is the temple. Many readers have recognized the usefulness of applying Jungian psychology to Blake's concept of the antithetical figures of the Zoas. Of Jung's description of the psyche, most applicable to Blake is the centricity of the archetypal mandala, a principle often overlooked when Jungian Blake readers focus on the archetypal antitheses. The center orients the poem structurally and imagistically as well as epistemologically. It is in Blake's vision of the center, rather than through an arbitrary balance of oppositions, that Albion is liberated from the Circle of Destiny.

Visualizing Night the Ninth as the center rather than the ending of the poem, one recognizes in Blake's universe Jung's description of the archetypal mandala:

> Almost regularly the outer rim consists of fire, the fire of *concupiscentia*, "desire," from which proceed the torments of hell. The horrors of the burial ground are generally depicted on the outer rim. Inside this is a garland of lotus leaves. . . . Then comes a kind of monastery courtyard with four gates. It signifies sacred seclusion and concentration. Inside this courtyard there are as a rule the four basic colours, red, green, white, and yellow, which represent the four directions and also the psychic functions, as the Tibetan Book of the Dead shows. Then usually marked off by another magic circle, comes the centre as the essential object or goal of contemplation. (1969, 356)

Jung describes in the mandala an archetypal design that is central to the study of *The Four Zoas* in terms of causality and the depiction of the quest beyond time.

It is further important to regard the paired oppositions of the Zoas in terms of the perceived missing center, a concept also present in all the variants of the archetypal mandala, which are

> based on the squaring of a circle. Their basic motif is the premonition of a centre of personality, a kind of central point within the psyche, to which everything is related, by which everything is arranged, and which is itself a source of energy. The energy of the central point is manifested in the almost irresistible compulsion and urge to *become what one is,* just as every organism is driven to assume the form that is characteristic of its nature, no matter what the circumstances. This centre is not felt or thought of as the ego but, if one may so express it, as the *self.* (Jung 1969, 357)

Jung's graphic distinction between the ego, or limited mind, and the self, or consciousness, is useful in describing *The Four Zoas*, where the ego is equivalent to the dualism of fallen consciousness superimposed on the self, the undifferentiated vision of the redeemed state. There are, nevertheless, significant limitations to using Jung's archetypal mandala exclusively to describe the poem's structure.

One limitation is the perceived *absence* of a central image, crucial to the poem's structural principle as well as to its narrative interest. A second and more important limitation is that the Jungian analogue cannot account for Blake's superimposition of the linear matrix onto the centric, or the fallen onto the redeemed. For Blake, to write an epic of intellectual battle in a linear narrative structure would not only impose false closure on the ever vacillating, ever active psyche, but it would leave no recourse for representing its relation to the ever knowing, ever still self.

Rudolf Arnheim's discussion of the interplay of centric and linear forces in the visual arts helps describe Blake's poetic play with linear and centric movement:

> With all its virtues, the framework of verticals and horizontals has one grave defect. It has no center, and therefore it has no way of defining any particular location. Taken by itself, it is an endless expanse in which no one place can be distinguished from the next. . . . For his geometrical analysis, Descartes had to impose a center, the point where a pair of coordinates crossed. In so doing he borrowed from the other spatial system, the centric and cosmic one. (1982, viii–ix)[5]

Arnheim discusses the power of the composition that combines the mystical centric principle with the worldly grid: "The power of the center can be exploited to create a teasing contradiction between an element kept deliberately small and its crucial importance for the story being presented" (1988, 113). The implication for understanding *The Four Zoas* is that the poem's power lies in the "understatement" of the center, which in narrative terms is the actual forgetting or abandoning of it, in the midst of the "vectors," to use Arnheim's term, of the worldly, agonistic cross firings of the Zoas. Arnheim further discusses the power of such a device in painting:

> [B]y omitting any direct reference to the center, the painter understates the basic stability of his composition. He entrusts it to the interaction of

his vectors and charges the viewer with organizing what he sees by referring it to the indirectly given center. This more dynamic type of composition calls for more sophisticated perception than is required by a work
safely and stably built around a visible center. (1988, 115, 119)

This fundamental challenge to linear thinking suggests a key to the
problem of causality in the poem. Urizen's part in the moment of Albion's
epiphany in Night the Ninth is crucial to understanding the poem's principle of causality, or, more accurately, its challenge to the assumption of
causality. From the poem's outset, Blake rejects the promise of narrative
beginning and continuity. A sequence of rejected beginnings culminates
with the introduction of the myth of the missing center.

The first of the poem's broken promises of a beginning-as-mythical-
source is Eno, who is a combination of a muse figure and mythical mother:

> The Song of the Aged Mother which shook the heavens with wrath
> Hearing the march of long resounding strong heroic Verse
> Marshalld in order for the day of Intellectual Battle
>
> (E. 300, 3:1–3)

Not invoked by the poet directly, Eno holds a vague position as bard. One
immediately stumbles over the syntax: The "which" of the first line con-
fuses the temporal relation of Eno's song to the intellectual battle, because
she appears already to have sung about an event that has not yet occurred.
From the orientation of Night the Ninth, this makes perfect sense. The
apocalypse points us in the direction of causality as an eternal birth, always
in tension with the continuous movement outward into the world of experience. In Night the Ninth, the apocalypse follows Urizen's epiphany that
futurity is not eternity:

> He ceasd for rivn link from link the bursting Universe explodes
> All things reversd flew from their centers . . .
> In pangs of an Eternal birth
>
> (E. 392, 122:26–30)

These two moments—the opening of the poem and the "birth" of eternity
at the apocalypse in Night the Ninth—create a dynamic interplay of the
poem's two matrices of the dual and nondual states.

Soon after her introduction in Night the First, Eno is abandoned for biblical citations, whose authority substitutes for the poem's own vague figure of authority. Blake's irony, as this illustrates, can be seen as a version of romantic irony:

> [T]raditionally defined as the deliberate destruction of the art work's illusion, [it] involves the reader in a process which, although occurring so swiftly as to be experienced instantaneously, actually consists of three stages. In the first stage of romantic irony, the reader is brought against the presence of the artifice itself when, through the craft of the author, he is forced to face the work as a purely mental creation, a merely fictive entity. Stage two proceeds naturally from stage one as the author, who has mocked himself as a creator by destroying the illusion of his "creation," requires the reader to ponder the absurdity of the artist as a creator-god figure. This stage is a threshold for the third step, the disturbing perception of the coalescence of illusion-reality levels within all existence, the reader's life included. Through the enforced distance from the work achieved in stage one, the reader has confronted the illusion of the work's "reality" in his own mind . . . ; he doubts the boundaries of his own existence as a separate entity, much as he questioned the hitherto hermetic "zone" within which the art work had its "life." (Daghistany and Johnson 1981, 53)

Each of these "stages" manifests simultaneously from the beginning of *The Four Zoas*, yet Blake's irony is more radical than this description: he ultimately calls the project of telling the story itself into question. Speaking now of "those Living Creatures" that "the Heavenly Father only" can know, the narrator separates himself from his created figures by disclaiming his own role as creator of what Wallace Stevens would call the "supreme fiction."

If it is not a story that has begun, then what *has* begun is the problem of beginning the epic of intellectual battle. Los is introduced as the hero and given priority over his three precursors: "Los was the fourth immortal starry one, & in the Earth / Of a bright Universe Empery attended day & night" (E. 301, 3:10–11). Yet in another confusing syntactical twist, the introduction of the prophet-hero is displaced by that of Tharmas, whose priority is of a wholly unexpected kind:

Daughter of Beulah Sing
His fall into Division & his Resurrection to Unity

> His fall into Generation of Decay & Death & his Regeneration
> by the Resurrection from the dead
> Begin with Tharmas Parent power. darkning in the West
>
> (E. 301, 4:3–5)

The verb "Begin" can either refer to the fall and resurrection, thus forming an authoritative causal connection between Tharmas as parent power and the fall, or it can be an imperative directed at Eno, who is now a daughter of Beulah rather than mythical mother. For Blake, this suggests a new ambivalence toward Eno, since the daughters as protectors of mankind inadvertently arrest regeneration. A third reading is implicit in the first two: it is an imperative directed at the reader, suggesting the arbitrariness of "situating oneself in eternity," the frustration of finding a place to begin.

The poem gravitates toward Tharmas as the progenitor of the paradox of fallenness, that perpetual "darkning in the West." Though the earlier false starts are important ways of establishing Blake's peculiar brand of romantic irony, the drama between Tharmas and Enion is where the story of representing fallenness and redemption opens, as intuitive vision literally has closed. The subject of Tharmas's dispute with Enion is his having hidden Jerusalem. He assures Enion, "It is not love I bear to [Jerusalem] It is Pity / She hath taken refuge in my bosom & I cannot cast her out" (E. 301, 4:13–14). This moment establishes the crucial gesture of fallenness.[6] Hiding vision is an impossibility recognized in Night the Ninth, but here the delusion of being able to hide divinity initiates the fallen state that is characterized by panic, secrecy, and fear.[7]

The introduction of the tragedy of fallenness thus plummets from the lofty biblical representation to the bathetic squabble that, one senses, is a conflict that has gone stale to the point of enraging the antagonists. This typifies the continual shifting in the poem between the apparently sublime and the painfully bathetic. Fallenness, the great delusion of dualism, is for Blake not merely a philosophical system; it is the basis of flawed human existence. Tharmas, therefore, believes that he has hidden a being apart from himself, which we learn in Night the Ninth is part of the Self that is never separate.

Blake's apparent vacillation between Enitharmon and Jerusalem here, witnessed by his having crossed out Enitharmon and substituted Jerusalem in the manuscript, reveals Blake's own difficulties with the overlapping of the narrative and the figurative. Enitharmon would have been the logical

choice in terms of the poem's dramatic interest, but Jerusalem appears to
have been the stronger candidate figuratively, since she is the significantly
undramatic, formless figure of centricity.[8] Tharmas thinks he has hidden
her, but she has always been within, and in turn embodies the Divine Lamb,
as Albion discovers in Night the Ninth: "Behold Jerusalem in whose bosom the Lamb of God / Is seen" (E. 391, 122:1–2).

Based on this delusion, Tharmas further refuses to take responsibility
for his part in the drama in which he participates with Enion. He claims
not to have anything to do with Jerusalem's presence in his heart. From the
perspective of Night the Ninth, which reveals that it is the welcoming of all
in one that recreates wholeness, this response is seen to perpetuate the fallen
state. Here in Night the First, the phenomenological effect is immediate:
"Trembling & pale sat Tharmas weeping in his clouds" (E. 301, 4:28). As
the deluge of anger begins, the universe of fallen consciousness comes to
reflect the dualistic tendency to cast out all but the shadow of one's identity.
The first deterioration of a Zoa the poem witnesses is Tharmas's after he has
accused Enion of literally ripping him to shreds: "Why wilt thou Examine
every little fibre of my soul" (E. 302, 4:29).

Tharmas's assurance that he will amend his error by building Enion a
labyrinth also initiates the crucial disjunction between intending to heal
and causing disintegration, for it immediately infects Enion, whose first
words are

> . . . Thy fear has made me tremble thy terrors have surrounded me. . . .
> Hide me some Shadowy semblance. secret whisprings in my Ear
> In secret of soft wings.
>
>   (E. 301, 4:17–25)

Tharmas and Enion now hold death and secrecy in a causal relation. Enion
says, "Farewell I die I hide from thy searching eyes / So saying—From her
bosom weaving soft in Sinewy Threads / A tabernacle for Jerusalem" (E.
302, 5:5–7), and Tharmas himself is splintered, "His spectre issuing from
his feet in flames of fire" (13–15).

Enion's paralysis of will provides the first lesson in the futility of seeking causality through memory. More specifically, this is the first "rereading," behavior that will be repeated by other figures throughout the first
eight Nights and which the poem opposes to the "rereading" through vision

in Night the Ninth. Enion thus wonders, "Is this a deed of Love I know what I have done. I know / Too late now to repent" (E. 303, 5:45–46). Her tabernacle has acquired a "will of its own perverse & wayward" (21–22), thus becoming "the Circle of Destiny." This is an ironic version of the redeemed. Through the apocalyptic "re-vision," it will be seen that Jerusalem is at the center of this circle, but forgotten in the chaos of the tabernacle grown out of control.[9]

"Terrified in her own creation," then, Enion cannot take action. The widening effect of Tharmas's panic is to invoke the Daughters of Beulah who, as agents of mercy, attempt to prevent the fall of sleepers into eternal death. Ironically, however, they precipitate the fall by closing the Gate of the Tongue in a misguided attempt to prevent the spread of the contagion of panic already begun.

For the Daughters of Beulah, a crisis has occurred because, for them, something has been lost that only an external divinity can redress:

> Then those in Great Eternity met in the Council of
> God . . . that one Man
> They call Jesus the Christ & they in him & he in them
> Live in Perfect harmony in Eden the land of life
> Consulting as One Man above the Mountain of Snowdon Sublime
> (E. 310–11, 21:1–7)

This golden world is no more outside of the human than it is temporally prior. The ambassadors from Beulah are "introducd to the divine presence," telling of "Wars of death eternal," which presumably are the events through the first eight Nights. Losing the divine vision, then, occurs perpetually. In this way, the end of Night the First recalls the opening. Here, the splitting of Urthona into the Spectre and Los echoes the fragmentation of Tharmas triggered by his hiding of Jerusalem:

> dividing from his aking bosom fled
> A portion of his life shrieking upon the wind she fled
> And Tharmas took her in pitying Then Enion in jealous fear
> Murderd her & hid her in her bosom embalming her for fear
> She should arise again to life Embalmd in Enions bosom
> Enitharmon remains a corse such thing was never known
> In Eden that one died a death never to be revivd

> Urthona stood in terror but not long his spectre fled
> To Enion & his body fell. Tharmas beheld him fall
> Endlong a raging serpent rolling round the holy tent.
>
> (E. 312, 22:20–29)

The serpent figure, which returns in Night the Seventh as Vala, here represents Urthona without the Spectre, a variation of the circle around the parodic "holy tent" that hides the corpse of Enitharmon. Jerusalem is now regarded as a city, civilization itself, rather than the female form hidden within Enion's tabernacle. Interestingly, Blake substitutes Enion's hiding of Enitharmon for Tharmas's hiding of Jerusalem. The decision to do so is significant on Blake's part, since Jerusalem is constructed by the characters in new ways now that she is "lost."[10] Enion transfers the sexual jealousy to Enitharmon, ironically imitating Tharmas's own gesture that had so infuriated her at the opening of Night the First.

Most surprising in the midst of seeking some narrative principle through this episode, however, is recalling that the ambassadors from Beulah are speaking all this to the Council of God. In other words, they assimilate the narrative voice, but the fact that this is pointedly an inner narrative emphasizes the questionable authenticity of the narrated events. Their conclusion, typically frantic, is not supported by an authorial voice but is rather the result of their own mental state:

> Jerusalem his Emanation is become a ruin
> Her little ones are slain on the top of every street
> And she herself le[d] captive & scatterd into the indefinite
> Gird on thy sword O thou most mighty in glory & majesty
> Destroy these opressors of Jerusalem & those who ruin Shiloh
>
> (E. 312, 19:1–5)

The rhetoric is the charged language of epic. It is crucial to see it as an inner narrative, since what is at stake is not whether the events are *real* but whether they are *true*. They are real in that they are any moment in world history, as the mythical-biblical names suggest. Yet they are not true to the poem's mythos because they exist in time, whereas the whole coexists with the "ruin" and the "indefinite," invulnerable to them.

The effect of the dramatically told story is that the Family Divine drew up

the Universal tent
Above High Snowdon & closd the Messengers in clouds around
Till the time of the End.

(E. 312, 19:7–9)

The caesura here, a rare device in the poem, emphasizes the finality of such
an end, which the poem itself rejects. This is the End conceived by conventional quest poetry, the escape from the fearful "unknown Space / Deep
horrible without End" that the messengers from Beulah describe to the
Family Divine (E. 312, 22:38–39). Until man recognizes his inner link to
divinity, he wanders in a labyrinthian natural world, expecting such an
End to redeem or free him. Illusion though the poem shows this to be,
it is Albion's reality as long as he perceives it as such. Thus, the Lamb of
God

followd the Man
Who wanderd in mount Ephraim seeking a Sepulcher
His inward eyes closing from the Divine vision

(E. 313, 19:12–14)

The second draft of the end of the first Night shows Blake's attempts to
emphasize the ironic futility of the message from Beulah:

The Emanation stood before the Gates of Enitharmon
Weeping. the Daughters of Beulah silent in the Porches
Spread her a couch unknown to Enitharmon here reposed
Jerusalem in slumbers soft lulld into silent rest

(K. 279)

This act follows the pattern established by Tharmas at the opening of Night
the First; but it is more insidious yet, for it professes to be one of salvation.
To emphasize the fact that it merely keeps fallen consciousness from moving toward redemption, or possibly even that it precipitates fallenness itself,
Blake juxtaposes this inertia of inward division with the chaos that Night
the Sixth explores more deeply:

Terrific ragd the Eternal Wheels of intellect terrific ragd
The living creatures of the wheels in the Wars of Eternal life

But perverse rolld the wheels of Urizen & Luvah back reversd
Downwards & outwards consuming in the wars of Eternal Death
(E. 313, 20:12–15)

Night the First ends with a return, like the Ouroboros itself, to the chaos
that surrounds the empty or sleeping center. Eternal life beheld as wheels
rushing uncontrolled from the center is none other than the wars of Eternal Death from which the messengers of Beulah have sought protection
but which, as the poem unfolds, are shown to be the fabrication of a dualistic mind.

Night the First, then, appears to function as a prologue to Night the
Second through Night the Eighth; it introduces the principle of fallen consciousness and ironically patterns the covering gesture of the ministers of
Beulah after the fallen Tharmas's covering of Jerusalem. One might then
ask how the relation between the end of Night the First and the opening of
Night the Second can be described, if it is not a temporally causal one. One
answer is that this opening describes the fall as perpetual or habitual rather
than as a single dramatic moment in a narrative line. This is conveyed
grammatically through the relentless use of gerunds at the critical moment:
"Rising upon his Couch of Death Albion beheld his Sons / Turning his
Eyes outward to Self. losing the Divine Vision" (E. 313, 23:1–2). The connection to Night the First is not temporally sequential. Because all the ac-
tivities occur outside of time, the contagion spreads without a single source
to blame for the disease of fallenness. Albion's accusation of Urizen sounds
uncannily like the accusations that were wielded in Night the First and are
echoed throughout the first eight Nights: "Thy brother Luvah hath smitten me but pity thou his youth / Tho thou hast not pitid my Age" (E. 313,
23:7–8). Albion hands Urizen control of consciousness, aware that Urizen
will abuse his power over the other Zoas. He perpetually chooses Urizen,
not only for the obvious reason that Urizen has energy while he is ener-
vated but, still more subtly, because of the perpetual intervention of the
Daughters of Beulah.

While one reads forward, asking what the causal relation is between
Night the First and what follows directly, namely Albion's turning from
Jerusalem, the point of view of the apocalypse illuminates such incom-
pletely narrated moments. The processes of moving forward in time and
reading retrospectively from Night the Ninth keep the reader engaged in
the dynamic of apprehending experience from the two forces of temporal

logic and of vision, or linear and centric in Arnheim's terms. The poem describes a tension between two concepts of origin: the source of divine vision and the traditional quest for a golden world, in which the preoccupation with finding the source of fallenness as a specific moment in time throws such a paradise "downwards and outwards." Fallen consciousness remains caught in the Wars of Eternal life while vision transpires at the center regardless of the chaos of fallen consciousness.

When the poem is read from beginning to end, then, it appears as a sequence of the characters' self-proclaimed epiphanies of causality, one supplanting the next. Yet when one reaches Night the Ninth, the apocalypse does not call the reader back to the poem's beginning for a historical moment of origination, but rather reverses time in an eternal birth. The search for causality in time is a blindness of fallen consciousness. Edward Said's definition of beginnings helps to describe Blake's representation of origination:

> With regard to what precedes it, a beginning represents . . . a discontinuity. . . . What are the conditions that allow us to call something a beginning? First of all, there must be the desire, the will, and the true freedom to reverse oneself, to accept thereby the risks of rupture and discontinuity; for whether one looks to see where and when he began, or whether he looks in order to begin now, he cannot continue as he is. (1975, 34)

To adapt such a statement to the poem, however, one would have to add the crucial point that Blake's mythos emerges whole from the discontinuity. This means that, according to the dream vision that frames the poem, knowledge must be experienced rather than merely comprehended discursively. Through memory, fallen consciousness constantly modifies eternity so that the fictions of fallenness continuously replace one another.

Albion's revelation, in Night the Ninth, of the nondual nature of divinity parallels and redeems not only Tharmas's assumed covering of Jerusalem but also Albion's own fallen gesture introduced in Night the Second. There, he beholds a deathly universe by turning his eyes outward: "Rising upon his Couch of Death Albion beheld his Sons / Turning his Eyes outward to Self. losing the Divine Vision." In traditional terms, this is a curious opening for the second section of the poem, since the first did not introduce Albion on a Couch of Death surrounded by Sons. Blake's manuscript revisions regarding the relationship of the first two Nights are key here.[11] By adding the present Night the First to what was originally the opening, now Night the Second, Blake problematizes the assumption of temporal sequence, challenging likewise its implicit assumption of causality. Albion has been on a Couch of Death throughout the rift between Tharmas and Enion, yet in a sense, because of the placement of this critical moment after Night the First, it suggests that Tharmas's hiding of Jerusalem has culminated in Albion's deathly state. The relation of the two gestures, covering and turning the eyes outward and so losing the divine vision, are associated even as the narrative challenges the attempt to connect them causally.

In the introduction to his facsimile edition of *Vala*, Margoliouth discusses the editorial difficulty of relating Night the First and Night the Second:

> The Nights were to be nights of Dream. Whose dream? Man's, the Eternal Man's: and it does not clearly begin until the present Night II, which helps to explain why that was once Night I. (1956, xvi)

This description does not answer the question of why Blake substituted the present Night the First for what is now Night the Second. Blake actually undoes the linearity of the present Night the Second by beginning the epic instead with what reads more as a parody of epic beginning and narrative continuity. To return to Huizinga and Gadamer, Blake's interest is in the play element that is both nondual and nonlinear.

An example of this subversion of traditional causality is found in the next episode. Luvah, imprisoned in Urizen's furnaces, says of Vala:

> And I commanded the Great deep to hide her in his hand
> Till she became a little sleeping Infant a span long
> I carried her in my bosom as a man carries a lamb
> I loved her I gave her all my soul & my delight
> I hid her in soft gardens & in secret bowers of Summer
> Weaving mazes of delight along the Sunny Paradise
> Inextricable labyrinths, She bore me sons & daughters
> (E. 317, 27:1–7)

Luvah's feeling of betrayal here echoes Tharmas's hiding of Jerusalem in Night the First. In Night the Ninth, this sense of separation is shown to be the distorting tendency of the fallen mind, not only from the perspective of Albion's discovery of the interiority of the divine but from that of Vala's

revelation that the world and the Lord that she has projected outside herself, and from which she felt separate, are actually her Self. The poem shows
that the notion of an inextricable labyrinth is a creation of the bound mind,
just as the power to hide that which is already part of the Self is a mental
creation.

Luvah's self-defense would apparently attest to the "times of innocence
& youth" that Vala, imprisoning him now, has forgotten. Yet Luvah betrays
his own participation in the fall, namely the covering or hiding that was
introduced as Tharmas's primary gesture as "parent power" of human limitation. Now, indeed, Luvah seems to be serving a punishment that fits his
own crime against Vala:

> They have surrounded me with walls of iron & brass, O Lamb
> Of God clothed in Luvahs garments little knowest thou
> Of death Eternal that we all go to Eternal Death
> To our Primeval Chaos in fortuitous concourse of incoherent
> Discordant principles of Love & Hate I suffer affliction
> Because I love
>
> (E. 318, 27:9–14)

Luvah claims that he is a victim because of his love. He separates himself
from the "Lamb of God," a figure that embodies the divine, because, he
claims, he is vulnerable to that which the Lamb is not. The incoherence is
the creation of his own contracted state, however, which becomes clearer as
the authorial voice emerges from behind Luvah's pathos. Following Luvah's
words, "O Urizen my enemy I weep for thy stern ambition / But weep in
vain O when will you return Vala the Wanderer," is the narrator's ironic
assessment: "These were the words of Luvah patient in afflictions / Reasoning from the loins in the unreal forms of Ulros night" (E. 318, 27:19–22).

Luvah's testimony-confession follows the building of the Mundane Shell.
His covering of Vala proleptically repeats the covering of Jerusalem, which,
in turn, follows and suggests a causal relation with the problem of perception that accompanies the completion of the Mundane Shell:

> Reuben slept on Penmaenmawr & Levi slept on Snowden
> Their eyes their ears their nostrils & tongues roll outward   they behold
> What is within they behold now seen without
>
> (E. 314, 25:21–23)

Night the Second opened with Albion turning his Eyes outward to Self and losing the divine vision. The completion of the Mundane Shell literalizes this gesture, suggesting that to behold the natural as separate from the self is an illusion.

The poem does not make explicit causal connections but suggests them through repetition, whether prolepsis or echo; it is never clear which is the main event and which refers to it. Thus, in another refusal to engage in grammatical subordination, the poem describes the ages of torment following Luvah's imprisonment:

> With trembling horror pale aghast the Children of Man
> Stood on the infinite Earth & saw these visions in the air.
> In waters & in Earth beneath they cried to one another
> What are we terrors to one another Come O brethren wherefore
> Was this wide Earth spread all abroad. not for wild beasts to roam
> But many stood silent & busied in their families
> And many said We see no Visions in the darksom air
>
> (E. 318, 28:11–17)

The statement echoes Albion turning eyes "outward to Self. losing the Divine Vision" and Reuben and Levi, who later "behold / what is within now seen without" a "dark Land" (E. 314, 25:21–25).

History seemingly moves forward in a sequence of self-fulfilling prophecies. Those who see no visions become "Others" (those who experience otherness), living out their visionlessness by building Ulro: "Others arose & schools Erected forming Instruments / To measure out the course of heaven" (E. 318, 28:20–21). The separation and opposition of Luvah and Urizen here suggest the difference between dualistic antithesis and what is equipoise in redeemed vision. The parts must be described in terms of the whole and vice versa, but beyond the veil of dualism one beholds the very principle of the superimposition of fallenness and redemption, of fragmentation and wholeness.

The Mundane Shell is the result of Urizen's ordering of perceived chaos. It is important that this genesis does not open the poem, but rather follows the causal relation set up at the opening of Night the Second between Albion turning his eyes outward and his beholding a dark, dismal world of nonentity: "Rising upon his Couch of Death Albion beheld his Sons / Turning his Eyes outward to Self. losing the Divine Vision" (E. 313, 23:1–2). As the gerunds suggest, this description reenacts rather than follows sequentially the episode between Tharmas and Enion.

The reaction of building a world of physical light and geometric order is the genesis of dualism associated with the gesture of covering:

> While far into the vast unknown, the strong wing'd eagles bend
> Their venturous flight, in Human forms distinct; thro darkness deep
> They bear the woven draperies; on golden hooks they hang abroad
> The universal curtains. . . .
>
> (E. 319, 29:8–11)

This too is a gesture repeated from the building of a tabernacle for Jerusalem in Night the First. The fabric of the universe becomes an ensnaring net binding and "condensing the strong energies into little compass" (30:5). The image of contraction is essential to Blake's nondualistic conception of the relationship of fallenness and redemption, suggesting further the paradox that controlling apparent chaos has dire consequences.[12]

The building of the Mundane Shell has a powerful effect on Ahania, echoing the motif of the female caught in "Labyrinthine porches" that had been introduced by Tharmas in his original covering of Jerusalem. Now, the effect of entrapment is compounded through the ritualistic worship of an absent God:

> His Shadowy feminine Semblance here reposed . . .
> Or hoverd oer his Starry head . . .
> . . . & when he turnd his back
> Upon the Golden hall & sought the Labyrinthine porches
> Of his wide heaven Trembling, cold in paling fears she sat
> A Shadow of Despair therefore toward the West Urizen formd
> A recess in the wall for fires to glow upon the pale
> Females limbs in his absence
>
> (E. 319–20, 30:23–31)

Urizen's altar in the labyrinth of the Mundane Shell parodically and proleptically echoes the redeemed recognition of the sacred center embodied by Jerusalem in Night the Ninth. Urizen creates the altar as an image of himself to comfort Ahania as he pursues his epic explorations of his dens. This parodies as well Vala's seeking her "Lord" Luvah at the point of epiphany in Night the Ninth, in which she recognizes that it is her own voice she has heard as God, and so lifts the veil of dualism between self and other and human and divine.

Mystery, Urizenic religion, is thus the parodic inversion of recognized divinity. Urizen is Nobodaddy, the absent God who commands worship through ritualistic self-denial, the very opposite of wholeness at the apocalypse.

If, according to the premise here, the poem represents the interplay of fallenness as the illusion of dualism and redemption as wholeness, how is such a distinction different from dualism itself? How can one avoid a reduction of this relation between fallenness and redemption to antithetical terms? The answer lies in the containment of each within the other, the hermeneutic circle that for Blake is the Ouroboros that is transformed, with a trick of the eye, to the quincunx or mandala.[13] In other words, it transposes the construct of the whole and its parts to the whole and its center; the whole never attempts to blend its parts but is rather held in equipoise by the center.

Here in Night the Second, Ahania "covers" Urizen, "folding him around/ In bright skirts." This echoes Los and Enitharmon in Night the First: "two wills they had. . . . / [Urizen] drave the Male Spirits all away from Ahania / And she drave all the Females from him away" (E. 320, 30:47–52). In spite of the fallen Urizen's role as tyrannical god, it is crucial to observe that he is not portrayed as the embodiment of pure evil, but rather as operating from the contracted awareness of the senses. He perceives what is happening to him and by him, but does not consider how to reverse the fragmentation: "This Urizen perceivd & silent brooded in darkning Clouds / To him his Labour was but Sorrow & his Kingdom was Repentance" (E. 320, 30:49–50).

Urizen does not consider praying to a higher power, since he has proclaimed himself God. It is Vala who appears in order to plead for salvation: "O Lord wilt thou not look upon our sore afflictions / Among these flames incessant labouring" (E. 320, 31:4–5). What Lord is she praying to? Clearly she has accepted Urizen as God, though the poem presents their relationship of master-slave in contradistinction to that of the Daughters of Beulah and the Council of Heaven. From the perspective of Night the Ninth, both versions of God are flawed, though antithetical to each other. The Daughters of Beulah behold God as distinct from humanity, and one fragment worships the other without perceiving the whole. What both lack is the wholeness that dispels duality. Again, the authorial voice ironically takes on Vala's perspective, referring to Urizen as "King of Light" while he has just recognized his own very human helplessness at what he perceives to be his fallen labor.

The echoing chain of responses is "in vain." Each acts out his part in the fall, lamenting futilely; most enigmatic is Luvah's urge to act out of love, useless now without Vala's understanding: "[I]n vain his love / Brought him in various forms before her still she knew him not" (E. 321, 31:18– 19). We do not know until Night the Ninth what Vala's right understanding of Luvah is. Here, no matter how many forms he takes, she does not "know" him because she does not even know her present state. She describes it as slavery, the consequence of a tyrannical god:

> The times are now returnd upon us, we have given ourselves
> To scorn and now are scorned by the slaves of our enemies . . .
> Furrowd with whips . . .
> Forgive us O thou piteous one whom we have offended
> (E. 321, 31:11–15)

Vala continues to see herself as separate from Luvah: "Still she despisd him, calling on his name & knowing him not / Still hating still professing love, still labouring in the smoke" (E. 321, 32:1–2). In Night the Ninth, when Vala calls Luvah's name, her own voice echoes back. At this point she understands that there is no difference between inner and outer realms; Luvah is present in herself and is of herself.

Curiously, in the midst of the completion of the "Golden World" of the Mundane Shell, "The heavens were closd and spirits mournd their bondage night and day / and the Divine Vision appeard in Luvahs robes of blood" (E. 321, 32:13–14). As the sons of Urizen "beheld Heaven walled round," Urizen "comforted saw / The wondrous work flow forth like visible out of the invisible" (E. 321, 33:10). By this point in Night the Second, this is seen again to echo Albion turning his eyes outward and losing the divine vision, for Urizen has created an illusory fortress against illusory Non Entity. It immediately follows, therefore, that the divine vision, embodied in Christ, permits the illusion of fallenness as the paradoxical means toward reintegration:

For the Divine Lamb Even Jesus who is the Divine Vision
Permitted all lest Man should fall into Eternal Death
For when Luvah sunk down himself put on the robes of blood
Lest the state calld Luvah should cease. & the Divine Vision
Walked in robes of blood till he who slept should awake
                                            (E. 321, 33:11–15)

In contrast to the agency of the Daughters of Beulah, the divine vision
permits the fragmentation, since it is paradoxically through movement that
one discovers that which is unchanging.

Through Urizen's acting out his dualistic fantasies in the building of
the Mundane Shell, he must confront his own fear most dramatically. Paradoxically, godhead is detached. In this sense, the Council of God is not
illusory, but the fact that it is within the consciousness of Albion implies
that the detached godhead is also an innate capacity of the human.

The creation of the golden chain follows the building of the Mundane
Shell, though whether it is an antithetical architecture to the Mundane
Shell or an outgrowth of it is unclear. It appears to be both, as so much
repetition in the poem is both parody and echo. Blake's irony allows the
capacity for redemption in the fallen. The golden chain is a consequence of
the Mundane Shell, even as the golden chain appears to redeem it. In fact,
however, it is a further complication of the dualistic universe. Urizen's fear
deepens as the universe is spatialized, while the plotting of Los and
Enitharmon intensifies as they irreverently treat the Miltonic universe as a
boundless playground:

For Los & Enitharmon walkd forth on the dewy Earth
Contracting or expanding their all flexible senses
At will to murmur in the flowers small as the honey bee
At will to stretch across the heavens & step from star to star.
                                            (E. 322, 34:9–12)

They make stepping stones of the golden chain of stars, earlier described as
a manifestation of the compassion of the Divine Vision.

Enitharmon's song following the "death" of Los is a rhapsody celebrating her newfound power: "The joy of woman is the Death of her most best
beloved / Who dies for Love of her. . . ." (E. 324, 34:62–63). It distorts as
it foreshadows Vala's song in Night the Ninth, in which her recognition of

Luvah as part of herself signals the transcendence of separation and the breaking of the illusion that love means losing oneself in another. Yet even as Enitharmon's song is parodic of Vala's, it glimpses and therefore foreshadows the divinity Vala uncovers:

> The fading cry is ever dying
> The living voice is ever living in its inmost joy
>
> Arise you little glancing wings & sing your infant joy
> Arise & drink your bliss
> For every thing that lives is holy for the source of life
> Descends to be a weeping babe
>
> (E. 324, 34:75–80)

It glimpses the absolute understanding of Night the Ninth that consciousness contracts to form the human. Yet without transition, it plummets back into dualistic delusion:

> I faint beneath these beams of thine
> For thou hast touchd my five senses & they answerd thee
> Now I am nothing & I sink
> And on the bed of silence sleep till thou awakest me
>
> (E. 324, 34:89–92)

Clearly, without an understanding of the oneness of subject and object, Enitharmon quickly "loses the divine vision," thus repeating again the principle of fallenness in her own variation.

Los, participating in this version of otherness, sends Enion and Ahania into Non Entity. Characteristically, Ahania experiences the fear that Enion's manifestation of the vacuum creates:

> Thus livd Los driving Enion far into the deathful infinite
> That he may also draw Ahania's spirit into her Vortex
> Ah happy blindness Enion sees not the terrors of the uncertain
> Thus Enion wails from the dark deep, the golden heavens tremble
>
> (E. 324, 34:97–100)

Enion here represents the power to transform the perceived world through the mind's uncertainty. In this way another difference between the fallen and redeemed is the difference between uncertainty and the conviction that results from epiphany.

Though Enion does not experience the "terrors of the uncertain," she experiences the defeat of the fallen world of toil. As opposed to Los and Enitharmon, who plunder the universe "at will" (E. 322, 34:11, 12), Enion feels victimized by her own participation in the fallen world: "I am made to sow the thistle for wheat; the nettle for a nourishing dainty / I have planted a false oath in the earth, it has brought forth a poison tree" (E. 324–25, 35:1–2). Enion's voice hearkens back to the aphoristic speakers of the *Songs of Experience,* yet her more complex character deepens the implications of the voice of experience, for she perceives herself as innocent victim to the fallen world even as she has participated in its creation:

> What is the price of Experience do men buy it for a song
> Or wisdom for a dance in the street? No it is bought with the price
> Of all that a man hath
>
> (E. 325, 35:11–13)

The rhetorical question parodically foreshadows Urizen's epiphanic "Where shall we take our stand" in Eternity in Night the Ninth because it comes of wrong understanding: the price of experience is not the issue when one considers that she means loss of prior innocence. From the hindsight of Night the Ninth, divine vision permits experience to bring consciousness toward that which it already always is—organized innocence.

At this point, however, Enion does not have the perspective of organized innocence. For this reason, her lament for the ease of the unfallen world distorts the pastoral vision at the end of Night the Ninth:

> To see a god on every wind & a blessing on every blast
> To hear sounds of love in the thunder storm that destroys our enemies
>   house
> To rejoice in the blight that covers his field
>
> (E. 325, 36:5–7)

As with Enitharmon's abrupt pivoting from joy to terror, Enion's lament contains the germ of redemption in a phrase like it is easy "to see a god on every wind," since this becomes true of Vala in Night the Ninth. Nevertheless, Enion's lament points to the disparity between the fallen characters' vision of innocence and Blake's portrayal of organized innocence in Night the Ninth.

Enion's lament thus reveals the limitation of the fallen state: although seeing God in the suffering of others might appear as the authorial voice speaking out against injustice through Enion, in this context it betrays Enion's limited understanding of human suffering and conflict. From the perspective of Night the Ninth, her bitter lament, "It is an easy thing to rejoice in the tents of prosperity / Thus could I sing & thus rejoice, but it is not so with me!" (E. 325, 36:12–13) perpetuates the dualism of the fallen state. By Night the Ninth, the very notion of enemies, slaves, and soldiers as separate entities dissolves. The effect of Enion's lament, indeed, is a vibration that sends Ahania to "the margin of Non Entity," ending Night the Second with the dire consequence of otherness: the perceived absence of the Self.

CHAPTER III

Prophecies, Visions, and Memories:
Fictions as Mental Contraction

AS CHAPTER 2 HAS DISCUSSED, the frame story of a conventional dream vision is set in the persona's waking life, allowing the reader to maintain a wakefully discursive distance from the dream. The unreal elements of the dream are thereby mediated for the reader by this frame of a solid reality. By contrast, Blake's departure from the traditional dream vision turns the dream inside out so that the waking life of the fallen world is the dream of a formless consciousness: consequently, the reader is thrown into the dream without footing in the familiar.* Blake's implicit frame of an undifferentiated consciousness is a vehicle for representing the atemporal relation of the fallen and redeemed states, and more technically, for superimposing the centric eternal onto the worldly matrix of space and time.

The present chapter takes up the narrative problems of the voicelessness of this elusive stage manager, consciousness. *The Four Zoas* redistributes the authorial voice so that it is not in the sole power of an objectified narrator. Instead, the speaking and acting figures of the poem form a collectively distorted mythology through their memories, visions, and prophecies. The inner narratives, which tell conflicting versions of the origin of the fallen state and its outcome, establish an embedded and therefore qualified level of narrative within Albion's dream that is, in turn, within the outermost dream being staged by a consciousness free of voice and history.[1] By exploring the relation of the embedded narrative to the poem's narrator, this chapter addresses the problem of how the authorial voice can be gleaned from the conflicting versions by these self-proclaimed authorities of what has been, what is, and what will be.

Chapter 2 has explored the poem's quest for the origin of the fallen world through the relation between the epiphany in Night the Ninth of "the infinite and unbounded" and the development of the dualistic universe in Night the Second through the building of the Mundane Shell. Complicating the poem's spatial representation of the contraction of consciousness is the temporal matrix of mental contraction manifested in the inner narratives. Hayden White's study of "narrativity" has significant implications for Blake's intricate embedding of narrative. White suggests that "the cultural function of narrativizing discourse [is] an intimation of the psychological impulse behind the apparently universal need not only to narrate but to give events an aspect of narrativity" (1987, 4). The figures of *The Four Zoas* play out their collective mythology in a sequence of episodes. This "bloody chain of nights & days" temporalizes and thereby parodies the golden chain that "bind[s] the Body of Man to heaven from falling into the Abyss." At the poem's structural middle is the nadir of this bloody sequence: Out of the projections of Los as the fallen "prophet of Eternity" and Los-Urthona's building of the universe of Death emerge the Limits of Opacity and Contraction, forming the parallel in temporal architecture to Urizen's building of the Mundane Shell. The present chapter explores the ways that such a nadir at the poem's structural or "linear" center stands in contrast to the "centric" center of the poem as labyrinth, namely Night the Ninth.

If one takes the premise that, from the perspective of undifferentiated consciousness, there is no beginning or end to fallenness, then it follows that a history of the fallen world with a beginning, a middle, and an end is a fiction, real as it may become for those who act out what they conceive to have already taken place. This forms the contraction of the infinite into time. The reader, trained to seek out a coherent story line, attempts to derive such a fiction of the fall through the versions told by various characters. Yet such a reader is left with inconsistencies and loose ends that are often dismissed through the interpretive deus ex machina of the unfinished state of the text.

In her discussion of the unreliability of the narrator, Helen McNeil asks, "If action and causality are distorted in *The Four Zoas*, can the poem be said to have a history?" (1970, 389). McNeil attempts to piece "history" together through evidence from the different accounts:

> The variety of true, untrue, and ironic histories proposed by the Zoas makes even the reader armed with a knowledge of *Milton* and *Jerusalem* fear that no one story will ever triumph over any other. Since *The Four Zoas* is an epic of situations with only the most perfunctory exposition, the reader is tempted to believe that the "true" account, the one he should believe, is simply situational truth, as it is presented at any given point. . . . Eventually a fairly reliable history of the Zoas' fall and recovery can be patched together, but not before the reader has been tricked into believing a dozen false ones. (389–90)

Though this speculation raises important issues concerning the unreliability of the narrator, it is not clear how a true account can be gleaned from the conflicting reports and, more significantly, how any can be privileged as "true" as opposed to false or, even more ambiguously, ironic.

In spite of his claim to "re-vision" *The Four Zoas*, Ault similarly does not allow for an authorial voice, asserting instead that the reader maintains "a state of failed imaginative judgment" (1986, 128). Contending that there is no wholeness to the text, Ault opposes the unified vision of "Newtonian narrative" to Blake's fragmented narrative structures:

> In the poem Blake experiments with creating a text that cannot sustain its authentic existence independent of and prior to the narrative world in the process of being constituted through sequential acts of reading, thereby creating a reader whose perception is able to alter the very being of the text's supposedly fixed facts and devising a narrative world that, although it comes into existence temporally through the mutual interconstitution of reader and text, functions as the primary agent by which the reader and text are able to transform one another mutually. (109)

Though this accurately describes the characters as readers of each other's fictions in the first eight Nights of the poem, what of Night the Ninth? There, the disjointed narratives and narrative interruptions are replaced by a sequence of epiphanies that depend one upon the other and, in turn, radically revise the narrative problems of the first eight Nights. The broken

narrative form of the first eight Nights needs to be distinguished from the
wholly different narratology of Night the Ninth, whose revelations not only
depend one upon the other but in turn reread the fragmentation of the
earlier Nights. The limitation of Ault's approach, by contrast, is its absolute
duality: according to Ault, narrative either subscribes to Newtonian unity,
which one easily agrees Blake does not, or it has no center and is therefore
fragmented.

The complexity of Blake's narrative method lies in its representation of
wholeness as intrinsic to the same consciousness that loses sight of its own
integrity in its fallen state. Norman Wacker's treatment of Blake's revision
of epic is useful in describing Blake's narrative principle. Wacker compares
the traditional neoclassical unities with Blake's notion of unity:

> For Blake [neoclassical Aristotelianism] is a fallacious kind of unity asso-
> ciated with the enforced formal closure of the classics and of mathemati-
> cal or rational conceptions of form. . . . In reflecting on the possibilities of
> new forms of unity inherent in the destabilization of formal closure, Blake
> returns the neo-classical reification of unity and epic practice to a sense of
> living forms derived from particular characters, i.e., from a composition's
> particulars rather than genre conventions or pre-existing models. (1990,
> 128)

One needs to suspend neoclassical choices such as unity versus chaos in
order to describe Blake's mythos accurately.

Taking the premise that the narrator does not represent authorial consciousness, one begins to see a design behind assigning the poem's storytelling
to a narrator who defers to the conflicting memories and forecasts of the
fallen characters.[2] In such a refusal to mediate between the inner narratives
and the reader, the authorial voice represents the intricate relationship between such fictions and the liberation from "progression" into which such
"Contraries" dissolve at the apocalypse. Thus, the statement from *The
Marriage of Heaven and Hell*, "Without Contraries is no progression," is
often cited as evidence for Blake's dialectical depiction of history (E. 34,
pl.3). One critic, arguing for a dialectical reading of Blake's myth, states
that Blake "finally learned to apply to paradise itself the central principle by
which he analyzed human history: 'Without contraries is no progression'.
. . . Blake reformulated the notion of paradise so that it allows for an alter-
nation of states, inspiration and recuperation. . . ." (Cantor 1984, 68).

Here, by contrast, the aphorism is taken as the limited perception of fallen understanding that does not regard the ever still Self underlying the world of change.

Blake establishes his peculiar brand of irony in *The Four Zoas* by providing a narrator who refuses to take command of a narrative that promises to tell the story of the fall of humanity. This narrative irony suggests, as chapter 2 has argued, that the fallen state is one which perpetuates itself in spite of an ever present state of redemption. Chapter 3 explores the narrative phenomenon in which the story of the fall is relegated to the storytelling characters. By so de-authorizing the words of the narrator, Blake effectively takes out of the narrator's hands his own paradoxical mythos of the fallen state as the contraction of undifferentiated consciousness. The effect of the subversion of the narrator's authority from the poem's outset, with its sequence of false starts, is a series of erasures of one elevated beginning by a lesser one. The epic beginning is thus successively deflated until a story of the fall of humanity apparently unfolds not with an act in time but rather by instituting a pattern of behavior with the quarrel between Tharmas and Enion.

Crucial to the developing usurpation of the narrative line is the conversation between Ahania and Urizen that opens Night the Third. It complicates the pattern of domestic behavior instituted by Tharmas and Enion at the opening of Night the First, in which the inception of the fallen state paradoxically associates a fear of separation with casting out an "other." Ahania's vision immediately follows the end of Night the Second, in which Urizen simultaneously casts and casts out the physical world in the form of the Mundane Shell. This sequence, from the projection of a dualistic universe to Ahania's myth of its inception and its historical outcome, forms a crucial link in the chain of episodes leading to Los's creation of a world of Death, a movement that traces the contraction of consciousness even as the characters seek causal explanations behind the movement from one event to another.

Ahania's "vision" in Night the Third taps into the narrative voice by claiming authority as to the cause of the fall.[3] She locates a moment in which, she claims, Luvah has usurped Urizen's power. At the center of this "vision," Ahania's version of Albion tells Vala, "I am nothing when I enter into judgment with thee / If thou withdraw thy breath I die & vanish into Hades," a statement that, parodic of the center of the revelations of Night the Ninth, ironically foretells what Urizen is about to do to her, namely withdraw part of himself—Ahania as his emanation—by casting her into his created hell (E. 327, 40:13–14). This is not mere foreshadowing, but rather a perversely self-fulfilling prophecy, since Ahania suggests to Urizen not only reasons for his jealousy—and, in so doing, exacerbates his fallen fear of separation—but also ways for Urizen to "punish" her and so further complicate the dualistic universe. By extension, it describes the pattern of behavior that could apply to any of the domestic antagonists, beginning in the poem with the anxious sense of separation that Tharmas and Enion invoke in their quarrel. From the point of view of Night the Ninth, the notion of the limited self—the character "Urizen" who has a distinct identity from Ahania, for instance—dissolves in an ecstatic liberation. At the apocalypse, this limited self that was threatened by the externalized world is discovered to be the same Self as that which it has projected as Other.[4]

In Night the Third, Ahania's vision, fictional though it may be, is characterized from the beginning by its uncanny though distorted forecast of the apocalypse. She tells Urizen to "leave all futurity" to Albion or "the Eternal one," an unwitting description of Night the Ninth, since only in conjunction with Albion's emerging from the sleep of death can Urizen realize the error of confusing eternity with futurity, and only then can he leave his fallen fear of futurity for the wholeness of Albion he is a part of in eternity.

However, here in Night the Third, "vision" is far from revelation, and so confusion and fragmentation spiral in Ahania's attempt to fix blame for and a date on the fall of humanity from the apparently "obliterated" Divine Vision:

Why didst thou listen to the voice of Luvah that dread morn
To give the immortal steeds of light to his deceitful hands
No longer now obedient to thy will thou art compell'd
To forge the curbs of iron & brass to build the iron mangers
To feed them with intoxication from the wine presses of Luvah
Till the Divine Vision & Fruition is quite obliterated
                                                        (E. 326–27, 39:2–7)

Ahania speaks of Urizen giving up his power to Luvah on "that dread morn," thus isolating a moment and elevating it to the mythical level of the fall. It is crucial to note that the text itself never authorizes such a privileged moment.

In fact, Luvah's usurpation of Urizen's power is problematized upon its introduction in Night the First, in which it is embedded in Enitharmon's "Song of Death" to Los:

> The Fallen Man takes his repose: Urizen sleeps in the porch
> Luvah and Vala woke & flew up from the Human Heart
> Into the Brain; from thence upon the pillow Vala slumber'd.
> And Luvah siez'd the Horses of Light, & rose into the Chariot of Day
> (E. 305, 10:10–13)

Enitharmon's use of the simple present tense in her introduction to the narrative is crucial in the same way the series of gerunds that opens Night the Second is: "Rising upon his Couch of Death Albion beheld his Sons / Turning his Eyes outward to Self. losing the Divine Vision" (E. 313, 23:1–2). Luvah's usurpation is represented as a perpetual tendency rather than an act in time. Underscoring the poem's antilinearity is the narration in present tense of this act in the apparently historical past. Like Eno's song at the poem's outset of an event that has not yet taken place, the device disorients the reader seeking temporal linearity.

Urizen's "sleep" in Enitharmon's song stands in stark contrast to Albion's sleep and the sleep that gives rise to the poem's dream. Kathleen Raine's humorous point regarding the national hero's tendency to fall asleep is a fitting description of these inner narratives, in which the hero's power is snatched away while his eyes are closed.[5] To reinforce this effect of calling into question the narrative's authenticity as a historical pinpointing of the fall, it is also important to note that the context of its telling is highly polemical. Enitharmon wants to frighten Los through her Song of Death, another instance of the contrast between the fallen mythmaking that is motivated by dualism and the poem's mythos that subsumes it.

If the context of the narrator's own elusiveness is not enough, Los's response to Enitharmon immediately throws the authenticity of Enitharmon's tale into question:

> He answer'd, darkning more with indignation hid in smiles

> I die not Enitharmon tho thou singst thy Song of Death
> Nor shalt thou me torment For I behold the Fallen Man

Seeking to comfort Vala, she will not be comforted
She rises from his throne and seeks the shadows of her garden
(E. 306, 11:4–8)

Los's response is too insidious to be called the righteous indignation of the prophet of vision. From the perspective of Night the Ninth, though, it is clear that Los here proleptically, if not prophetically, describes the moment in Night the Ninth leading to Vala's epiphany. His "forecast" is flawed because he cannot see that she will be comforted by a knowledge neither he nor Vala herself can know through the bound mind, namely that the "shadows" she seeks are the projections of her own light. At this point in Night the First, the contagion of fearful possessiveness infects the poem's cosmos. Tharmas and Enion introduce the domestic context while Eno, who sings of an event that has not yet taken place, introduces narrative embeddedness.

Enitharmon's Song of Death in Night the First thus anticipates Ahania's "vision" in its contribution to self-fulfilling prophecy. This foreshadowing is crucial in its subversion of the apparent hero, Los, the "fierce prophetic boy" introduced at the opening of the poem as the potential hero but upstaged by the quarrel between Tharmas and Enion (E. 305, 9:35). As though this scene of domestic strife is the more revealing link to introducing Los than the promise at the outset that he is the epic hero, the poem only returns to him when his prophetic role is charged with irony in the context of the banal quarrel with Enitharmon. His first prophecy is upstaged by Enitharmon who, with a rhetorical question, answers what should be the rhetorically unanswerable prophetic voice of Los: "[W]ilt thou slay with death him who devotes himself to thee" (E. 306, 10:24).

As opposed to Urizen's violent response to Ahania's "vision" in Night the Third, Los's reaction, "indignation hid in smiles," is less directly threatening. It recalls the insidious impulse of hiding or covering that begins with Tharmas when he hides Jerusalem in the name of pity. Here, the antagonism is cloaked by a smile.[6] The immediate narrative effect, though, is that the interaction deflates Los's prophetic power. His response to Enitharmon is closer to that of the taunting child who has powers dangerously disproportionate to his ignorance: "I die not Enitharmon tho thou singst thy song of Death." He foresees the destruction of Ulro:

. . . I see the invisible knife
I see the shower of blood: I see the swords & spears of futurity

Tho in the Brain of man we live, & in his circling Nerves.
Tho' this bright world of all our joy is in the human Brain.
(E. 306, 11:13–16)

This introduction of Los immediately defines the relation of prophecy and fulfillment as self-willed, just as Enion's casting destiny out in her own created "tabernacle" underscores the self-fulfillment of prophecy. Los cannot foresee the apocalypse of Night the Ninth beyond the destruction of Ulro because it requires the power of insight rather than foresight, vision rather than anxious anticipation.

In contrast to the dramatic irony of Los's prophecy in Night the First, in which he simply cannot see beyond Ulro, Ahania intentionally distorts her vision in Night the Third. Blake suggests this distortion by framing the vision with the conversation between Ahania and Urizen, thus paralleling her relationship with Urizen to the one she describes between Vala and Albion. The effect is that the reader, hoping for narrative coherence, learns more about the teller of the tale than about the characters and situation of her narrative.

One recognizes, for instance, the panic that betrays Urizen behind Albion's emotional dependence on the shadowy Vala. Like Urizen, he clings to fixed values to ensure longevity. Such a notion of immortality stands in contrast to the nondual state of eternity realized in Night the Ninth. In Ahania's narration, Albion says:

O I am nothing when I enter into judgment with thee
If thou withdraw thy breath I die & vanish into Hades
If thou dost lay thine hand upon me behold I am silent . . .
O I am nothing & to nothing must return again
(E. 327, 40:13–16)

In contrast to the tradition of the biblical fall and punishment, Ahania's version is wrought with domestic manipulation, revealing more about her preoccupations with Urizen as a mate than it does about the mythical fall of which reader and figures alike quest through the labyrinthian poem for authentication.

Narrative anarchy results from the blurring of boundaries between the episode in which Ahania is a character and the inner story she narrates. For instance, one thinks that the phrase "the shadowy voice was silent" must refer to Ahania, but a closer look shows that it is Ahania's shadowy voice describing Albion's "shadowy voice" (E. 327, 40:19) In effect, she is a character blinded by the fallen world in which she participates, yet she momentarily attains authority rivaling that of a third-person narrator.

Ahania's diction, in fact, borrows liberally from the narrator's. In the frame to the vision, the narrator describes Urizen and Ahania in elevated language: "Now sat the King of Light on high upon his starry throne / and bright Ahania bow'd herself before his splendid feet" (E. 326, 37:1–2). Echoing this, Ahania describes her "bright hair" wet by her tears, and Urizen addresses her as "bright." The effect of Ahania's borrowing deflates the narrator's dazzling description of the two. The distortion not only of Ahania's use but of the narrator's is clear from the hindsight of Ahania's resurrection in Night the Ninth. There, "bright Ahania took her seat by Urizen in songs & joy." She is restored to an equal status to Urizen, sitting beside him rather than kneeling before him (E. 395, 125:35). By contrast, Ahania's assurance here that Urizen has nothing to fear subjects the elevated language of the narrator to further irony through the use of rhetorical questions: "Why sighs my Lord! are not the morning stars thy obedient sons / Do they not bow their bright heads at thy voice?" (E. 326, 37:5–6).

Ahania's description of her story of Albion and Vala as "Divine Vision" is most clearly a distortion of the divine vision of Night the Ninth when she concludes, "Prophetic dreads urge me to speak. futurity is before me / Like a dark lamp. Eternal death haunts all my expectation" (E. 327–28, 41:7–8). The vision is self-fulfilling. Her forecast fills Urizen with dread, who sends her plummeting through space "Saying Art thou also become like Vala. thus I cast thee out. . . . Wherefore hast thou taken that fair form / Whence is this power given to thee!" (E. 328–29, 43:5, 11–12). The power is self-begotten: One might respond that Ahania has created a portrait of Vala that Urizen has ironically mistaken for a "real" woman in the sense in which the dualistic mind figures the real as other and the other as real, as outside the limited self and therefore a threat to that limited self. Urizen literally paves the way for his own descent when he casts out Ahania as a literalized fallen emanation.

The effect of Ahania's embedded narrative, then, is to steal from a narrator vulnerable to the suppositions of fallen consciousness some of the ostensible story line and surface logic that accumulate along the forward-moving matrix. By complicating in this way the titanic proportions the narrator keeps attempting to set up for the Zoas, the authorial voice has more flexibility relating the redeemed state to the fallen so that they are not merely antithetical. For instance, the immediate effect of problematizing the fallen Urizen so that he is not merely a parodic inversion of the redeemed Urizen in Night the Ninth is that, though he succeeds in ejecting his troublesome mate from his territory, her narrative raises for him the would-be rhetorical question, "Am I not God . . . . Who is equal to me / Do I not stretch the heavens abroad or fold them up like a garment" (E. 328, 42:19–20). In his image of folding up the heavens "like a garment," Urizen recalls the motif of covering begun with Tharmas. As in the earlier episode, it is a potentially protective act that nevertheless insidiously perpetuates the fallen state, since it creates the veil of dualism. Urizen asserts his power as male over the emanation by casting her out, recalling further the paradoxical relation between covering and casting out. Albion's looking outward to self and losing the Divine Vision establishes this sequence in Night the Second.

As a result of her narrative, then, Ahania falls into Non Entity and Urizen pursues a yet more deathly quest to ensure his supremacy; both illusory states result from the dualistic fear of otherness. Only at the apocalypse, where he recognizes that eternity has no context, can Urizen transcend the would-be rhetorical question, "Am I not God." He attains true wonder in a question that opens the gates of nonduality: "Where shall we take our stand to view the infinite & unbounded / Or where are human feet for Lo our eyes are in the heavens" (E.391, 122:24–25).

What keeps Urizen from divinity in the fallen world, then, is his fear of others or otherness. The dramatic irony of Urizen's "Am I not God" powerfully illustrates Northrop Frye's analysis of the presence of the divine in the fallen world and the fallen blindness to it:

> There must . . . be another dimension of experience, a vertical timeless axis crossing the horizontal flow of time at every moment, providing in that moment a still point of a turning world, a moment neither in or out of time, a moment that Blake in the prophecies calls the moment in each day that Satan cannot find.
>
> The worst theological error we can make, for Blake, is the "Deist" one of putting God at the beginning of the temporal sequence as a first cause. . . . The only God worth worshipping is a God who, though in his essence timeless, continually enters and redeems time, in other words an

incarnate God, a God who is also Man. . . . Attempts to approach the
Father directly produce what Blake calls "Nobodaddy. . . ." [W]hen we
invent such Gods as Nobodaddy, we place them "up there," in the sky
and out of sight. But as "eternal" means really present, so "infinite" means
really here. Christ is a real presence in space as well as a real presence in
time, and the poet's imagination has the function of bringing into ordi-
nary experience what is really here and now, the bodily presence of God.
Just as there is no God except a God who is also Man, so there is no real
man except Jesus, man who is also God. (1987, 30–32)

The inverse, in temporal terms, of the fallen forecasting exemplified
through Los and Ahania is a reliance on memory, that failed faculty which
Blake opposes to vision in *A Vision of the Last Judgment*: "Vision or Imagi-
nation is a Representation of what Eternally Exists. Really & Unchangeably.
Fable or Allegory is formd by the Daughters of Memory. Imagination is
Surrounded by the daughters of Inspiration who in the aggregate are calld
Jerusalem" (E. 554). The narrative effect of memory as hindsight gone awry
is the fabrication of the myth of origin. One of the poem's most dramatic
enactments of memory's distortion is in Night the Seventh[a] when
Enitharmon longs to recount the mythical fall but understandably has a
failure of memory. Speaking to the Spectre, Enitharmon begins her own
fiction of the fall. She emphasizes the moment of her own begetting in a
solipsism that conflates priority with origin. Being perhaps the least imaginative of all the poem's storytellers, she admits what the others are not
willing to in their respective fictions: "In dark confusion mean time Los
was born & Enitharmon / But how I know not" (E. 359, 83:27–28).

The Spectre eagerly picks up the narrative thread, but in so doing he
substitutes his own version of the story in which he figures as the central
character: "This thou well rememberest listen I will tell / What thou
forgettest" (E. 359, 84:9–10). Rather than seeing the Spectre as a mouth-
piece for the author, one can see his manipulation of Enitharmon's "memory"
when he says,

> Listen O vision of Delight One dread morn of goary blood
> The manhood was divided for gentle passion making way
> Thro the infinite labyrinth of the heart. . . .
> I was divided in darkness & oblivion thou an infant woe
> And I an infant terror in the womb of Enion . . .

Thou & that demon Los wert born . . .
Ah poor divided dark Urthona now a Spectre wandering
(E. 359, 84:12–30)

The Spectre's "response" to Enitharmon is not a response, but one of the most startling enactments of the poem's play with the usurpation of the narrative voice.

Readers have understandably tended to be as susceptible to the Spectre's authoritativeness as is Enitharmon. One, for instance, writes,

> The Spectre has a more vivid memory, in his account, of events closer to the present, of the enclosure of Los and Enitharmon in the arteries of Generated life. . . . He stresses, however, not the separation of the sexes into Luvah and Vala, but a separation of another more spectrous kind. . . . These two accounts of the Fall, then, clearly develop the two aspects of a fallen "separation" which will occupy Blake's imagination for a long time to come. The Spectre's withdrawal from life is especially important because it develops eventually into Blake's mature vision of Satan. (Wagenknecht 1973, 223)

Such a reading is useful in pointing out this moment as a version of the fall. However, suggesting that the Spectre here is a prototype for Satan reduces Blake's use of biblical mythology. Ernest Jones's definitive use of the term "decomposition" for describing the way Shakespeare breaks down aspects of a single personality into different characters is useful in illuminating the complexity of Blake's figuration. Decomposition, Jones claims, is a mechanism of myth formation in which

> various attributes of a given individual are disunited, and several other individuals are invented, each endowed with one group of the original attributes. In this way one person of complex character is dissolved and replaced by several, each of whom possesses a different aspect of the character which in a simpler form of the myth was combined in one being. (1949, 131)

With this "mechanism of myth" in mind, one can see the limitation of attempting to reduce the poem's figures to characters in other works. The *Zoas* "decomposes" figures like Satan in far more complex ways than Jones's approach would suggest; it does so through states, such as opacity, as well as through figuration. The above reading, for instance, transposes Luvah and Vala into Miltonic characters:

> [W]hen they mate they paradoxically produce a new, doubly fallen Vala, the birth of whom from the body of sleeping Enitharmon is even more painful than was the birth of Orc. . . . The birth of the renewed, doubly fallen Vala is based upon Milton's description of Sin's delivery of Death in *Paradise Lost*. . . . Blake is loading the image of a new Vala with all the ambiguity of the old. But surely the breaking of the gates of Enitharmon's heart may also be a hopeful omen, suggesting that she is open to pity at long last and can never return to the ways of courtly love and sexual torment.(Wagenknecht 1973, 223–24)

Problematizing this reading is the emphasis in Blake's mythos away from a clear-cut moral choice between sexual or idealized love. Not only is pity in the poem as ambiguous as sexual love, but as problematic as taking the Spectre as a prototype for Satan is reducing Vala to an allusion to Milton's Sin. As is the case with much criticism of the poem, this reading disregards the relation between Vala's state here and her epiphany in Night the Ninth. Vala is clearly a more complex figure than Urizen's daughters, for instance, who seem more directly allusive of Milton's allegorical figure of Sin. Narrative authority is further complicated by the passage's containment in one of the poem's embedded narratives.

Leslie Brisman's reading of the interaction between Enitharmon and the Spectre more fruitfully links the problem of Enitharmon's forgetting to the relationship between the Spectre and Enitharmon:

> Such little oblivions are the special province of poetry and help it to the same transcendence of formulaic thought that the whole creative mind has over pure consciousness. Forgetfulness covers not just the birth of Enitharmon but the relation between Enitharmon and the shadow of Enitharmon speaking. When the Spectre hails her, "Listen, thou my vision, / I view futurity in thee," he collapses in the appositive "my vision" just the temporalizing difference that is allowing this whole episode to take place. "My vision" could be said to mean, literally, "she whom I now see." It also means "she in whom I foresee," or "she with whom I foresee." If the Spectre made clear just what he would lose through clarification,

his statement might go something like this: "You are the only one through whom (granted the awareness I have but can lay aside that you are 'lovely / Delusion') I can create." (1978, 272)

The reading parallels this chapter's earlier discussion of Urizen's creating of Ahania by casting her out. The difference between the two interactions, though, is that the question of the Spectre's interruption of Enitharmon seems to involve the problem of not only what they are remembering as the mythical origin but how memory itself works and is distorted by present context.

A useful critical perspective in teasing out the elements of memory and the context of the storytelling is Peter Brooks's discussion of narrative interruption and the displacement of the authorial voice in a different context:

> A narrative account that allows the inception of its story to be either event or fiction—that in turn opens up the potential for another story, anonymous and prehistoric—perilously destabilizes belief in explanatory histories as exhaustive accounts whose authority derives from the force of closure, from the capacity to say: here is where it began, here is what it became. (1984, 277)

This could well describe the narrative move between Enitharmon and the Spectre, in which a hazy "memory" is replaced by a more elaborately constructed myth.

Looking back in the poem for an "explanatory history," one finds further testimony to Blake's refusal to engage in "the force of closure" that Brooks discusses. The poem introduces Los and Enitharmon after they have been infected by the contagion of panic and deceit. Los is scornful of Enitharmon, and so, too, "scorn & Indignation rose upon Enitharmon." Inadvertently, perhaps, they carry out her "prophecy" toward Los's claimed end. What neither sees is the interiority of the divine vision, as Enitharmon and Los look outward for paradise due, in part, to Eno's windows created at their birth:

She also took an atom of space & opend its center
Into Infinitude & ornamented it with wondrous art
Astonishd sat her Sisters of Beulah to see her soft affections
To Enion & her children & they ponderd these things wondring

And they Alternate kept watch over the Youthful terrors
They saw not yet the Hand Divine for it was not yet reveald
(E. 305, 9:12–17)

The dynamic of reading forward in the poem to Night the Seventh[a] for continuity in plot and backward to this point to seek causality reveals the ambiguity of pity in Night the Seventh [a]. The narrative roots of "pity" can be traced back to the opening of Night the First in which Tharmas hides Jerusalem, he says, out of pity. Here, then, in the poem's earliest portrayal of the infants Los and Enitharmon, their protection by the so-called pity of the Daughters of Beulah is implicitly ironic. As custodians of divine protection, their authority cannot be taken at face value, since they look outward for a Divine Hand they cannot yet see. According to Night the Ninth, externalized divinity, particularly the synecdochally limited view, is the fragmented perspective of a dualistic mind of which they themselves are a projection.

From the hindsight of the end of the poem, then, the authorial voice of consciousness that awakens from the dream is the perspective that includes all the limited ones. Husserl's discussion of pure consciousness and its relation to context helps illustrate this quality of Blake's voices in the poem:

> [N]o concrete experience can pass as independent in the full sense of the term. Each "stands in need of completion" in respect to some connected whole, which in form and in kind is not something we are free to choose, but are rather bound to accept.
>
> For instance, if we consider any outer perception, shall we say this definite perception of a house taken in its concrete fullness, there then pertains to it as a necessary part of its determination the experience-context; but it is a particular, necessary, and yet "non-essential" part of its determination, being such, namely, that changes in it alter nothing in the experience's own essential content. Thus the perception itself changes according as the determination of the context changes, whereas the lowest specific difference of the genus "perception", its inner uniqueness, can be thought of as remaining identical with itself. (1962, 221)

The analysis that essential content is unaffected by changing perception could well describe the narrative and epistemological problems of causality in Blake's depiction of fallen consciousness. In the dialogues between Enitharmon and the Spectre in Night the Seventh [a] and Ahania and Urizen in Night the Third, the relation of prior events to their recollections and prophecies to their fulfillment suggest that the fallen figures shape the collective perception of limited consciousness.

In contrast to the problematic relationships between inner stories and the poem's narrator, the development of Tharmas at the opening of Night the Fourth sets the stage for new complications in relation to the narrator as limited consciousness plummets toward the universe of Death. The embedded narrative of Ahania, in her pleading with Urizen, and that shared between Enitharmon and the Spectre, in their alternative versions of their inception, suggest that the fallen state transpires through dialogue as much as it does through other forms of interaction. Tharmas provides an alternative mode of communication, getting his message across through pure emotionalism. This is literalized in his excreting over the "dark Abyss":

> the voice of Tharmas rolld
> Over the heaving deluge. he saw Los & Enitharmon Emerge
> In strength & brightness from the Abyss his bowels yearned
>   over them
>
>   (E. 331, 47:1–3)

Tharmas's principal emotions introduced in Night the First are love and pity. But now he is obsessed with knowing their cause, even recognizing that they are arbitrarily named rather than attempting to explain through them the presence of Jerusalem in his bosom. The poem, in this way, moves backwards in its tracing of causality:

> And he said Wherefore do I feel such love & pity
> Ah Enion Ah Enion Ah lovely lovely Enion
> How is this All my hope is gone for ever fled
>
>   (E. 331, 47:7–9)

Night the Fourth, more specifically, contrasts Ahania's vision in Night the Third of Albion seeking an emotional hold on Vala.[7]

At the opening of Night the Fourth, the narrator directly depicts Tharmas seeking freedom from the endlessly fragmenting emotionalism at the core of his plastic being: "Deathless for ever now I wander seeking oblivion / In torrents of despair in vain" (E. 331, 47:12–13).

It is Tharmas's idiosyncrasy among all the figures to weave a causal structure into the protean world of emotion he projects through his "blue watry eyes" (E. 366, 93:40; K. 339, line 230). Night the Fourth thus opens with the familiar torrent of Tharmas's engulfing emotionalism, whose source he cannot fathom, related in earlier moments of the poem to his relentless search for death. Tharmas's dogged movement forward is contrasted to Enion who, at the end of Night the Third, wanders like Ahania, without identity: "Only a voice eternal wailing in the Elements" (E. 331, 46:7).

The narrative complication arises first when the narrator explains that Tharmas feels "mighty scorn" as he observes Los and Enitharmon in their "strength and brightness," yet Tharmas's lamentation that follows contradicts the narrator's suggestion of simple envy:

> Wherefore do I feel such love & pity. . . .
> How is this All my hope is gone for ever fled. . . .
> Deathless for ever now I wander seeking oblivion
> In torrents of despair in vain.
>
> (E. 331, 47:8–13)

The frustrating indeterminacy of Tharmas's feeling complicates the narrator's assessment of "scorn" in his reaction to Los and Enitharmon. However, a moment of parodic epiphany follows this protean moment in which the fallen Tharmas appears to have usurped narrative authority:

> Are love & rage the same passion? they are the same in me
> Are those who love. like those who died. risen again from death
> Immortal. in immortal torment.
>
> (E. 331, 47:18–20)

Tharmas refashions the ever stultifying emotionalism, converting love and pity to indignation.

A key to the difference between Tharmas's effect on the narrative and that of the figures discussed earlier lies in his questions. The fallen Urizen, it was seen, asks rhetorical questions that indicate a will to defy what is already out of the character's control ("Am I not God"). Irony on the part of this creator-consciousness, rather than the limited narrator, invariably lies behind the dare to suggest otherwise than the affirmative answer. In the above passage, Tharmas asks questions that, by contrast to Urizen, reveal his frustration with indeterminacy, underscored by the caesuras in lines 19 and 20.

The answer to his question, "Are love & rage the same passion?" (E. 331, 47:18) can be glimpsed through the association of the fallen Luvah in Night the Second with Christ: "I suffer affliction / Because I love" (E. 318:27, 13–14). This earlier episode helps explain the developments in Tharmas's character and their relation to the narrator in Night the Fourth. Luvah, imprisoned in Urizen's furnaces, says of Vala,

> And I commanded the Great deep to hide her in his hand
> Till she became a little sleeping Infant a span long
> I carried her in my bosom as a man carries a lamb
> I loved her I gave her all my soul & my delight
> I hid her in soft gardens & in secret bowers of Summer
> Weaving mazes of delight along the sunny Paradise
> Inextricable labyrinths, she bore me sons & daughters
>
> (E. 317, 27:1–7)

Tharmas's hiding of Jerusalem is echoed here through Luvah's ironic feeling of betrayal. This is clear from the perspective not only of Albion's discovery but of Vala's revelation in Night the Ninth that the world and the Lord that she has projected outside herself, and from which she therefore felt separate, is actually her Self. The poem shows that the notion of an inextricable labyrinth is a creation of the bound mind, just as is the power to hide that which is already part of the Self.

This retrospective irony may help explain why Luvah's speech reads like testimony in a self-defense. But in one of the poem's most astonishing examples of a character stealing the narrative, the judge to whom Luvah pleads is a collective: "Ye O sons of Men / The workmanship of Luvahs hands" (E. 317, 26:5–6). His addressing the reader in itself is out of character for the poem. Even more interesting, however, is that he is addressing future readers. The poem suddenly throws the collective reader into the drama as Luvah's descendants in a dramatic enactment of nondualism, reaching beyond its temporal boundaries to future readers.

Blake has, in fact, qualified the statement in an ambiguous "if" clause that trails away, replaced by Luvah's emphatic insistence on Vala's guilt and his own innocence: "If I indeed am Valas King & Ye O sons of Men / The workmanship of Luvahs hands." This is reminiscent of the vague grammar of the opening of the poem, "Begin with Tharmas," a phrase whose construction makes unclear whether we are enjoined to begin or the fall begins with Tharmas. As chapter 2 has discussed, this superimposition suggests the arbitrariness of beginning. Here too, Luvah addresses the reader as his creation, though we are conditionally related to him in a phrase that heightens the crisis of causality. The construction *"if" Luvah is Vala's king* is followed not by *then*, but by *and*, subverting any attempt at its own logical subordination with parataxis. Logical, grammatical subordination would state a causal relation between our inheritance and Luvah's power over Vala.

Because he addresses the reader directly, Luvah appears to be vindicating himself not to Urizen—as it might at first appear, since the opposition is so set up—but to the "history" that he implies the reader witnesses in order to understand his own fallenness. Moreover, from the hindsight of Vala's epiphany in which she herself is the divinity she had sought as Luvah, the conditions of Luvah's leaving his Zoic estate to the reader heightens the irony of the split between his words and the authorial voice behind them.

Nelson Hilton describes Blake's relationship to the reader in terms useful in the discussion of the relation of narrator to characters:

> Blake annihilates his (and the reader's) "authority": he will not be a selfhood talking to itself or to other selfhoods while there is the waiting (self-) communication of Albion and Jerusalem, of language and Divine Imagination. (1983, 8)

This aptly describes the way *The Four Zoas* problematizes the relationship. Hilton warns readers against labeling Blake "ambiguous," since *The Four Zoas* condemns "ambiguous words blasphemous" (E. 336, 53:26). Yet the context, as is always the case with this poem, is itself ambiguous. The authorial voice also refers, in the preceding line, to "Tharmas his God." The ironic narrator never allows us to rest on his authority.

In an interesting variation on Husserl's discussion of the relation between perception and context, Hilton discusses the impact of the reader's perception in determining context:

> The issue, evidently, is not the context but the kind of perception brought to bear by the reader. The reader's perception must educate itself through the multiple possibilities of a context that continually attempts to raise the reader to its expanding field of reference. Ambiguity is not an appropriate word to apply to Blake because the very word and its associations

presuppose the binary logical thought process that Blake targeted for transformation: ambiguity is in the mind of the beholder. (1983, 10)

As mentioned in chapter 2, Luvah betrays his own participation in the
fallen state. His participation in fallenness is not merely usurping Urizen's
power, which Ahania claims in her "Vision," but rather the gesture of covering or hiding, as seen in Tharmas's primary gesture as "parent power" of
human limitation: "They have surrounded me with walls of iron & brass,
O Lamb / Of God clothed in Luvahs garments" (E. 318, 27:9–10). Cloth-
ing God in "Luvahs garments" takes on still more complex significance in
light of the fact that Luvah's testimony-confession immediately follows the
building of the Mundane Shell. The covering impulse that intensifies the
dualistic world is the foundation for the Mundane Shell, the world of time
and space. Regardless of the figures' conscious understanding, Jerusalem as
the human divine is unchanged by the fictions that "surround" her. The
characters create fictions and then seek meaning, interpretation, and causality. To put this in narrative terms, the myth exists as myth. The poem
represents history as the creating of fictions and of reading them, of searching for the rational in the nonrational, while divinity remains silently unaffected by the vicissitudes called history.

Luvah's covering of Vala proleptically repeats the covering of Jerusalem. Further, the covering of Jerusalem follows and suggests a causal relation with the problem of perception that accompanies the completion of
the Mundane Shell, as the sleep of Reuben and Levi reveals: "Their eyes
their ears their nostrils & tongues roll outward they behold / What is within
now seen without" (E. 314, 25:22–23). As chapter 2 discusses, Night the
Second opens with Albion turning his eyes outward to Self and losing the
divine vision. The completion of the Mundane Shell is the realization of
this gesture which, as the gesture itself suggests, is but an illusion, for beholding that which is within as without does not mean that divinity is
actually lost.

In light of these interplays, the ironic development of the fallen world
of Ulro in Night the Fourth is that Tharmas disowns both Urizen and
Luvah and empowers Los, echoing Albion's command to Urizen to build
the Mundane Shell. His version is to build a world of Death to fend off
oblivion, paralleling and complicating Urizen's building of the Mundane
Shell to fend off infinity and futurity:

> Go forth Rebuild this Universe beneath my indignant power
> A Universe of Death & Decay. Let Enitharmons hands
> Weave soft delusive forms of Man above my watry world
> Renew these ruind souls of Men thro Earth Sea Air & Fire
> To waste in endless corruption. renew thou I will destroy
> Perhaps Enion may resume some little semblance
> To ease my pangs of heart & to restore some peace to Tharmas
>
> (E. 332, 48:4–9)

Los does "go fourth." Here, in Night the Fourth, "the fourth immortal starry one" (E. 301, 3:9) comes of age in Zoic terms; it is his turn to complicate the drama of fallenness by fulfilling the fears and desires of Tharmas, "parent power."

Tharmas's recipe for a world of delusion is to have Enitharmon "cover" his watery world of inchoate emotion with delusions of discrete human forms. In order for him to fulfill his fantasy of being destroyer-god, he needs Los perpetually to create. In this way, so his illogic goes, Enion may become distinct and thus he will find peace.

The splitting of Los and Urthona is one of the most problematic developments of the dualistic state from this point to Night the Seventh. Here, Los refuses Tharmas's offer, making it clear that Tharmas cannot follow Urizen's act as God. This is Los's opportunity, he reasons, to rule alone:

> We have drunk up the Eternal Man by our unbounded power
> Beware lest we also drink up thee rough demon of the waters
> Our God is Urizen the King. . . .
> And he is falln into the Deep rough Demon of the waters
> And Los remains god over all. weak father of worms & clay
> I know I was Urthona keeper of the gates of heaven
> But now I am all powerful Los & Urthona is but my shadow
>
> (E. 332, 48:13–20)

With this fallen reasoning, Los becomes distinct from Urthona. It should be emphasized that events tend to occur in this poem after they are declared to have been so: Here, Los suggests that he was separated earlier from Urthona, as Night the First proclaims, but it is not until this point in the poem that their separation is enacted in a yet more complicating version of covering by Tharmas:

. . . in a Wave he rap'd bright Enitharmon far
Apart from Los. but coverd her with softest brooding care
On a broad wave in the warm west. balming her bleeding wound

(E. 332, 49: 4–6)

The play on wrapped/rap'd conflates the two seemingly antithetical acts, the first of protection, the second of violence. This reinforces the previous suggestions that the fallen Tharmas cloaks his sexual destructiveness under the veil of parental covering.

From the hindsight of Night the Seventh[a], the irony of Tharmas's promise / threat to labor at the universe of Death and decay is that the building of Golgonooza will reverse this process of fragmentation, reuniting Los, Enitharmon, and Urthona. Tharmas's promise that this labor will constitute "works of joy" is complex even in its own context, though. Not only is it ironic in itself, but Tharmas immediately adds the understanding that it will heal Urthona's shattered limbs: "So shall the spungy marrow issuing from thy splinterd bones / Bonify & thou shalt have rest when this thy labour is done" (E. 333, 49:16, 17).

The pattern with Tharmas from the beginning of the poem emerges as a sequence of violation and consolation. In dealing with Urthona, though, his political skills have sharpened with the developments of the fallen state. Not only does Tharmas offer the Spectre a godlike position, but in case this does not appeal to the vanity of the Spectre, Tharmas quickly follows with a threat: "If thou refusest dashd abroad on all / My waves. thy limbs shall separate in stench & rotting" (E. 333, 49:21–22). The dislocating of Urthona's limbs, like a statue falling from a tower, follows a similar sequence of violence and apparent consolation to the rending of Enitharmon. Tharmas subsequently promises that his bones will soften and re-"Bonify." Urthona, in other words, will proceed from spectre to leaden statue to human to God *if* Urthona agrees. Implied is that if not, Tharmas will make the torture even more severe.

Urthona's response to such a hyperbolic set of alternatives is interesting in relation to his response to Enitharmon in Night the Seventh. Here he is no less bombastic than Tharmas, though true to the narrative interest he shows again in the dialogue with Enitharmon. In Night the Fourth, he responds with a different fiction of the Fall: "I well remember the Day," he says. What Day in this series of Nights, in which eons pass unnoticed by the monolithic figures? The Day is of his own creation: "My loins begin to break forth into veiny pipes." The irony is that this act of dismemberment of a newly defined entity occurs simultaneously with the moment of his narrative. This disparity between the present and the fictionalizing of the characters dramatizes the way the narrative modifies and contracts the absolute and formless.

Tharmas needs Urthona to help Los bind Urizen, referring to Urthona as Shadow and Los as Son. In this way, ironically, they reunite toward Golgonooza:

> But my Sweet Enion is vanishd & I never more
> Shall see her unless thou O Shadow. wilt protect this Son
> Of Enion & him assist. to bind the fallen King.
>
> (E. 334, 51:1–3)

Curiously, Tharmas causally connects Enion's vanishing to Urizen's tyranny, whereas the reader might trace her vanishing to Night the First. The authorial voice suggests this but does not impose it, only pointing out that Tharmas's logic is thrown into question as well as the reader's own need to impose a sequential order on the movement of the poem.

Tharmas, it might appear, comes closest thus far to understanding wholeness and nonduality: "O Los thou art Urthona. . . ." (E. 334, 51:14). Yet just as redemption seems to be around the corner, Blake uses enjambment to reveal the more likely plunge the reader must make in the inevitable twist of fallen logic: "O Los thou art Urthona & Tharmas / Is God."

Tharmas's effect on Urizen is less explicit. Its dynamic, however, can be gleaned through the effect of Tharmas's watery world on the desiccated Urizen. At the opening of Night the Sixth, Urizen's insatiable thirst cannot be contained in his silver helmet. Though he does not recognize the three women as his daughters, Urizen is struck by their bountiful water: "And wherefore dost thou pour this water forth in sighs & care" (E. 345, 67:10). The second "Draws all into a fountain" (E. 345: 67:14–15), while of the third it says, "With labour & care thou dost divide the current into four / Queen of these dreadful rivers." Their watery abundance and power strikingly contrast with Urizen's stance: "dry the rocky strand beneath his feet" (E. 345, 68:3).

Upon their mutual recognition, there is a surprising chiasmus: "Hiding themselves in rocky forms from the Eyes of Urizen / then Urizen wept &

this his lamentation poured forth." He proceeds to re-create his fathering of them and reverses the "benedictions," an event the reader has not witnessed firsthand:

> For labourd fatherly care & sweet instruction. I will give
> Chains of dark ignorance & cords of twisted self conceit . . .
> That they may curse Tharmas their God
>
> (E. 345, 68:21–24)

It is here that some causal hinge is suggested. The watery world of emotion is controlled by Tharmas, whom Urizen's daughters have accepted as their god: "Tharmas heard the deadly scream across his watry world . . . / froze to solid were his waves" (E. 346, 68:28–30). Urizen, this suggests, crosses over into the power over the fluid world of emotion:

> Silent in ridges he beheld them stand round Urizen
> A dreary waste of solid waters for the King of Light
> Darkend his brows with his cold helmet & his gloomy spear
> Darkend before him.
>
> (E. 346, 69:1–4)

Tharmas, knowing that Urizen's greatest fear is unbounded fall, threatens Urizen with a diabolical combination of vertigo and dehydration:

> If thou refusest in eternal flight thy beams in vain
> Shall pursue Tharmas & in vain shalt crave for food I will
> Pour down my flight thro dark immensity Eternal falling
> Thou shalt pursue me but in vain till starvd upon the void
> Thou hangst a dried skin shrunk up weak wailing in the wind
>
> (E. 346, 69:18–22)

Although the threat of desiccation alone would seem great after Urizen's inability to quench his thirst at the opening of this Night, Urizen ignores Tharmas and seeks out Urthona (with whom he will war by the end of Night the Sixth). Los's world is horrific in its monstrous inhabitants and deathly landscape. Ironically, the phrase describing his state—"cruel delight"—echoes his childhood attitude as he played in the pastoral world.

In an epic simile, the reader is reminded that this is a universe of projection:

Scard at the sound of their own sigh that seems to shake the immense
They wander Moping in their heart a Sun a Dreary moon
A Universe of fiery constellations in their brain. . . .
Beyond the bounds of their own self their senses cannot penetrate
As the tree knows not what is outside of its leaves & bark
And yet it drinks the summer joy & fears the winter sorrow
So in the regions of the grave none knows his dark compeer
Tho he partakes of his dire woes
                                        (E. 347, 70:7–16; my emphasis)

Urizen's question in Night the Ninth, "Where shall we take our stand to
view the infinite & unbounded / Or where are human feet for Lo our eyes
are in the heavens" appears yet more dramatic with this moment in mind,
in which Urizen passes through the hell of his own creation (E. 391, 122:24–
25). Here, questioning is pointless and despairing:

Oft he stood by a howling victim Questioning in words
Soothing or Furious no one answerd everyone wrapd up
In his own sorrow howld regardless of his words, nor voice
Of sweet response could he obtain tho oft assayd with tears
                                        (E. 347, 70:41–44)

Tharmas, ironically, suggests Urizen's projection of infinite hell. Even though
he pretends to ignore Tharmas, Urizen lives out Tharmas's curse. He sees
the way his curse has taken on a life of its own:

He could not take his fetters off for they grew from the soul
Nor could he quench the fires for they flamed from the heart
Nor could he calm the Elements because himself was Subject
So he threw his flight in terror & pain & in repentant tears
                                        (E. 348, 71:11–13)

Urizen's repentance is charged with irony. The fact that he "threw his flight,"
suggests that he continues his outward projection in a vertiginous chaos of
suffering. The irony is more pointed when comparing this moment with
that of Night the Ninth in which, just after his epiphany, Urizen bursts the
chains—not only those literal chains binding him to earth but even the
figurative golden chain of externalized divinity, in other words, of all duality.

Urizen thus acts out Tharmas's curse: "[T]urning round he threw / Himself into the dismal void. falling he fell & fell." He creates the most direct inversion of the mandala, the vortex:[8]

Whirling in unresistible revolutions down & down
In the horrid bottomless vacuity falling falling falling
Into the Eastern vacuity the empty world of Luvah

(E. 348, 71:21–24)

Appropriate to the parody, Luvah, whose redeemed state manifests as Christ, inhabits a vortex in his fallen state.[9] The "ever pitying one," a Beulah-like divinity rather than a compassionate God, "seeth all things . . . / And in the dark vacuity created a bosom of clay" (E. 348, 71:25–26). This is the externalized force that grants Urizen the oblivion for which he longs (cf. E. 348, 71:10). This oblivion is a death until he undergoes "another resurrection to sorrow & weary travel" (E. 348, 71:34).

Los's gesture of redemption begins the apocalypse which destroys dualistic perception. Just as Los rends the veil of duality that his building of the Universe of Death institutes, Tharmas declares an end of Mystery. Appropriately, the redeemed vision that comes as a sequence of epiphanies ends with Tharmas, just as the story of the fall begins with his gesture of secrecy. In Night the Ninth Tharmas, as a child, comes before the redeemed Vala, who asks why he feels such sorrow. Vala urges him to bring Enion before her, giving rise to a dramatic redemption of their fragmented relationship:

a Whirlwind rose up in the Center & in the Whirlwind a shriek
And in the Shriek a rattling of bones & in the rattling of bones
A dolorous groan & from the dolorous groan in tears
Rose Enion like a gentle light & Enion spoke saying
O Dreams of Death the human form dissolving. . . .
I shall cast off my death clothes & Embrace Tharmas again

(E. 400–401, 132:14ff., 22ff.)

The dreamer-as-hero passes through the apocalyptic ring of fire, undoing the chain that had been the precipitous sequence of fallen gestures. Appropriately, this undoing begins at the center: it is not a linear chain, but an eternal movement toward the center.

New life ensues so that even traditionally grotesque figures attain the innocence of regeneration without losing their power. In other words, they are not softened or idealized, but shown to be perfect as they are:

> They cry out in joys of existence. the broad stems
> Rear on the mountains stem after stem the scaly newt creeps
> From the stone & the armed fly springs from the rocky crevice
> The spider. The bat burst from the hardend slime crying
> To one another What are we & whence is our joy & delight
>
> (E. 401, 132:28–32)

How do we winnow (as the redeemed Tharmas literally does in Night the Ninth) the glimpses of redemption from the parodic forms? Night the Fifth complicates the proliferation of unreliable narrators; the sublime rhetoric of the narrative draws the reader in only to reveal at the end of the passage that this myth of the fall, of how the current situation originated, is sung by the Demons of the Deep:

> Concenterd into Love of Parent Storgeous Appetite Craving
> His limbs bound down mock at his chains for over them a flame
> Of circling fire unceasing plays to feed them with life & bring
> The virtues of the Eternal worlds ten thousand thousand spirits
> Of life lament around the Demon going forth & returning
> At his enormous call they flee into the heavens of heavens
> And back return with wine & food.
>
> (E. 341, 61:10–16)

This can be compared with an earlier passage, in which the Demons of the Deep decree Luvah to be the antithesis of Love, king of rage; they blame Vala directly for the fall: "where the lovely form / That drew the body of Man from heaven into this dark abyss" (E. 340, 59:1–2). It is crucial to note that the descriptions of Vala as the source of evil come from both Ahania in Night the Third and from the projections of Los's fear. The Demons prophesy the emergence of Vala as warrior at the time of Orc's fiery birth: "Clarions of war / call Vala from close recess" (E. 340, 59:18–19). It is thus important to separate this demonic prophecy from authorial voice, which can be derived through the retrospective reading of Night the Ninth. There

Vala initiates the process of transformation with her affirming vision of divinity from the nondual perspective.

Blake thus presents the dualistic definitions of character through pointedly secondhand, self-appointed authorities. Because their accounts conflict and seem to piece together a distorted whole, the stories cannot be "true" as mirrors of a reproducible, phenomenal world. What they tell becomes real through fearful projection:

> the fiery boy grew fed by the milk
> Of Enitharmon. Los around her builded pillars of iron
> And brass & silver & gold fourfold in dark prophetic fear
>
> (E. 340, 59:27–28; 60:1)

It is in this atmosphere of fear and self-fulfilling prophecy that Golgonooza is conceived, but not completed:

> For now he feard Eternal death & uttermost Extinction
> He builded Golgonooza on the Lake of Udan Adan
> Upon the Limit of Translucence
>
> (E. 340, 60:2–4)

The "Limit of Translucence" suggests permeation of light, a significant change from the building of the Mundane Shell, which was motivated by pure dread when Albion's eyes turned outward. Here, a potential equilibrium between inner and outer realms is suggested, giving hope for Golgonooza's realization as a city of redeemed imagination.[10]

Clearly, Los-Urthona's architecture is set against Urizen's. Imagination, however, is divorced from inner divinity. This results in as flawed a conception of the universe as Urizen's Mundane Shell, motivated by fear of change or fear of understanding eternity. The difference is revealed in Urizen's question in Night the Ninth of where one takes a human stand in eternity. Los now has his fear of Orc with which to contend:

> Enitharmon beheld the bloody chain of nights & days
> Depending from the bosom of Los & how with griding pain
> He went each morning to his labors with the spectre dark
> Calld it the chain of Jealousy.
>
> (E. 341, 60:19–22)

Los's building of chains focuses his labor of the Universe of Death and Destruction on the single threat of Orc. The implication is that as long as Los represses Orc he cannot attain the City of Art, and so he creates the destiny he fears.

CHAPTER IV

Centricity and the Vortex

THE TRANSFIGURATION OF SPATIAL IMAGES in *The Four Zoas* plays a key role in conveying the relationship of the dual and nondual states. Not only do individual images correspond but whole motifs echo each other, the fallen often parodying the redeemed. Blake's symbolism has been a constant source of debate among scholars, prompting Northrop Frye to dismiss its significance entirely:

> [W]e find ourselves confronted at once with the word "symbolism," just as in dealing with his thought we found ourselves confronted with "mystic." Blake, we said, does not call himself a mystic but a visionary, and we are now in a position to see that it is much safer not to call him a mystic at all. He does not use the word "symbolism" either: we do not propose to draw the very radical conclusion that his poetry is not symbolic, but we do say that most of the meanings attached to the word are irrelevant to Blake. (1947, 106–7)

Rather than avoiding either Blake's mysticism or his symbolism, this study regards both as crucial elements of the relationship between the dual and nondual elements of Blake's mythos.

As Damrosch notes in his extensive study of Blake's symbolism, the subject cannot be avoided since "it is useless to claim that the poems function symbolically rather than doctrinally [or vice versa]. The doctrines are

97

symbols, the symbols doctrines" (1980, 8). Because his central concern is the conflict between dualism and monism in Blake's work, Damrosch reopens the important discussion of the mystical element, noting that "It has been too customary to deny that Blake was a mystic. . . . 'Mysticism' is an arbitrary descriptive term rather than the name of a specific thing" (47–48). By looking at mysticism in this light, further, Damrosch points to the commonality between Blake's symbolism and Western mystical writers such as Meister Eckhart and Jacob Boehme. Indeed, Blake's figuration can be described through Gadamer's discussion of the Greek symbolon, whose primary characteristic is "the dividing of what is one and reuniting it again" (1993, 78).

Damrosch points out that for Blake, "[s]ymbols are seriously compromised by their status in a fallen world and in a sense are illusory, but at the same time they participate in a reality whose existence cannot be doubted except by corrupted minds" (1980, 12). Such an approach is key to regarding the relationship between the fallen and redeemed. Nicholas Halmi provides another useful analogy for this relationship in his comparison between the symbolism of gnosticism and that of romanticism:

> Gnosticism's emanationism was a consequence of its radical dualism, which had presented the problem of explaining how man could be saved by a God who had not even created him. Romanticism's symbolist doctrine, in contrast, was a consequence of its desire precisely to overcome dualism. (1993, 15–16)

Though of course Blake stands apart from the "symbolist doctrine" of high romanticism, one can apply Halmi's statement to Blake's twin representation of dual and nondual figuration.[1] The fusion of the two states, for instance, is literalized in Night the Ninth by Los's reunion with the Spectre of Urthona and Enitharmon to create Golgonooza, the city of redeemed art.[2] Huizinga, describing the "sacred identity between two things of a different order," states that

> [t]his relationship is not adequately expressed by calling it a "symbolical correspondence" as *we* conceive this. The identity, the essential oneness of the two goes far deeper than the correspondence between a substance and its symbolic image. It is a mystic unity. The one has *become* the other. (1950, 25)

The redemption of images at the apocalypse involves dissolving the differentiation characteristic of these figures in their fallen states. Thus, the integral relationship between mysticism and symbolism in Blake's mythos needs to be addressed.

The transfiguration of fallen and redeemed images is best demonstrated by the vortex, one of the most ubiquitous motifs in *The Four Zoas*. From the perspective of fallen consciousness, the vortex is an image of chaotic movement toward an empty center. From the perspective of nondual consciousness, the vortex takes on the characteristics of the mandala, which Kathleen Raine notes as "typical imagery" of the regenerate Albion (1968, 2:263).[3] However, beyond the movement toward a sacred center, what is crucial to Blake's mandala is that, like the vortex, the center is empty. As the fallen form of the mandala, then, the vortex shares the mandala's defining attributes, or lack thereof. While both have empty centers, one is associated with fear, chaos, and annihilation, the other with peace, equilibrium, and liberation. In the vortical state, centers are thrown off in a vertiginous, undirected movement in which the arbitrary, comforting boundaries—the Limits of Translucence, Contraction, and Opacity—come to naught. This suggests that redemption does not mean filling the anxiety-producing vacuum of the vortex but rather perceiving the same vortex, including its empty center, from the nondual perspective.[4]

Not only do the vortex and the mandala comment on each other, but with even more complex implications, these fallen and redeemed images of centricity correspond to the motifs of the chain and the Ouroboros, forming a dense fabric of imagery. The image of the chain and its relationship to the endless cycle of the vortex correspond as well to the chained, serpentine Orc and to Vala. Their extreme fallen state is figured as the Ouroboros, the snake eating its tail and signifying the endlessly self-perpetuating self-destructiveness of contraction. In the redeemed state, however, the Ouroboros signifies eternity.[5] Because states are aspects of a single consciousness, for Blake, he does not represent these forms as antithetical. Instead, he transforms the figure itself. The state of the Self, whether contracted or free from duality, transforms the figure. Thus, the central paradox of the journey to the unbounded center is that one must move, in vortical chaos, past set boundaries in order to "view the infinite and unbounded" (E. 391, 122:24). This manifests spatially with the superimposed images of centricity so that, imageless and inarticulate, the empty center seems to be hell itself in the contracted state. But when imagelessness and emptiness are liberated from duality at the apocalypse of Night the Ninth, they contribute not to a living hell, but to an eternal Elysium. Whether the culmination of the epic quest is a descent into inferno or Elysium depends on the state of the quester.[6]

The relationship among these motifs extends to the boundary lines that help define the fallen world. The "discovery" of the Limits of Opacity and Contraction is associated with the emergence of Orc, "terrible child," who in turn is associated with "solemn revolutions" and wheels of turning darkness (E. 339, 57:8–17). After the limits of Opacity and Contraction are found, the spatial boundaries represent limitation of more abstract imaginings:

> so Los & Enitharmon
> Shrunk into fixed space stood trembling on a Rocky cliff
> Yet mighty bulk & majesty & beauty remain but unexpansive
>
> As far as highest Zenith from the lowest Nadir so far shrunk
> Los from the furnaces a Space immense & left the cold
> Prince of Light bound in chains of intellect among the furnaces
>   (E. 339, 57:11–16)

As the pulsation of Los's hammer that builds the world of Death paradoxically becomes the heartbeat of the fallen world, the chains that bind Orc begin a new motif of fallen centricity:

> . . . grew a chain beneath the Earth
> Even to the Center wrapping round the center & the limbs
> Of Orc entering with fibres. became one with him a living Chain
>   (E. 342, 63:1–3)

Orc's "formative" years literalize revolution. The adolescent Orc is Luvah's fallen form, embodying the passion for liberation from stasis not through the ec-stasy of vision, which Luvah embodies as Christ at the apocalypse. Instead, since inward vision is lost when Albion's eyes turn outward, Orc embodies the struggle for liberation through contrariety.

The vortical chaos of revolution literalizes bound consciousness viewing itself solely through its political context and historical progress. Thus, when the aphorism in *The Marriage of Heaven and Hell* "Without Contraries is no progression" is seen as ironic rather than as authorial dictum, one can trace Blake's indictment of dualistic limitation to earlier works often considered to be grounded in dialecticism (E. 34, plate 3). Readings that rely on a dialectical description of the poem's structure cannot account for the moments and images that elude historical progress and so conclude, as one reader states, that

> [i]n rethinking the path from the creation to the apocalypse, Blake found himself rethinking the nature of the two poles of his myth as well. While Blake conceived of the apocalypse as resulting from political events, he pictured it as a specific moment in history, and hence a state that could be reached once and for all, like the Biblical Last Judgment. If history has a definite end, then it is plausible to think of it as having a definite beginning too. In short, the focus on political-historical events in Blake's original conception of his myth gave it a neat structure, a linear narrative shape similar to the Bible's. But as Blake's conception of his myth became increasingly psychological, the linear shape of his narrative began to break down. (Cantor 1984, 63)

The insistence on "neat structure" that involves an apocalypse stemming from history impoverishes Blake's myth, which develops through the matrices of figuration as well as narrative structure. One of the most striking instances of this multiplicity of dimensions is the echoing of the structural, narrative centricity with the imagistic interplay of vortex and mandala.

As the parodic form of the mandala whose center unifies the whole, the vortex is the formal manifestation of thought without vision. As Mitchell notes of the vortex or spiral, "its very structure suggests continuous transformation and denial of closure, coiling inward toward a perpetually vanishing center and outward toward a never attained boundary" (1983, 126–27) . It is both appropriate and ironic that the image is associated with Urizen, since it is he who seeks boundaries to fend off futurity. His compulsive activity, in fact, creates the tormenting and chaotic universe he fears. The downward spiral of Night the Fifth and Sixth culminates in Urizen's descent. In this episode, the vortex most pointedly contrasts with the archetypal movement of the quester through the labyrinth to the sacred center.

The temporal manifestation of Urizen's Mundane Shell is the Universe of Death that Los and Urthona build. Their labor, however, simultaneously temporalizes the golden chain, whose links are pulsations:

the thundering
Hammer of Urthona. forming under his heavy hand the hours
The days & years in chains of iron round the limbs of Urizen
Link hour to hour & day to night & night to day & year to year
In periods of pulsative furor.

(E. 335, 52:28, 29; 53:1–3)

The golden chain that appears after Urizen's creation of the Mundane Shell and along which Los and Enitharmon play, in their state of unorganized innocence, here by contrast becomes the prison of Los and Enitharmon:

But Enitharmon wrapd in clouds waild loud. for as Los beat
The anvils of Urthona link by link the chains or sorrow
Warping upon the winds & whirling round in the dark deep
Lashd on the limbs of Enitharmon & the sulphur fires
Belchd from the furnaces wreathd round her. chaind in ceaseless fire

(E. 335, 53:5–9)

The phrase "Enitharmon wrapd in clouds" recalls Tharmas "rap'd bright Enitharmon" at the sundering of Los and Urthona (E. 332, 49:4). Here "wrapd," in a chiastic reversal of letters, becomes warp[ing], suggesting both the literalized distortion of the act of covering as well as its paradoxical violence.

Complicating Los's epithet "Prophet of Eternity" is his activity at the nadir of his fallen state in which he, "absorbd in dire revenge," binds Urizen and bastes Enitharmon: "[F]rom ladles huge / He pourd the molten iron round the limbs of Enitharmon" (E. 336, 53:15-16). Indeed, the passage with the privileged epithet is charged with irony that has accrued from the inception of the dualistic universe:

The Prophet of Eternity beat on his iron links & links of brass
And as he beat round the hurtling Demon. terrified at the Shapes
Enslavd humanity put on he became what he beheld

(E. 336, 53:22–24)

The last phrase of this passage echoes Albion losing the divine vision when he turns his eyes outward.

Los's epithet, Prophet of Eternity, is easily and often taken as authorial in conjunction with the opening description of Los as "fourth immortal starry one." However, the phrase is ambiguous even on the grammatical level: is being Prophet of Eternity possessive or descriptive? In other words, is Los eternally a Prophet, or is he one who prophesies about eternity or, for another reading, is he a prophet in eternity? Because the phrase is followed by Los's creation of the temporal chains that bind, "Prophet of Eternity" has yet another twist, as an oxymoron: eternity transcends futurity even as Los creates a world of time with the pulsations of his beating hammer. Fallen prophecy must be self-fulfilling and illusory rather than actual and providential, while the redeemed Prophet of Eternity can strip the veil of temporality that covers the eternal. Los can only take on this role at the opening of Night the Ninth, when all the fragments move toward their eternal roles.

As becomes increasingly clear, the text does not show causal relationships through grammatical construction. Instead, it suggests a subversion of grammatically demonstrable causality, reflecting linguistically the ironic attitude the text takes toward fictions that are assumed to be truth. One significant example is the statement, "he became what he beheld / Raging against Tharmas his God" (E. 336, 53:24–25). There is a complex causal chain implicit in this run-on sentence: "Because" could be placed at the end of line 24 so that he became [the terror] he beheld because of his rage against Tharmas and because he holds Tharmas as his God in the Nobodaddian sense of Godhead. In this way Los fulfills Albion's turning eyes outward to self in Night the Second, now associated with the fallen poet of prophecy: "uttering/Ambiguous words blasphemous filld with envy."

The labor of creating the fallen chain ensnares "the Eternal Mind," which

> bounded began to roll eddies of wrath ceaseless. . . .
> Forgetfulness dumbness necessity in chains of the mind lockd up
> In fetters of ice shrinking disorganized rent from Eternity
> (E. 336, 54:1, 4–5)

The fallen prophecy is no more than Los's fear, which he fulfills by creating a chain of ages of dismal woe. To be rent from Eternity, however, is not a rupture in time. By reading this episode as an irreversible act in time, one is subject to the same "forgetfulness dumbness necessity in chains of the mind" since even as the "fetters of ice" are contracting they break when they are recognized as unreal. This recognition is a privilege the reader has over the fallen figures, since Blake creates a retrospective reading that does not rely on memory.

Where God is perceived outward, an antithetical figure of evil is created. Hence, opacity is Satan, yet it gives rise to the mythical God. Los does not confront God as such, but rather the fearfulness that rules his mind. This is due to the Limit of Opacity that stands as the end-frame of Night the First's covering impulse and connects it with Night the Second's gesture of casting perception outward: "And first he found the Limit of Opacity & namd it Satan / In Albions bosom for in every human bosom these limits stand" (E. 338, 56:19–20). Limits, the poem tells us, bind the heart. The Limit of Opacity is related to the covering impulse also associated with the veil. It is related as well to the inability to recognize divinity within, which leads to casting reality out. Thus God's hand, interpreted by the fallen characters as providential, is an aspect of opaqueness.

This self-subverting quality of protection is illustrated by Blake's design for page 63 of Night the Fifth. There Los "covers" the infant Orc in a parodic version of the protective agents of Beulah (see figure 5). Los stretches his right hand over the infant who is passively and openly stretched between Los and Enitharmon. Los's left hand is over his heart, reminiscent of Tharmas's gesture of taking Jerusalem into his heart. These gestures of simultaneously taking in and casting out characterize the fallen state. As will be seen later in this chapter, Blake parodies the image in a reversal of poses in Night the Seventh (figure 6).[7]

Los's perpetuation of opacity from the earlier moments is manifested in the externalization of divinity:

> And Los beheld the hand of God over his furnaces
> Beneath the Deeps in dismal darkness beneath immensity
> In terrors Los shrunk from his task.
>
> (E. 338, 54:26–27, 55:1)

The shapes he fears, calling them God, are his own creation. Thus he perpetuates fallen imagining by fearing what is created by his fear:

> terrifid at the shapes
> Enslavd humanity put on he became what he beheld
> He became what he was doing he was himself transformd
>
> (E. 338, 55:21–23)

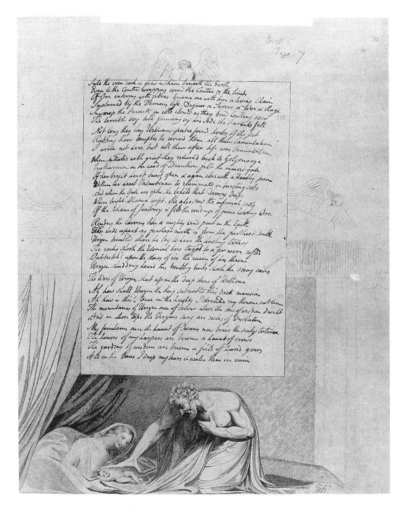

Fig. 5. Night the Fifth. *The Four Zoas.* MS. 39764, folio 32, reprinted with permission from the British Museum, London.

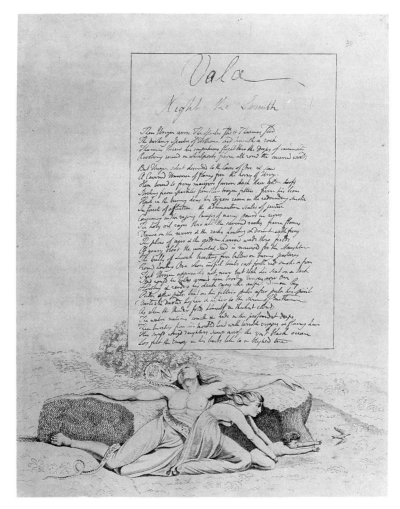

Fig. 6. Night the Seventh. *The Four Zoas*. MS. 39764, folio 39, reprinted with permission from the British Museum, London.

The poem's shift to the Council of God watching over Albion's body gives rise to the most blatant failure of the Daughters of Beulah to recognize what is not causal. This, in turn, results in the inwardly blinded art of Los. The Daughters of Beulah pray, "Lord. Saviour if thou hadst been here our brother had not died" (E. 337, 56:1). The Saviour urges their patience, for the price of experience, even more perhaps than the fall of intellect, is the fall of imagination. Thus, "he became what he beheld / He became what he was doing he was himself transformed" (E. 338, 55:22–23).

Night the Fourth completes the paradoxical, twofold movement of covering and casting out that together comprise fallen consciousness. Hence Night the Fourth ends with the nascent dualism of the fallen world: "While yet those beings were not born nor knew of Good or Evil." It is crucial to hear the authorial irony in such a statement. The setting of limits on infinity is an impulse of unorganized innocence as well as of fallenness. The difference this particular comparison points out is that "wondrous art" is innocent in intention, though it veils Truth as problematically as does Urizenic allegory.

The world projected outward through the Mundane Shell creates the illusion, begun by Urizen and perpetuated by Los, that fixed borders fend off the infinite. Hence, Night the Fifth opens with a literalization of "shrinking" consciousness:

> Infected Mad he dancd on his mountains high & dark as heaven
> Now fixd into one stedfast bulk his features stonify
> From his mouth curses . . .
> His feet shrink withring from the deep shrinking & withering
> And Enitharmon shrunk up all their fibres withring beneath. . . .
> . . . So Los & Enitharmon
> Shrunk into fixed space stood trembling on a Rocky cliff
> Yet mighty bulk & majesty & beauty remaind but unexpansive
> As far as highest Zenith from the lowest Nadir. so far shrunk
> Los from the furnaces a Space immense . . .
> (E. 338-39, 57:1–15)

With a causality that challenges Dante's punishments for the sinners of the *Inferno*, Blake has Los immediately experience the effects of "discovering" the Limits of Contraction and Opacity, a fallen movement whose repercussions are as powerful as any, since they form the principal limitations of human experience.[8]

Los, literally shrinking and contorting, immediately experiences the effects of setting these limits (E. 338, 55:16). The unfolding of the fallen state thus formalizes Los's terror "at the shapes / Enslavd humanity put on he became what he beheld / He became what he was doing he was himself transformd" (E. 338, 55:21–23).

In Los's limited perception of the forms he beholds, he simultaneously projects and introjects those forms. Blake literalizes this process through Los's shrinking and contorting:

> Spasms siezd his muscular fibres writhing to & fro . . .
> . . . the bones of Los
> Twinge & his iron sinews bend like lead & fold
> Into unusal forms dancing & howling stamping the Abyss
> (E. 338, 55:28–35)

The Limits of Contraction and Opacity are the result of Los's insanity, the extreme contraction of consciousness characterized by the shrunken forms it projects.[9]

By fulfilling his role as prophet of eternity at the opening of Night the Ninth, Los redeems his earlier fallen labor of instituting the Limit of Contraction. However, this fulfillment is powerfully ironic: Los's fury at the murder of Jesus is deflated by the revelation that Los does not see Christ standing beside him. His outrage at separation and death paradoxically causes him to tear the veil of dualism.

Blake counterpoints Los's desire for external salvation with Urizen's recognition that Luvah is somehow Orc. Urizen's bafflement at seeking causal explanations, in this case how Luvah could be Orc, is likewise a significant turn from the parodic into the redeemed. Thus, as Los and Enitharmon despair over the thought of salvation beyond the sepulcher, Urizen makes a series of associations to try to account for the identity of the Lamb of God, metamorphosed incomprehensibly from the serpent Orc:

> When Urizen saw the Lamb of God clothed in Luvahs robes
> Perplexd & terrifid he Stood tho well he knew that Orc
> Was Luvah But he now beheld a new Luvah. Or One
> Who assumd Luvahs form & stood before him opposite

But he saw Orc a Serpent form augmenting times on times
In the fierce battle & he saw the Lamb of God & the World of Los
Surrounded by his dark machines for Orc augmented swift
In fury a Serpent wondrous among the Constellations of Urizen
                                                    (E. 373, 101:1–8)

The phenomenological moment is charged with irony: Orc appears here a
creation of Urizen's universe, mapped out in Urizen's stars but realizing a
fabulous existence of his own through the fearful fantasy of his creator:
"Still Orc devourd the food / In raging hunger . . . Stretching to serpent
length / His human bulk" (E. 373, 101:17–20).

The relationship between Urizen and Orc thus unfolds through the
snake image, which is in turn redeemed by the transfiguration of Luvah
into Christ, as Daniel Hughes notes:

> Just as Urizen's repressive law is a protective exclusion, denying the minute
> particulars of human existence, so Orc's reaction creates the Druid Snake,
> the same dull round in which Orc and Urizen will repeatedly become
> each other. That Orc, hung on the Tree, recalls the Crucified and can be
> identified as Luvah, the Zoa of the passions, as Urizen suspects, does not,
> by itself, redeem the serpent symbol. It is essential to understand that the
> snake cannot be lifted up, "identified," until the whole creation comes to
> the Last Judgment. (1969, 79)

Complicating the task of defining the redeemed form of the serpent is its
redeemed form as the Ouroboros, shared not only between Urizen and
Orc, but with Vala as well.

By linking the serpent to the vortex through the Ouroboros, Blake
challenges the traditional representation of the serpent of Eden. Damrosch
points out the ambivalent nature of the serpent, noting that "[s]ince the
serpent sheds its skin it is also symbolic of immortality, an ideal which can
be negative if it means endless cycles of death-in-life, positive if it suggests
spiritual immortality" (1980, 106). Though Damrosch rightly argues that
its meanings "all conform to a single pattern," which he refers to as "iconic,"
Blake's Ouroboros figure takes on a plasticity of form that moves it beyond
the iconic (111). Suggesting a larger and more fluid implication for Blake's
representation of fallen and redeemed humanity, DeGroot explores the dichotomy between the "tail-eating snake (time or the year, represented by

the closed circle) and the snake touching its tail with its mouth (eternity, represented by the circle which has become a line and also symbolized by the scroll without beginning or end)" (1969, 556). Hazard Adams offers yet another suggestive association of the Ouroboros with Blake's use of typology:

> The crucifixion of Orc in Blake's prophetic books takes up this whole curious tradition. . . . In the later prophetic books, Orc has become a cyclical concept, tied to linear history, and we find much irony in his gnostic connections, his activity being circular and confining like the tail-eater. Blake's texts are not Gnostic or occultist, but in the crucified serpent and the tail eater he employed two venerable devices and took advantage of the ambiguity that over time they began to harbor. To read Blake is to discover many such usages . . . , but Blake's texts are not Cabalistic, nor was he an alchemist any more than he was a Gnostic. . . . Above all, it appears that Blake's intention was to open up typological method, which traditionally saw its process as expressing fulfillment in history and closure of the text. Blake's notion was to free the figure to evoke new possibilities from the vestiges of its typological usage that are carried into his text. In this sense, Blake's use of typology is a contrary to the type/antitype relation and yet assimilates it as a part, making us read the part as implying a new sort of whole. (1987, 56)

These observations underscore the importance of Blake's Ouroboros in his revision of traditional allegory, in which prior events are types of later events. Despite the distinction between the fallen and redeemed, Blake's figuration does not privilege a single form in the process of transformation. The complication of allegorical associations is thus shared among various figures, such as the serpent being shared among Orc, Luvah, and Vala.

To add to Urizen's confusion about the mutual identity of the Lamb of God and the Serpent, Vala is introduced as serpentine: "Gathring the fruit of that mysterious tree circling its root / She spread herself thro all the branches in the power of Orc" (E. 373, 101:24–25). Vala, speaking Orc's language and appealing to his own vortical thinking, urges him to disclose Luvah's whereabouts:

> But happiness can never [come] to thee, O King, nor me
> For he was source of every joy that this mysterious tree

Unfolds in Allegoric fruit. When shall the dead revive
Can that which has existed cease or can love & life Expire

Urizen heard the Voice & saw the Shadow. underneath
His woven darkness & in laws & deceitful religions
Beginning at the tree of Mystery circling its root
She spread herself thro all the branches in the power of Orc
A shapeless & indefinite cloud in tears of sorrow incessant
Steeping the Direful Web of Religion swagging heavy it fell
From heaven to heavn thro all its meshes altering the Vortexes,
Misplacing every Center

(E. 375, 103:17–28)

This motion appears to forecast the apocalypse. The relationship between the Ouroboros here and the eternal birth in Night the Ninth, in which all objects are flung from their centers, is archetypal in its symbolism:

> Shakti is represented as a snake wound three and a half times round the *lingam,* which is Shiva in the form of a phallus. This image shows the *possibility* of manifestation in space. From Shakti comes Maya, the building material of all individual things; she is, in consequence, the creatrix of the real world. This is thought of as illusion, as being and not-being. It *is,* and yet remains dissolved in Shiva. Creation therefore begins with an act of division of the opposites that are united in the deity. From their splitting arises, in a gigantic explosion of energy, the multiplicity of the world. (Jung 1969, 357)

Blake's fallen and redeemed are essentially the same figure, the transformation coming much as it does in Jung's description of mandala, namely, with the vision of the recognized center. The eternal form of the Ouroboros thus coexists with the fallen form as the snake eating its tail in inevitable, time-bound mortality.

Through the apocalypse of eternal birth, by contrast, "every one of the dead" rises. This eternal birth is not literal rebirth or resurrection, for epiphany occurs even as the deathly sleep of fallen consciousness transpires. With newfound vision, the risen dead "magnify themselves no more against Jerusalem" (E. 392, 123:21). By contrast to Urizen's question about taking a stance in eternity, the redeemed Ouroboros, touching its tail to its mouth, implicitly and immediately apprehends its stance in eternity:

And now fierce Orc had quite consumd himself in Mental flames
Expending all his energy against the fuel of fire
The Regenerate Man stoopd his head over the Universe & in
His holy hands recievd the flaming Demon & Demoness of Smoke
And gave them to Urizen's hands

(E. 395, 126:1–5)

In her comparison of this transformation to Jung's discussion of mandalas, Gallant explores the "disturbed" mandalas that exclude irreconcilable elements:

The vast majority of individual mandalas have as their center the Anthropos, or Universal Man. . . . Generally appearing in dreams or fantasies when a person is experiencing the worst kinds of dissociation, they attempt to unify seemingly irreconcilable elements. This is characteristic even of what Jung calls "disturbed" mandalas—"disturbed" because they reveal attempts to exclude what Jung calls "the dark principle." Such attempted mandalas fail to symbolize the psychic totality of the true mandala that incorporates all parts of the self—the unprincipled and formless unconscious as well as consciousness. (Gallant 1978, 56)

The disunity characteristic of "disturbed mandalas" has fascinating implications for Blake's representation of fallenness. Gallant, however, going on to discuss the vision of Ezekiel alluded to at the end of Night the First, problematically links the external divinity of the Council of God with the redemption of the disturbed mandala:

These mandalas at the conclusion of Night One are all successful in form and function. . . . This casts light on the Council of God. . . . [T]he council appears after Enion laments the existence of "Eternal Death," summing up the story of the Zoas' fall. The Council "dr[aws] up the Universal tent . . . & closd the Messengers in clouds. . . . Till the time of the End" (I.19.7–9), suggesting that the apparent chaos that the Zoas are experiencing is part of a larger pattern of order known to the Council. (57)

Though the Jungian analogue sheds light on the transmutations of the archetypal mandala figures in the poem, Gallant's conclusion regarding the Council of God reduces the poem to a Jungian case study: "In *The Four*

Zoas, mandalas appear when the 'Abyss' or 'Non Existence' seems over-whelming to a Zoa or Emanation. The Council of God appeared when 'Eternal Death' seemed dominant to all." When the Council of God is regarded as a projection of the wishes of Beulah, it becomes instead an instrument of Blake's version of romantic irony rather than a literally sav-ing providence.

Complicating the Jungian analogue further, Blake interweaves moments of hope with the perpetuation of fallenness. Thus, in contrast to the causal connection between the hopefulness of the fallen figures and the projection of an externalized providence, Night the Fifth suggests an immediate causal reaction between Los's physical contraction and his building the Universe of Death. In the rapidly transforming cosmos of the fallen state, Los sees the appearance of Orc as the fulfillment of both Enitharmon's Song of Death and his own dreaded prophecy of the end of Ulro. Los's "prophetic fear" of "Eternal death and "uttermost Extinction" is his own fulfillment of Eni-tharmon's prophecy in Night the Second. In the context of Los's binding of Enitharmon in Night the Fifth, the double image of labyrinth and vortex complicates the image of the chain:

> Los folded Enitharmon in a cold white cloud in fear
> Then led her down into the deeps & into his labyrinth . . .
> Concenterd into Love of Parent Storgous Appetite Craving
> His limbs bound down mock at his chains for over them a flame
> Of circling fire unceasing plays to feed them with life & bring
> The virtues of the Eternal worlds
>
> (E. 341, 61:7–13)

Los, folding Enitharmon in fear and love, echoes the pattern Tharmas sets at the opening of the poem by hiding Jerusalem. Los has now taken on Tharmas's former role as "Parent power" (E. 301, 4:7).

By introducing the image of the labyrinth here, Blake spatializes the effect of the arbitrary emotionalism that Tharmas brings into the fallen world. At the opening of Night the Fourth, Tharmas's confused emotion at beholding Los and Enitharmon has significant implications for the birth of Orc and his association with his parents. Blake weaves together this dense network of parent-child relationships through the motif of covering, now connected imagistically to centricity. The natural world, an "orb of eccen-tric fire," imitates the gesture of covering: "And there the Eagle hides her young in cliffs & precipices / His bosom is like starry heaven expanded all the stars / Sing round" (E. 342, 61:26–28). The eagle, traditionally a symbol of fearlessness and epic heroism, is here fearful for its young.[10] Blake reverses the traditional symbol in order to show Los and Enitharmon's blindness to Orc's innate divinity in their supposition of his evil. Upon returning to Golgonooza, Los and Enitharmon thus "felt all the sorrow Parents feel," that totality of emotion now suggesting tremendous ambivalence.

The fallen images of chain and vortex merge most dramatically in the melding of Orc into the rock. In fact, the episode intensifies the pattern and elements of Tharmas and Enion's interaction at the opening of Night the First:

> Fibres had from the Chain of Jealousy inwove themselves
> In a swift vegetation round the rock & round the Cave
> And over the immortal limbs of the terrible fiery boy
> . . . the infernal chain . . . had taken root
> Into the iron rock & grew a chain beneath the Earth
> Even to the Center wrapping round the Center & the limbs
> Of Orc entering with fibres.
>
> (E. 342, 62:23–32, 63:1–3)

The "wrapping" first seen in Tharmas's hiding of Jerusalem now describes the vortex, whose center is empty. The fibrous melding of Orc into rock recalls and reverses the atomization of Tharmas by Enion in Night the First: "Why wilt thou Examine every little fibre of my soul" (E. 302, 4:29).

In the course of these transfigurations, the question necessarily arises of why Luvah must undergo such a painful and elaborate transformation as fallen Orc? The answer can only be seen retrospectively. At the opening of Night the Seventh, Urizen's fortress of books and the "burning pastures round howling Orc" create two simultaneous and mutually consuming perversions of the mandala as labyrinth of fire to the sacred center. Urizen's circle is a fixed covering as opposed to that of Orc, who, as a ring of fire, anticipates and parodies the apocalypse of Night the Ninth.[11] This spatial relation of the two is further complicated when a root from Urizen's Tree of Mystery appears, forming "intricate labyrinths":

> Amazd started Urizen when he found himself compassd round
> And high roofed over with trees. he arose but the stems
> Stood so thick he with difficulty & great pain brought

His books out of the dismal shade. all but the books of iron
Again he took his seat & rangd his Books around
On a rock of iron frowning over the foaming fires of Orc
(E. 353, 78:9–14)

The Urizen-Orc antithesis, represented thermally through the dichotomy of "cold snow/fierce fire," is qualified by the visual suggestion that they are merely two versions of the archetypal structure of the quest toward the center. The redeemed form of the structure represents them as joined points surrounding Jerusalem, the visionary center.

When entrapped by a dominating force Orc tends toward rage, the seeds of which are sown by his relationship with Los in Night the Fifth. In the extreme state of his rage, Orc transfers his parent Los's rage to Urizen, whose fallen state directly opposes Orc's. This transference is figured in the more complex image of Orc in Night the Seventh, at which point his center becomes so volatile that he bursts free of his chains:

His soul was gnawn in sunder
The hairy shoulders rend the links free are the wrists of fire
Red rage redounds
(E. 363, 91:16–17)

The retrospective reading from Night the Seventh back to Orc's "formative" stage in Night the Fifth thus underscores the ironic similarity of fallen and redeemed forms.

The Zoas, in their fallen state, find fault with the "other's" failure of consciousness but not their own, as Orc demonstrates when he sees that Urizen's covering is an illusion of solidity:

thou sitst closd up
In that transparent rock as if in joy of thy bright prison
Till overburdend with its own weight drawn out thro immensity
With a crash breaking across the horrible mass comes down
Thundring & hail & frozen iron haild from the Element
(E. 354, 79:5–9)

Urizen's covering is transformed from sterile snow to "the dismal shade" of trees. The natural world thus contaminates his controlled, lifeless protection of a sovereign intellect.

Urizen blames Orc for his entrapment in fire on the grounds that "No other living thing / In all this Chasm I behold" (E. 353, 78:18). His interrogation of Orc is a moment of metamyth typical of this Night: "Image of dread whence art thou whence is this most woful place / Whence these fierce fires but from thyself" (E. 353, 78:17–18). Urizen questions not only how Orc got there and whether Urizen himself is responsible for Orc's entrapment, but he doubts that Orc is real. These questions are charged with irony from the perspective of Night the Ninth: the "woful place" is Urizen's creation, the fallen form of the labyrinth surrounding the sacred center. When Orc becomes Luvah-as-Christ-as-Divine Lamb, he is at the center of Jerusalem, who is the center of Albion.

Blake's design echoes the inverse pictorially: the child Orc is stretching his arms outward, away from his parents, while Enitharmon grasps him (see figure 6, p. 105). Now in the passive position that the infant Orc had been in the earlier design (see figure 5, p. 106), Los is "wrapped" by a snake, Orc's extreme fallen form. Parodic of the wholeness achieved at the apocalypse, the family appears in this image as one figure, suggested by Enitharmon's robes, which cover and literally connect them.

Urizen's description of Orc at the center of fire suggests the illusory quality of form the intense play of light and darkness creates:

> Bound here to waste in pain
> Thy vital substance in these fires that issue new & new
> Around thee sometimes like a flood & sometimes like a rock. . . .
> And now a rock moves on the surface of this lake of fire
> To bear thee down beneath the waves in stifling despair
> (E. 353–54, 78:21–29)

Thus, he says, "Pity for thee movd me to break my dark & long repose" (E. 354, 78:30). He proclaims himself hero, having rescued Orc, only to be perplexed by Orc's joy. The irony is again implicit in his demand for solidity and permanence of the protean forms that he cannot control. Orc, in turn, sees himself made a worm round Urizen's Tree. Upon recognizing the "grey obscure . . . beyond the bounds of Science," he is transformed into a serpent. Through his own limited understanding, Orc glimpses freedom from Urizenic boundaries by which he perceives that he has become transformed.

Orc bursts the chains of Mystery in Night the Seventh in a moment of liberation parodic of Urizen's epiphany:

No more remaind of Orc but the Serpent round the tree of Mystery
The form of Orc was gone he reard his serpent bulk among
The stars of Urizen in Power rending the form of life
Into a formless indefinite

(E. 365, 93:24–27)

Orc is not only transfigured into a creature distant from his human form but he is projected in the expanse of Urizen's created universe as a constellation of mythical proportions. One of the most surprising transformations at the apocalypse, in light of this relationship and its imagistic representation, is Urizen's bursting of chains in Night the Ninth, which plays a key role in liberating consciousness from the bondage he himself helped to create.

In Night the Seventh, then, Urizen's power to turn form into "a formless indefinite" complicates the power of contraction with which one comes to associate him in his creation of the Mundane Shell. Returning to the end of Night the Fifth, one can now trace Urizen's development to this point. Here, contraction is literalized most vividly as Urizen declares his intention in rhetoric charged with ambiguity:

I will arise Explore these dens & find that deep pulsation
That shakes my caverns with strong shudders. perhaps this
     is the night
Of Prophecy & Luvah hath burst his way from Enitharmon
When Thought is closd in Caves. Then love shall shew its
     root in deepest Hell.

(E. 344, 65:9–12)

The image of thought buried in caves ironically anticipates vision at the center of the human. Thought without vision is the deadly power of Urizen in the fallen state. His causal "when . . . Then" statement in line 12, above, is thus parodic of the epiphany of Night the Ninth. Burying Love's roots in deepest hell is an act of Urizenic Mystery. Urizen's is the rhetoric of entrapment, recalling the opening of the poem in which Tharmas hides Jerusalem within himself. Urizen's act, intended to protect, proves instead to be the dreaded one he has sought to fend off. In this way, his behavior, typical of the fallen pattern, is self-subverting.

Though Urizen's vortical progress through his dens in Night the Sixth sounds much like the apocalypse of Night the Ninth, the crucial difference is Urizen's anxiety about the self-created chaos surrounding the empty center:

> His dismal voyage eyeing the next sphere tho far remote
> Then darting into the Abyss of night his venturous limbs
> Thro lightnings thunders earthquakes & concussions fires & floods
> Stemming his downward fall labouring up against futurity
> Creating many a Vortex fixing many a Science in the deep
> And thence throwing his ventrous limbs into the Vast unknown
> Swift Swift from Chaos to chaos from void to void a road immense
>   (E. 349, 72:9–15)

Here, the futurity that Urizen later recognizes as delusion presses down on him with what seems an undeniable physicality. Pushing back against futurity, he creates the vacuous center surrounded by chaos that comes to define his vortical movement.

The narrator introduces the divine hand leading Urizen. The image of providential agency is reminiscent of the earlier intrusions of covering cherubs, such as the closing of the Gate of the Tongue. Here too, Urizen's unregenerate mind, which buries love in deepest hell, perceives divinity as external and providential rather than emanating from the center. Urizen is nevertheless nonplussed by his own fallen labor:

> For when he came to where a Vortex ceasd to operate
> Nor down nor up remaind then if he turnd & lookd back . . .
> The unpassd void upward was still his mighty wandring
> The midst between an Equilibrium grey of air serene
> Where he might live in peace & where his life might meet repose
>   (E. 349, 72:16-21)

Juxtaposed to his epiphanic "Where shall we take our stand to view the infinite & unbounded" in Night the Ninth, this desire for an "Equilibrium grey" suggests again the self-subverting impulse of the unredeemed, which includes unorganized innocence as well as fallenness. Urizen tries to control destiny and yet does not realize that the very act of throwing destiny outward in space and forward in time causes the chaos of fallenness.

Thus, parodically anticipating Urizen's innocent wonder in Night the Ninth is his rhetorical question in the midst of his own created chaos:

> Can I not leave this world of Cumbrous wheels
> Circle oer Circle, nor on high attain a void
> Where self sustaining I may view all things beneath my
>   feet . . .
> Here will I fix my foot & here rebuild
>
> (E. 349–50, 72:22–73:14)

Imagistically, Urizen's fallen "world of Cumbrous wheels" involves a circularity parodic of the redeemed center. Here, Urizen includes and complicates the paradoxically Beulah-like perception of externalized divinity. It is a central moment in Blake's parody of conventional allegory that "establishes a hierarchy of more and less powerful agents and images" (Fletcher 1964, 113).

Urizen's quest, then, parodies his epiphany in Night the Ninth. The culmination of the interplay of vortex and chain appears at the crucial moment in his quest:

> Endless had been his travel but the Divine hand him led
> For infinite the distance & obscurd by Combustions dire
> By rocky masses frowning in the abysses revolving erratic
> Round Lakes of fire. . . .
>   his venturous limbs . . .
> Creating many a Vortex fixing many a Science in the deep. . . .
> Swift Swift from Chaos to chaos from void to void a road immense
> For when he came to where a Vortex ceasd to operate
> Nor down nor up remaind then if he turnd & lookd back
> From whence he came twas upward all. & if he turnd and viewd
> The unpassd void upward was still his mighty wandring
> The midst between an Equilibrium grey of air serene
>
> (E. 349, 72:12–20)

The ambiguous use of "infinite" is charged with irony: Urizen lives out his created fear, suggested by the synecdoche of Urizen's "venturous limbs" visually echoing the providential divine hand. Urizen's agoraphobia thus reaches an extreme as he moves through his literalized fear in the form of his self-created chaoses. These chaoses parody the golden chain that, in Urizen's desperation, become more explicitly linked (so to speak) to the bound intellect.

The nostalgia for inexperience is distorted memory (cf. E. 350, 73). It contrasts with the pastoral in Night the Ninth, which is not nostalgia but rather the epic nostos itself. At the apocalypse, reintegrated consciousness returns home to wholeness.

To ask where one takes a stand to view the infinite, as Urizen does in Night the Ninth, is thus to recognize that human limitation is somehow related to unbound consciousness. Subsuming Albion's dream within the dream of undifferentiated consciousness confounds the habit of dualism, since any dualistic "interpretation" of fallenness in this context dissolves, as do the boundaries between characters as others and between the human and divine. In this way, the most direct parody of Night the Ninth comes at the end of Urizen's lament for the loss of innocence: "Here will I fix my foot & here rebuild / Here Mountains of Brass promise much riches in their dreadful bosoms" (E. 350, 73:14–15). Though the stance is arbitrary, it is connected parodically to the wealth in the "bosom," which in turn parodically foreshadows Albion's "Behold Jerusalem in whose bosom is the lamb of God."[12]

At the extreme of the imagistic parody of redemption, Urizen declares himself king of his own illusion: "His will where none should dare oppose his will himself being King / Of All & all futurity be bound in his vast chain" (E. 350, 73:19–20). This is the chain that bursts at the apocalypse just as he asks the epiphanic question. Urizen's efforts, frustrated because of the self-perpetuating nature of his fearful projections, give rise to one of the poem's most explicit references to the invulnerability of inner divinity regardless of a human lack of awareness or even belief in it: "For every one opend within into Eternity at will/But they refusd because their outward forms were in the Abyss" (E. 350, 74:1–2).

The portrayal of providence outside the human is a function of Blake's revision of prelapserian innocence or temporal priority in traditional, biblical theodicy. Unorganized innocence is contemporaneous with both fallenness and redemption. The framing of Urizen's "hideous pilgrimage" with the synecdoche of the divine hand is less puzzling in light of this relationship between nondual vision and the illusion of separateness:

Endless had been his travel but the Divine hand him led
For infinite the distance & obscurd by Combustions dire
By rocky masses frowning in the abysses revolving erratic

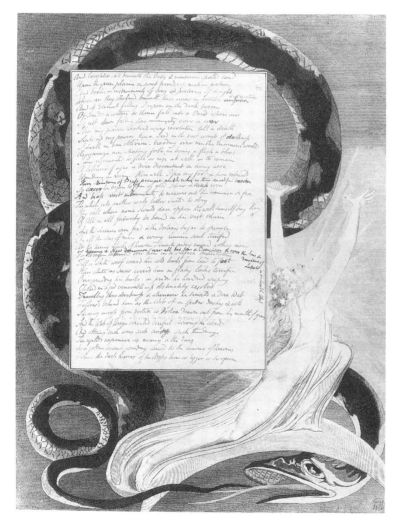

Fig. 7. Night the Sixth. *The Four Zoas*. MS. 39764, folio 37, reprinted with permission from the British Museum, London.

Round Lakes of fire in the dark deep the ruins of Urizens
    world
                           (E. 349, 72:2–5)

The problem for the limited human mind is that, though the Council of God is the perfect balance of all in one and one in all, it is located beyond the limit of perception, later called the Limit of Translucence. The name indicates a permeation of light despite its seeming inaccessibility. This contrast to the Limit of Opacity is significant, as Merleau-Ponty's discussion of borders in painting illustrates: "[N]o lines [are] visible in themselves. . . . [Borders are] always between or behind whatever we fix our eyes upon" so that, though they are implicated, "they themselves are not things" (1964, 183). Limits as optical illusions, or here, delusions, are important to keep in mind as Albion seeks boundaries from the chaos of infinitude. Albion's desire for closure is motivated by Urizen's control over him, as Urizen says: "I remaining in the porches of the brain / Will lay my scepter on Jerusalem the Emanation" (E. 311, 21:29–30).

The double meaning of Blake's "bounding line" has significant implications for the relation between the mandala/vortex motif and boundaries, as Mitchell discusses:

> The peculiar life and quality of Blake's linear style may best be summarized in the oxymoronic pun on "bounding" (i.e., closing, holding in, confining; or, contrarily, leaping, springing over boundaries), which he loved to play with verbally and which informs his graphic technique. . . . It was also the sign of the resolution of the "boundary" paradox in Blake's aesthetics: every line must define, set off, enclose a form in a firm, determinate "bounding line"; but every line must also leap, and cause the pictured form to leap into life. (1983, 152)

Eno's action in Night the First, in which she "took an atom of space & opend its center / Into Infinitude" initiates the poem's complex relation between boundary markers and images of the center (E. 305, 9:12–13).

After most of the action of the poem has taken place, though, what does it mean for Night the Eighth to begin with what appears to be the birth of fallen Albion: "Then all in Great Eternity Met. . . . / Upon the Limit of Contraction to create the fallen Man" (E. 371, 99:1–2)? Apparently, creating in this sense is not the equivalent of originating new life, for

"The Fallen Man stretchd like a Corse upon the oozy Rock" (4). As another incarnation after another death, the fallen Man's perpetual movement through eternity is both a literal depiction of reincarnation and symbolic of the movement of consciousness from its binding notions and constructs toward liberation. It is therefore appropriate that the glimpse of eternity at the end of Night the Seventh affords Albion a new birth.

The Vision of Beulah consists of the nightmares imagined by those who cannot fall. It suggests that one extreme always implies its opposite. Even the Daughters of Beulah are not beyond duality, since the state of redemption, or nonduality, is beyond contraries, beyond virtue as well as vice. The state of human regeneration involves a more evolved understanding of the nature of redemption than the state of Beulah, which frets over fallenness and merely tries to avoid further error. This representation of human regeneration is likewise more evolved than the state that proclaims, "Without Contraries is no progression" (*MHH*, E. 34, pl. 3). It becomes clear in *The Four Zoas* that progress through contraries is not inevitable historical reality but is rather a contraction of consciousness.

The Daughters of Beulah, setting the Limit of Contraction, negotiate not only boundaries—contraction as the opposite of expansion—but the "contract," or the debt humanity owes. Their negotiations result in Albion waking from his death, not into eternal life as liberation from the Mundane Shell but into waking life that is still part of the dream. The proleptic echo of Albion's epiphany in Night the Ninth moves beyond mere parody when Los beholds

> the Divine Vision thro the broken Gates
> Of thy poor broken heart astonishd melted into Compassion & Love
> And Enitharmon said I see the Lamb of God upon Mount Zion
> Wondring with love & Awe they felt the divine hand upon them
> (E. 372, 99:15–18)

The limited perspective of Beulah here echoes their earlier interceptions; the divine is a synecdoche rather than the whole vision of divinity. The Daughters of Beulah plead for man's salvation to a wholly externalized divinity.

Golgonooza is far from a replication of the mandala whose labyrinth leads to the sacred center. It is founded rather on both Beulah's pity and

Urizen's mystery, the two forces competing for domination of fallen consciousness. In spite of this twofold limit that would appear to make redemption impossible, it is in this state that Jesus appears:

> Los loved [the poor wandring spectres]
> With a parental love for the Divine hand was upon him
> And upon Enitharmon & the Divine Countenance shone
> In Golgonooza Looking down the Daughters of Beulah saw
> With joy the bright Light & in it a Human form
> And knew he was the saviour Even Jesus . . .
> Astonishd Comforted Delighted in notes of Rapturous Extacy
> All Beulah stood astonishd Looking down to Eternal Death
> They saw the Saviour beyond the Pit of death & destruction
> For whether they lookd upward they saw the Divine Vision
> Or whether they lookd downward still they saw the Divine Vision
> Surrounding them on all sides beyond sin & death & hell
>   (E. 372, 100:5–16)

Though the fallen mind contains divinity, it can only conceive divinity in
limited form. With the vision of the Savior, it glimpses the "extacy" of the
undifferentiated Self that literally dissolves the boundaries the fallen mind
has created (11). Yet such grace is causally inexplicable according to all that
the fallen mind has set up in its construct of reality. In this way, divinity can
only be perceived synecdochally by limited consciousness. An interesting
detail in the manuscript is the faint pencil drawing of what Magno and
Erdman call "Saviour in globe" on page 9 of Night the First (see figure 8).[13]
The detail is worth noting because it portrays the centric nature of divinity,
watchful and silent at the center of its globe in the midst of the fallen chaos
that casts divinity upward and outside the self.

The Limit of Translucence, perhaps the most dynamic of boundaries,
can be described through the analogue of Heidegger's Transcendent Dasein:

> Characterizing transcendence as the basic structure of subjectivity—be-
> ing *there*—will help us little in exploring the constitution of Dasein. On
> the contrary, since we are now expressly forbidden to introduce a concept
> of subject either explicitly or inexplicitly, transcendence can no longer be
> defined as a "subject-object relationship." Transcendent Dasein . . . sur-
> passes neither a "boundary" which stretches out before the subject and
> forces it to "remain in" (immanence) nor a "gap" which separates it from

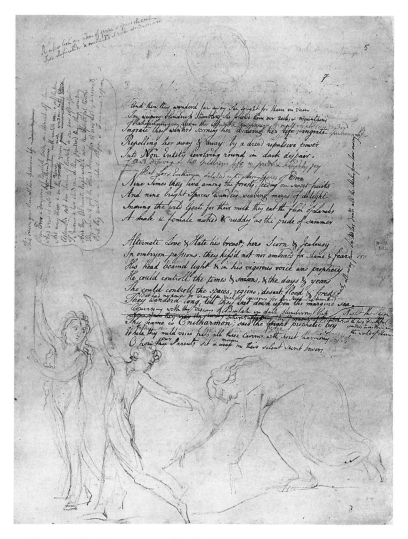

Fig. 8. Night the First. Pencil and chalk drawing. *The Four Zoas*. MS. 39764, folio 5, reprinted with permission from the British Museum, London.

the object. Moreover, objects—objectified beings—are not that *toward which* surpassing happens. *What is* surpassed is simply *being itself,* i.e., every being which can be or become unconcealed to Dasein, *even and precisely* the very being as which Dasein "itself" exists. (1969, 37, 39)

Blake spatializes transcendence as an equipoise between immanence and the "Being" projected outward by the association of liminality with movement from the center.

When such equipoise is thrown off, one has incomplete and distanced glimpses of divinity. In the same way that the synecdoche of the divine hand and the metonymy of the Council of God represent this distortion, the Daughters of Beulah create the limits of Translucence and Opacity, which stand in important relation to the disparity between the unredeemed perception of the cosmos and that revealed in Night the Ninth.

This contrast in the way different states of consciousness represent the relation of the human and the divine is crucial to understanding the larger design of Blake's mythos. Divinity regarded as either the disembodied hand or the Council in Heaven is the creation of a dualistic consciousness that thrusts divinity outside itself and, appropriately, cannot perceive divinity as a whole Self. Fletcher notes that these types are teleologically controlled tropes, with the metonymic giving the effect of our having "trouble distinguishing agent and image." (1964, 87). Yet Blake associates these synecdochal or metonymic representations of divinity with the Daughters of Beulah, who plead to the externalized omniscience for grace. The synecdoche thus appears as a symbolic representation of fictions that project the modifications that fallen consciousness imposes on the Truth—whole and centric, but elusive when reality is thrust outward.

Externalized divinity must therefore be distinguished from an epiphanic moment like Los's vision of the Savior beyond boundaries. The opening of Night the Eighth, for instance, reintroduces the Beulah view of the cosmos, arbitrarily linking causality and time. This association appears ironic after the watershed effect of Night the Seventh's two versions:

Then all in Great Eternity Met in the Council of God
as one Man Even Jesus upon Gilead & Hermon,
Upon the Limit of Contraction to create the fallen Man.
(E. 371, 99:1–3)

The creation of fallen humanity is a paradox, with the poem's irony at the expense of the Daughters of Beulah anxiously "hov'ring over the Sleeper." What the retrospective reading from Night the Ninth and back to this moment teaches is that time and causality are not commensurate. According to Eliade, "death is often only the result of our indifference to immortality"—for the Daughters of Beulah, not recognizing it as the eternal present, or for the fallen Urizen, fearing it as futurity (Eliade 1969, 56).

The Council of God literally realizes the bad dreams of fallen consciousness. Just as divinity is projected outward by the fallen Zoas, so too is the nightmare of fallenness realized physically as weeds that sprout from the floating corpse of Albion's deathly sleep. Said's analysis of the linguistic implications of temporality and significance in Heidegger and Merleau-Ponty illuminates Blake's own representation of time and causality:

> Heidegger and Merleau-Ponty have effectively argued for the equivalence of temporality and significance, yet philosophically and linguistically their view requires us, I think, additionally to acknowledge the mind as providing self-concerned glosses on itself over time, the mind as comprising its own philosophical anthropology. (1975, 43)

This tendency of the mind aptly describes the perpetual reinterpreting by Blake's figures of what the text insists is a fictional origin.

Los's vision of the divine hand thus contributes to the delusion that thrusts divinity outward. He enters Enitharmon's bosom through the broken heart gates and, like Urizen exploring his dens, he can "explore / Its intricate Labyrinths" (E. 372, 99:26–27). In this way, "Los loved [the poor wandering spectre] with a parental love for the Divine Hand was upon him." Los projects his own motives as those of an externalized deity rather than recognizing, as he does in Night the Ninth, divinity within.

The interpretive problem of deciding whether seeing "the Saviour beyond the Pit of death & destruction" (E. 372, 100:13) as a moment of affirmation in the midst of chaos or a misapprehension of divinity can be addressed through Cassirer's analysis of mythical thinking: "Because myth lacks the form of causal analysis it cannot know the sharp dividing line which only this form of thought creates between the whole and its parts" (1955, 51). Though Los, seeing the divine vision "on all sides beyond sin & death & hell (E. 372, 100:16), seems typical of mythical thinking according to

Cassirer, Blake does not apply to nondual consciousness the sharp dividing lines that he would attribute to fallen consciousness. It seems that the fallen figures seeing divinity everywhere they look makes the internal link conspicuous in its absence. If one allows both versions of Night the Seventh influence on what comes after, the suggestion is that redemption necessitates the reintegration of divinity.

CHAPTER V

City of Art, Temple of Mystery:
The Divided Path to Apocalypse

BLAKE LEFT TWO VERSIONS OF NIGHT THE SEVENTH, a source of interpretive controversy for readers of the manuscript. Editors and readers have suggested solutions to the problem by either yoking the two together in a continuous Night or choosing one over the other in an attempt to imagine which Blake preferred or wrote later.[1]

Peter Otto aptly describes the relationship between the two versions through the metaphor of embrace based on that between Los and his Spectre:

> [A]s soon as the Nights are seen to be parallel and contemporaneous and themselves enacting, within the form of the text, "the spectrous embrace," we are able to see that much of the debate that has raged around these Nights is spurious and misleading. . . . In *The Four Zoas* the recognition that good and evil, spirit and flesh, Night the Seventh[a] and [b], are entangled with one another, and the experience of the tension that this duality introduces into the world, will push Los and provoke the reader until there remains no option but the embrace of the whole Man. (1987b, 142–43)

Otto's description is valuable in aligning the spirit of the poem so closely with the textual state of the manuscript.[2] Although in the essay Otto could not develop the larger structural implications of the contemporaneity of

129

the two versions, there are many worth pursuing, particularly the link Otto discovers between the twofold state of Night the Seventh and the dualities of the fallen world.

It is possible then, in fact truer to Blake's design, to consider both versions of Night the Seventh in a single reading without one being subsumed by the other or without attempting to impose a temporal sequence upon them. In Night the Seventh, the fork in the road to apocalypse, fallenness reaches its most dire state while glimpses of eternity promise wholeness. In terms of the poem's concern with representation and mythos, Night the Seventh is the pivotal moment in which the poem must confront its central paradox, the problem of how to represent the imageless. The two versions present two paths to wholeness. Both contain failed architectures of art, the building of which leads in dramatically diverse though not mutually exclusive ways to apocalypse.

Version [a] emphasizes both the building of Golgonooza and the dramatic antagonism between Urizen and Orc that has been intensifying since the rumored usurpation of Urizen's power by Luvah. It thus continues the dynamic between Tharmas and Los-Urthona that was the central concern of Night the Fourth. Night the Seventh [b], on the other hand, de-emphasizes the Zoic contraries, concentrating more on the problems of representation that become literalized as the fallen state grows more elaborate. Blake represents this in the [b] version with the exfoliation of Urizen's Tree of Mystery into the Temple of Allegory.

Representation, specifically the tension between allegory and Blakean symbolism, plays a key role in the crisis that manifests as the two versions of Night the Seventh. Gadamer's comparison of symbol and allegory is useful in isolating the essential difference between the two modes of figuration:

[T]he concept of symbol has a metaphysical background that is entirely lacking in the rhetorical use of allegory. It is possible to be led beyond the sensible to the divine. For the world of the senses is not mere nothingness and darkness but the outflowing and reflection of truth. (1993, 73)

Thus, while Urizen's brand of representation in the [b] version is set against the struggle of Los to enact an artistic labor akin to Gadamer's description, the building of Golgonooza in Night the Seventh [a] appears to be a move toward redemption opposing Urizen's vortical labor: "[T]he Spectre of

Urthona / Wondering beheld the Center open'd; by Divine Mercy inspir'd" (K. 329, VII[a], 373–74).

Golgonooza, however, is not merely antithetical to the earlier fallen architectures. The inability of Enitharmon and Los to create the City of Vision becomes apparent in a moment of ironic revelation on Enitharmon's part:

> I behold the Lamb of God descending
> To Meet these Spectres of the Dead. I therefore fear that he
> Will give us to Eternal Death, fit punishment for such
> Hideous offenders: Uttermost extinction in Eternal Pain. . . .
> Lest any should in futurity do as we have done in heaven.
>
> (K. 330, VII [a], 424–30)

Enitharmon's prophetic exclamation echoes her Song of Death in Night the Second, which usurps the prophetic power of narrative that Los claims. However, it also proleptically glimpses Albion's epiphany in Night the Ninth, beholding Jerusalem and the Lamb of God within her. Nevertheless, with Enitharmon's imposition of faulty logic on her irrational fears ("I therefore fear . . ."), it appears that her vision is delusion. Enitharmon regards divinity as an external justice that punishes man's sins with "uttermost extinction in eternal pain" (K. 330, VII[a], 424–26). In Night the Ninth, by contrast, Albion's eyes are no longer fixed solely outward as they become in Night the Second when he loses the inward connection to vision, "Rising upon his Couch of death Albion beheld his Sons / Turning his Eyes outward to Self. losing the Divine Vision" (E. 313, 23:1–3). The key to Albion's epiphany is that he beholds divinity as an imageless center embodied in the figure of the Lamb of God that is within Jerusalem, in turn within himself. Redeemed vision perpetually frees itself from its own images while fallen understanding, seen in Enitharmon's "vision" of the Lamb of God, clings to images that further distance the divine from the human.

Golgonooza itself raises problems as a city of redeemed imagination. Los and Enitharmon idealize Golgonooza in ways the retrospective reading shows to be distorted. This is clearest, perhaps, in Los's response to Enitharmon. Here, the pattern of their interaction repeats their early conversation, in which Enitharmon's Song of Death plants the seed of Los's "prophecy" of Ulro. There, Los cannot foresee Golgonooza, however flawed it may be. Here, by contrast, Los's description of centricity reveals his potential for playing his part as redeemed prophet in the move toward wholeness:

Stern desire
I feel to fabricate embodied semblances in which the dead
May live before us in our palaces & in our gardens of labour,
Which now, open'd within the Center, we behold spread abroad
To comfort Orc in his dire sufferings

(K. 331, VII [a], 440–44)

Centricity is at its most ambiguous here. This is appropriate, since the state it represents carries suggestions of both the fallen and the redeemed. Thus, Los forsakes the center by projecting Golgonooza outward into the physical world, leaving the center as empty as Urizen's labor does. Yet unlike Urizen, Los recognizes for the first time that he is choosing to comfort the suffering Orc with his images or "embodied semblances," a wholly different, limiting perspective of his role as prophet of imagination than he grasps at the opening of Night the Ninth, in which he no longer sees the function of his art as lifelike semblances of the dead. Instead, in Night the Ninth, the now "dead" Orc is resurrected in the form of Luvah-as-Christ to show him the eternal. At this pivotal moment of imagination, despite Los's desire to save Orc, he uses Urizenic thinking. This shift makes his labor more ambivalent yet, since it claims here to oppose the enslavement of Mystery while nevertheless perpetuating it.

The City of Art cannot stand as the achieved center or goal of the journey of imagination because Los and Enitharmon are still blind to vision, or the center itself. Returning to Jung, one finds that the "squared circle" reveals what is missing in the City of Art in Night the Seventh, particularly if one remembers that Los is the archetypal fourth, the promised hero who drops out of the opening of the poem after he is introduced as such:

> The "squaring of the circle . . ." is one of the most important of [the many archetypal motifs which form the basic patterns of our dreams and fantasies] from the functional point of view. Indeed, it could even be called the *archetype of wholeness*. Because of this significance, the "quaternity of the One" is the schema for all images of God, as depicted in the visions of Ezekiel, Daniel, and Enoch, and as the representation of the Horus with his four sons also shows. (Jung 1969, 388)

Blake disturbs the pattern by making it impossible for Los, the fourth, to complete the mandala by his presence alone. Completeness reveals itself instead in the collective recognition of the fifth point at the center. In this way, the "quaternity" is transformed into the quincunx that completes the mandala in Night the Ninth.

This, however, is where Jung must be abandoned, since Blake's center eludes the depiction by a single point. In one Jungian reading, for instance, the behavior of the Zoas is compared to case studies of patients who create mandalas. Yet this analogy suggests the misleading conclusion that Los completes the mandala in Night the Seventh when, through Los's agency, the circle is "divided into just proportions" (Gallant 1978, 78). Jung's discussion of the squared circle illuminates, instead, what is lacking in Los's role in Night the Seventh and, in turn, what it contributes at the opening of Night the Ninth. Because consciousness as a whole must find equipoise to redeem itself, it is not enough for Los to behold divinity or even to aspire toward an architecture antithetical to the one he built when Tharmas commissioned the Universe of Death. The difference becomes clear in the sequence of epiphanies that comprises the complete quincunx in Night the Ninth.

Los himself makes a significant turn toward wholeness in Night the Seventh [a] when he begins to see that the inner/outer dichotomy is an illusion:

> Los embracd the Spectre first as his brother
> Then as another Self; astonishd humanizing & in tears
> In Self abasement Giving up his Domineering lust
> 											(E. 367, 95:29–31)

But Los still regards the Spectre as "*another* self," outside and threatening the limited self, revealing the extent to which his understanding of wholeness is incomplete. So too, the Spectre claiming the voice of prophecy also has a limited vision of eternity: "If we unite in one, another better world will be / Opend within your heart & loins & wondrous brain" (E. 368, 85:43–44). Though this revelation prophesies the apocalypse, the Spectre has a distorted notion of union according to Night the Ninth, for he says that it will be the end of time.

In this way, the ambivalence of centricity, its power to signify different states, is based on the inability of contracted consciousness to behold eternity in time as long as it clings to its notion of duality. Los understands what he could not before, namely, the divinity within himself:

Even I already feel a World within
Opening its gates & in it all the real substances
Of which these in the outward World are shadows

(E. 368, 86:7–9)

Yet when he embraces Enitharmon and the Spectre, vision is qualified with the subjunctive: "clouds *would have* folded round in Extacy & Love Uniting / But Enitharmon trembling fled & hid beneath Urizen's tree." The word "extacy" is significant: Los is on the brink, so to speak, of "standing out of place," the etymology of "ecstasy." The fallen impulse to hide and flee, which has been the pattern since Night the First, however, prevents this from being the moment of apocalypse.

It is in this pivotal moment that they build Golgonooza, City of Art:

But mingling together with his Spectre the Spectre of Urthona
Wondering beheld the Center opend by Divine Mercy inspired
He in his turn Gave Tasks to Los Enormous to destroy
That body he created but in vain for Los performd Wonders of labour
They builded Golgonooza

(E. 368, 87:2–6)

It resembles the redeemed mandala, but the labor is also "in vain," for Los's labor is fallen. As another perhaps more insidious version of Ulro, this pivotal moment in the quest reveals most clearly Blake's method of signification. Blake's signifiers can represent a multiplicity of ideas, but the key to their meaning is derived by the state of the perceiver. The fact that the perceiver can be in the state of organized innocence, however, qualifies what most scholars have said about Blake's symbols. Damrosch, drawing on several theories of symbolism, ultimately denies that Eden, the redeemed state, is available to all humans:

The problematic status of symbolic meaning is not an occasion for celebrating the richness of human experience, but a demoralizing symptom of the Fall. In Eden, by contrast, experience and art, vision and speech, unite in a single harmony. . . . But we do not live in Eden, and it would be wrong to suppose that these lines . . . describe experience as Blake actually knows it. (1980, 72)

It is not experience but organized innocence that undeniably knows the state that Blake describes with such clarity. The state of the perceiver is a composite of all elements of the interpreter of the given moment, namely, the character, the narrator, the derived authorial voice, and even the reader.[3]

As Los stands under Urizen's tree, beholding his art as Urizen's fruit, he is "filled with doubts in self accusation" (E. 369, 87:13). This version of the fall is a radical revision of the Biblical myth. Although Enitharmon reenacts Eve's part, the fruit with which she tempts Los is the product of his collusion with Mystery:

> Urthonas Spectre terrified beheld the Spectres of the Dead
> Each Male formd without a counterpart without a
>   concentering vision
> The Spectre of Urthona wept before Los Saying I am
>   the cause
> That this dire state commences I began this dreadful state
> Of Separation
>   (E. 369, 87:29–33)

The fruit is the product of fallen imagination whose art is inevitably flawed. Prophetic art grafted with "Universal Ornament" is tainted because it hides and distorts truth rather than revealing it. In this way six thousand years of death pass until Urthona recognizes that his dualistic separation of time and eternity has contributed to fallenness.

Urthona's newfound understanding forms a new causal link in the chain of the temporal world. His glimpse of his own participation in the fallen world in turn heralds a glimpse of "Ransom" and redemption (E. 369, 87:34). Los can now say to Enitharmon,

> but look! behold! take comfort!
> Turn inwardly thine Eyes & there behold the Lamb of God
> Clothed in Luvahs robes of blood descending to redeem
>   (E. 369, 87:42–44)

This moment anticipates Night the Ninth's chain of epiphanies. Los redeems the early moment in Night the Second when Albion turns his eyes outward. In language proleptic of Albion's epiphany in Night the Ninth, Enitharmon here proclaims, "I behold the Lamb of god descending / To Meet these Spectres of the Dead" (E. 369, 87:52–53).

But because she attributes the power of this moment to fear, Enitharmon maintains a separation from rather than merging with the eternal. The apparent revelation of Los and Enitharmon at the end of Night the Seventh is yet an incomplete understanding according to the collective epiphany of Night the Ninth. It has all the elements of fallen thinking from Beulah's pity and nostalgia. Recognizing Enitharmon's flaws but being blind to his own, Los responds,

> Thy bosom translucent is a soft repose for the weeping souls
> Of those piteous victims of battle there they sleep in happy obscurity
> They feed upon our life we are their victims.
>
> (E. 370, 98:6–8)

Enitharmon describes Golgonooza as a place of sacrifice. Even though it is open within the center, fear still predominates. Los thus perpetuates fallenness even as he contributes to the building toward redemption:

> O Lovely terrible Los wonder of Eternity O Los my defence & guide
> Thy works are all my joy. & in thy fires thy soul delights
> If mild they burn in just proportion & in secret night
> And silence build their day in shadow of soft clouds & dews
> Then I can sigh forth on the winds of Golgonooza piteous forms
> That vanish again into my bosom
>
> (E. 370, 98:16–21)

Enitharmon's language is proleptic of Vala's epiphany in which Vala hears her own voice on the wind when she had been seeking the voice of the Other as Luvah. However, Enitharmon's understanding here is far from Vala's epiphany, since Enitharmon's pity heightens duality. Taking in the "piteous forms," she does not reclaim another as the Self. As the divine vision shows, they simply disappear, echoing Jerusalem's apparent disappearance when Tharmas "hides" her at the opening of the poem.

Night the Seventh [b] takes a divergent path, moving toward apocalypse through Urizenic Mystery. It is thus the more directly parodic form of vision as redeemed representation. Problematic in a different way from the

[a] version, Night the Seventh [b] underscores Urizenic Mystery, which had been manifested essentially in narrative terms in the [a] version, setting it against redeemed representation in Night the Ninth. Version [b] thus begins in the depths beneath the Tree of Mystery with Urizen musing over the significance of his conquests:

> The time of Prophecy is now revolv'd, & all
> The Universal ornament is mine, & in my hands
> The ends of heaven; like a Garment will I fold them round me,
> Consuming what must be consum'd; then in power & majesty
> I will walk forth thro' those wide fields of endless Eternity,
> A God & not a Man, a Conqueror in triumphant glory.
>   (K. 333, VII [b], 4–9; E. 360, 95:18–23)

Blake here has Urizen make the allegorical connection of the medieval *kosmos* and ornament. As Angus Fletcher explains of medieval allegory, "It termed the kosmos of Scripture 'difficult ornament.' 'Difficulty' implies here a calculated obscurity which elicits an interpretive response in the reader" (1964, 234). Urizen's "Universal ornament" is complicated by his being wrapped in the heavens, which is parodic of Jerusalem shrouded in Enion's tabernacle.

Owen Barfield's distinction between allegory and myth in relation to "ornaments" helps explain Blake's opposition of Urizenic representation to the redeemed as mythical:

> These [ornaments] are "based on a *synthesis of ideas,* rather than on immediate cognition of reality." "In fact the accidental metaphor [ornament] carries with it a suggestion of having been constructed upon a sort of framework of logic. . . . The distinction between true and false metaphor corresponds to the distinction between Myth and Allegory, allegory being a more or less conscious hypostatization of *ideas,* followed by a synthesis of them, and myth the true child of Meaning, begotten on Imagination." (Fletcher 1964, 75–76 n. 8)

Barfield's distinction raises an important qualification to Damrosch's conclusion that

> [t]his deep ambivalence toward symbols underlies many of the difficulties in Blake's myth. When it is most allegorical, he is trying to force it to

do its bidding; when it is most symbolic, he hopes that by sharing in the Divine Vision we can see the truth without constant signposts to show us the way. (1980, 96)

Blake's inclusion of Urizenic Mystery within his own myth suggests a similar distinction between allegory and myth, which for Blake constitutes the dynamic opposition of fallen and redeemed representation. The poem continually poses this opposition between the creation of the waking life of the discursive faculties and vision as the dream of undifferentiated consciousness.

Urizen's "universal ornament" is thus the created world of the limited mind. It is set against the imagery of Albion's revelation in Night the Ninth, which, contrasted to Urizen's "universal ornament," is closer to the ancient meaning of *kosmos:*

> *Kosmos* does not mean any particular being that might come to our attention, nor the sum of all beings; instead, it means something like "condition" or "state of affairs," i.e., the *How* in which being is *in its totality.* Thus, *kosmos houtos* does not designate one realm of being to the exclusion of another but rather one world of being in contrast to a different world of the same being. . . . The world as this "How in its totality" underlies every possible way of segmenting being; segmenting being does not destroy the world but *requires* it. (Heidegger 1969, 49)

For Blake's figures, this is the "extacy" of apocalypse seen in Urizen's questioning in Night the Ninth of how one stands in relation to eternity, the wonder that initiates the apocalypse that "does not destroy the world but requires it." "Eternal birth" is the crucial phrase in this moment of apocalypse, for origin becomes a state just as Kosmos is.

Fallenness, represented by Urizen's universal ornament, is a state coeternal with birth, or beginning. Urizen's founding the Center in the Deep with a command to reverse "all the order of delight" suggests that beginning demands a discontinuity. However, Blake represents infinity as the continuous underlying the discontinuous, so that Urizenic Mystery represents the contrary of redeemed causation. Though birth may be a discontinuity, to use Said's term, fallenness in Blake's mythos continuously rediscovers this discontinuity and, in so doing, discovers the underlying continuity.

In this way, Blake's emphasis on centers suggests the difference between Urizenic allegory and redemptive myth, Barfield's "imagination" being equivalent to Blake's "vision." Urizen continues his fantasy of conquest by carrying out the building of his Temple of Mystery. Significantly, his Temple is founded on a parodic center:

> And he commanded his Sons [to] found a Center in the Deep;
> And Urizen laid the first stone. . . .
> And in the inner part of the Temple . . .
> They form'd the Secret place, reversing all the order of delight,
> That whosoever enter'd into the temple might not behold
> The hidden wonders, allegoric of the Generations
> Of secret lust, when hid in chambers dark the nightly harlot
> Plays in Disguise in whisper'd hymn & mumbling prayer
> (K. 333, VII [b], 18–26; E.361, 95:31–96:6)

The secrecy of Urizen's universal ornament is his source of power in the fallen world. The poem initiates this secrecy with Tharmas's instinctive hiding of Jerusalem.

Thus, the parody of a universe with vision at its center is Urizen's temple whose inner secret is emptiness surrounded by allegorical representations of the fall, or in Barfield's words, false metaphor.[4] Blake's inclusion of Urizenic allegory within his own representation complicates Hazard Adams's distinction between Blake's and Vico's symbolism:

> [T]o be at a center is to be in a condition where one points outward *toward* everything, as allegory is always pointing us *to* something. To be at a circumference is to contain, as mathematical form contains physical reality or the poem its so-called meaning. (1983, 19)

Blake is able to represent both what Adams refers to as poetic and conceptual logic by opposing Urizenic allegory to the redeemed. Yet this is never a simple dialectic, for by telling of their relationship through poetic discourse Blake problematizes the causal connections in ways that other discourses— theological, philosophical, or theoretical—do not.

Night the Seventh can thus be seen as the fork, or more accurately cul-de-sac, in the path toward wholeness. Figuration reaches its most fallen state with Urizenic obfuscation in one and, in the other, the mistaken good-will of an imaginative tribute to the dead through Los-Urthona's "embod-ied semblances." It is perhaps more difficult to see Golgonooza as an errant center of art, because it is less distinguishable from Blakean vision than is Urizen's. Nevertheless, it is flawed in its perception of that which it repre-sents as other, and so it too explodes in the fire of apocalypse. In this way, the reader does not have to choose between them in the name of a coherent plotline. Blake's revision of traditional narrative suggests that the critical moment splits versions of narrative and figuration, bringing them back together to be transfigured by the vision of wholeness they lack in their dualistic enterprises.

Golgonooza, by Night the Eighth, is a structure that must defend itself against the forms of "self deceit" that Urizen causes, thus heralding the extreme state of Mystery. The harrowing of Ulro inspires Los's creativity:

> Enormous Works Los Contemplated inspird by the holy Spirit
> Los builds the Walls of Golgonooza against the stirring battle
> That only thro the Gates of Death they can enter to Enitharmon
> (E. 374, 101:39–41)

The fruit of the Tree of Mystery forms a constellation that grows out of Urizen's control. Just as Los and Enitharmon are ambivalent regarding their own created images at the pivotal moment between fallenness and redemp-tion, so too is Urizen. Although he beholds Luvah as the Lamb of God, he is still subject to the power of his own Mystery. Urizen therefore sees him as separate, even doubting that this creature could be the old Luvah:

> Perplexd & terrifid he Stood tho well he knew that Orc
> Was Luvah But he now beheld a new Luvah. Or One
> Who assumd Luvahs form & stood before him opposite
> But he saw Orc a Serpent form augmenting times on times
> In the fierce battle & he saw the Lamb of God & the world of Los
> Surrounded by his dark machines for Orc augmented swift
> In fury a Serpent wondrous among the Constellations of Urizen
> (E. 373, 101:2–8)

The description is of a creature formed out of the stars, a mythographic allusion to the universal attempt to know the universe by fictionalizing it.

The explanation for Urizen's massive assault upon the senses is made explicit here:

> The spirits of life to pervert all the faculties of sense
> Into their own destruction if perhaps he might avert
> His own despair even at the cost of every thing that breathes
> (E. 375, 102:20–22)

Paradoxically, the constellation giving rise to the serpent form of Orc is followed by the "Shadowy hermaphrodite," Satan. Urizen's perception of Luvah-Orc, then, splits into redeemer and destroyer. This is perhaps the most extreme moment in which the figure as signifier reveals its power to convey meaning that depends on the state of the composite interpreter, thus showing the extreme contrast between Blake's own representation and Urizenic allegory.

It is Vala who, acknowledging that Luvah and Orc are one, makes a direct appeal to Urizen:

> For he was source of every joy that this mysterious tree
> Unfolds in Allegoric fruit. When shall the dead revive
> Can that which has existed cease or can love & life Expire
> (E. 375, 103:18–20)

The caesura brings the two seeming non sequiturs together in a suggested causal relationship. Out of the convergence of mythic eternity and allegorical Mystery arises Vala's question of whether love and life can simply stop existing, suggesting that the answer will be different depending on one's state.

Blake confounds the simple dichotomy between allegory and myth by complicating the constellation out of which Urizen creates his perception of Orc. The result is a form of the inverted mandala:

> Urizen heard the Voice & saw the Shadow. underneath
> His woven darkness & in laws & deceitful religions
> Beginning at the tree of Mystery circling its root

She spread herself thro all the branches in the power of Orc
A shapeless & indefinite cloud in tears of sorrow incessant
Steeping the Direful Web of Religion swagging heavy it fell
From heaven to heavn thro all its meshes altering the Vortexes
Misplacing every Center hungry desire & lust began
(E. 375, 103:21–28)

It is important to keep in mind that, as the fallen form of the mandala, the
vortex shares with it the characteristic of the empty center. As chapter 4 has
discussed, the vortex associates this emptiness with fear, chaos, and annihilation, throwing centers off in a vertiginous, undirected movement, while
the mandala associates the empty center with peace, equilibrium, and liberation. The vortex, in this case, reveals how Urizen becomes trapped in his
own machinery of self-protection.

Bruno Snell's distinction between myth and logic helps explain the
difference between the Blakean myth at work in the poem and Urizenic
thinking:

Mythical thought is closely related to the thinking in images and similes.
Psychologically speaking, both differ from logical thought in that the
latter searches and labours while the figures of myth and the images of
the similes burst fully-shaped upon the imagination. (1960, 224)

The building of Golgonooza is the attempt to build a sanctuary in the
midst of perception that emerges from contracted consciousness. It promises the possibility of detachment even through the revolutions of such
dualities as attraction and aversion and desire and antagonism. The simultaneously antithetical impulses nevertheless torpedo the attempts to build
a sacred city of art. From Golgonooza, paradoxically, arises the "Direful
Web of Religion," which falls "From heaven to heavn thro all its meshes
altering the Vortexes / Misplacing every Center hungry desire & lust began" (E. 375, 103:27–28).

Just as fallen moments form flawed images and concepts, they also
contain the power to glimpse the imageless divine:

[Enitharmon] sighd forth on the wind the spectres
And wove them bodies calling them her belovd sons & daughters . . .
In Golgonoozas Furnaces among the Anvils of time & space

Thus forming a Vast family wondrous in beauty & love
And they appeard a Universal female form created
From those who were dead in Ulro from the Spectres of the dead
(E. 376, 103:33–39)

Jerusalem, conceived out of "the Spectres of the dead," redeems in unexpected ways Los's flawed art and Enitharmon's prophecy of Night the Seventh:

And Enitharmon namd the Female Jerusa[le]m the holy
Wondring she saw the Lamb of God within Jerusalems Veil
The divine Vision seen within the inmost deep recess
Of fair Jerusalems bosom in a gently beaming fire
(E. 376, 104:1–4)

Now the vision mirrors Albion's recognition of divinity as a circle whose center is everywhere and circumference nowhere. Northrop Frye discusses Blake's circle in similar terms:

The Bible begins with a world of watery chaos and a pair of spiritual infants in a garden who grow up in a wilderness. But by the time we have reached the end we realize that the Bible, like other epics, has started with the action fairly well advanced, and that the Book of Genesis needs a prelude about a fiery city in which a single divine and human body formed the circumference of the whole of nature. Such a prelude, if we could be sufficiently inspired to compose one, would turn out to be very similar to the conclusion of the existing Book of Revelation. All things have proceeded from a divine Man, the body of Jesus, and will be reabsorbed into him; and the total vision of life must have a circular form.

But if the Bible had begun where it now ends, it would have presented its vision in a *closed* circle, and a closed circle would have suggested, as some Indian visions are said to do, the indefinite recurrence, not only of natural cycles, but of the whole progression of life itself from fall to apocalypse. (1947, 386)

Frye uses the Indian analogy to compare historical circularity with Blake's circle. Like the symbolism of the center in Indian myth, Blake's center is the timeless Self from which radiates the spiraling chaos of life or, for Blake, fallen consciousness. Frye's discussion of the circle thus does not depart from linearity any more than the dialectical readings mentioned earlier, since it is absorbed in time. Frye goes on to say, "But the Jesus we attain by this process of pulling the Bible around in a circle is polarized by the Jesus who stands opposite him in the middle of the Biblical narrative. Here again is the contrast between the present Jesus of vision and the past Jesus of history." For Blake, vision is coeternal with history. God dwells within man as the play of his consciousness, the drama which is history. The ineffable stillness of the center, which is called Jerusalem, witnesses the drama even though the characters do not perceive her.

By contrast, though the Sons of Eden are well-meaning in their plea for an end to suffering, their dualism simply perpetuates fallenness. Their exclamation "We now behold the ends of Beulah" has a double meaning: the final stages of the state called Beulah as well as the motives of the equally well-meaning but dualistic Daughters. The Sons urge the Divine Lamb to take the Satanic body, an act that undoes Beulah's protective work to separate the Lamb and Satan:

> Glory Glory Glory to the holy Lamb of God
> Who now beginneth to put off the dark Satanic body
> Now we behold redemption Now we know that life Eternal
> Depends alone upon the Universal hand & not in us
> Is aught but death In individual weakness sorrow & pain
>   (E. 376, 104:5–10)

The Sons of Eden sing hymns of praise whose distortion might be missed out of context. The Lamb of God puts off the Satanic body. In the terms of Blake's myth, both forms emerge out of Luvah, human passion. Further, the enjambment at the end of line 9 suggests the Sons' wrong understanding of divinity: as in Beulah, eternity seems to depend upon an externalized and synecdochal divinity rather than a divinity "in us." Reading line 9 together with line 10 emphasizes this separation, the individual containing only the effects of his frailty: "not in us / Is aught but death in individual weakness sorrow & pain."

In this way, war, which Beulah attempts to arrest, is unleashed as "[t]he Lamb of God stood before Satan opposite." Just as redemption is continuous and God takes human form whenever consciousness is liberated from duality, so too does the historical crucifixion recur whenever duality and separation reach their extreme:

Jerusalem saw the Body dead upon the Cross She fled away
Saying Is this Eternal Death Where shall I hide from Death
Pity me Los pity me Urizen & let us build
A Sepulcher & worship Death in fear while yet we live
                                                    (E. 379, 106:7–10)

Evident here is the influence of Los-Urthona's art on Jerusalem; it distorts understanding of the liberation of God from incarnation by deeming it the worship of death.

Only at this point, in which the robes of Luvah are revealed to hold Satan and mystery, can Los understand that Satan is a state rather than "another." Los thus proclaims his renewed power as prophet by revising his version of the fall. He now carefully distinguishes moments in time from eternity, which is invulnerable to limitation:

There is a State namd Satan learn distinct to know O Rahab
The Difference between States & Individuals of those States
The State namd Satan never can be redeemd in all Eternity
But when Luvah in Orc became a Serpent he des[c]ended into
That State calld Satan Enitharmon breathd forth on the Winds
Of Golgonooza
                                                    (E. 380, 107 [115]:23-28)

The poem here plants the seeds of vision even as Night the Eighth signals the movement from Mystery into natural religion with the fallen world precipitating toward apocalypse. The understanding now emerges that casting out all but the limited self leads to idolatry: "The Lamb of God has rent the Veil of Mystery soon to return / In Clouds & Fires around the rock & the Mysterious tree" (E. 385, 114:1–2).

The reverse of the two phrases above, of course, is also true: Though Enion predicts the end of Mystery, delusive arts are the weapons of the Antichrist at the moment of harrowing. Blake again confounds the attempt to impose a teleology on the chain of events. The mixed state of the human mind will see horror or liberation at such a moment, depending on the composite state of the interpreter. In a sense, all imagery of contracted consciousness is merely a type of the apocalypse that is beyond imagery.[5] Blake would agree with Austin Farrer that redemption is the liberation of images from fixed signification:

Being externalized, the images taken for the reality of the divine became idolatry, and taken for the reality of nature became a false science. The rejection of idolatry meant not the destruction but the liberation of the images. (1949, 14)

For Blake, the reign of the Antichrist gives birth to natural religion. Poetically, worship of nature without vision is idolatry.

Urizen's epiphanic question in Night the Ninth of where one can take a human stand in eternity should be considered in relation to his fallen need to place himself at the center of a world he controls allegorically. Hazard Adams discusses this fallen aspect of Urizen:

Ultimately . . . the devourer is at the circumference of a kind of myth of his own, but actually what I shall call an antimythical fiction that insists paradoxically on placing him at the center of experience and surrounding him with infinite space and time. If he does not appreciate the powerful irony of this situation and bring in the contrary, he is in trouble. Thus the curious difficulties Urizen has in finding a place to stand in *The Four Zoas* and his inability to attain to a circumference. He does not grasp that his antimyth is a created fictive form. He makes it surround and determine him as a fixed "reality." (1983, 112)

Adams's point about Urizen's fallenness is crucial, revealing indirectly much about what transpires in Night the First through Night the Eighth. Urizen's is the same kind of need for authority found in the Spectre of Urthona in Night the Seventh [a]. Further, it speaks to the relation between Blake's myth and the fictions within it. However, the outer dream qualifies too substantially any commentary on the fictions within it for such commentary effectively to apply theories of traditional narrative method without acknowledging Blake's radical revision.

Urizen's Tree of Mystery represents the paradox of perpetuating ignorance by deluding itself as knowledge. Nevertheless, hope for renewed vision permeates even the grimmest moments. The fire that destroys one form to create another perhaps worse one is the same fire that in Night the Ninth razes all duality in a moment of ecstatic recognition. The dissolution of form, repeated over and over at this extreme stage in the crisis of imaging the other, represents the overcoming of limit lines:

The form of Orc was gone he reard his serpent bulk among
The stars of Urizen in Power rending the form of life
Into a formless indefinite

(E. 365, 93:25–27)

The poem, even when it represents experience at its most violently fallen, reaches beyond the duality of good and evil. The liberation from form is death as a release from the life that the Zoas experience perpetually, though with different valuations—some ecstatic, some terrified at the release from duality. Regardless of these differences in reaction, the essential self paradoxically longs for atomization and independence in its quest for wholeness and union.

In this sense, Blake's figures are more than just the potentiality of poetic naming, as Adams argues (1983, 107). Vala's discovery in Night the Ninth also suggests that the undivided Self is that apparent Other to which she calls and who responds: the realization of poetic naming within the dream. Vala, the figure most directly associated with the elusiveness of naming, delights in her infinite variety. Raine (1983) has compared Vala to Maya, the illusion of a separate phenomenal world. Naming Vala is one of the poem's central puzzles, because she takes so many forms in the course of the quest toward wholeness. Who, then, is the Vala that the Demons of the Deep invoke in Night the Seventh [b]? They urge her to prepare for battle, but what battle? Is it one the story has built toward in narrative terms?

For something to be called "fallen" according to the universe of the poem is not a moral judgment on Blake's part, a claim readers often make in their indictment of Vala by taking as authorial the words of the fallen characters. It rather represents her ignorance of the One behind the diverse, or the Self within the other, in contrast with her revelation in Night the Ninth. Thus, "[t]he Shadowy Female varied in the War in her delight / Howling in discontent black & heavy" (E. 365, 93:33–34). Ironically, Tharmas mistakes her for Enion. This confusion of the identities of the Emanations is symptomatic of the Spectres, forming a parodic version of the dissolving of difference at the apocalypse among all the separate figures. In the fallen state, however, the confusion reveals the Spectres' misogyny, made extreme in their claim that the Emanations are interchangeable. After hearing Ahania's story of Vala's seduction of Albion, Urizen expresses this confusion: "Art thou become like Vala."[6] Tharmas, however, says, "I hear thy voice but not thy form see" (E. 366, 94:8). This differs from Urizen's rhetorical question, since it is not a matter of confusing a tale-teller for her subject, but of not recognizing the form because of the transfigurations wrought by the vicissitudes of fallenness.

In contrast to her epiphany in Night the Ninth, Vala responds with the same imagery in a parodic misunderstanding: "Hast thou forgot that the air listens thro all its districts telling / The subtlest thoughts shut up from light in chambers of the Moon" (E. 366, 94:10–11). This is Vala's mythmaking, which is not evil, as the characters claim, but a modification of that which is uncontainable in image or word. Vala's epiphany in Night the Ninth is the recognition that she is speaker and auditor, subject and object. The distinction between inner and outer realms collapses in a moment of liberation.

The double transformation of Vala and Jerusalem brings wholeness to its culmination. By Night the Ninth, they are joined in the mutual redemption that is the poem's central epiphany. In Night the Eighth, however, it is crucial that this innocence provides a counterpoint to Urizen's vortical universe. The question that arises in light of the double perspective is how one regards Jerusalem's entrance:

Thus forming a Vast family wondrous in beauty & love
And they appeard a Universal female form created
From those who were dead in Ulro from the Spectres of the dead

And Enitharmon named the Female Jerusa[le]m the holy
Wondering she saw the Lamb of God within Jerusalems Veil
The divine Vision seen within the inmost deep recess
Of fair Jerusalems bosom in a gently beaming fire
                                   (E. 376, 103:37–39, 104:1–4)

Leibniz's "manifestation of being," as Heidegger explains it, has significant implications for Blake's depiction of organized innocence, whose nondifferentiation stands in contrast with the confusions of fallen understanding: "Truth, then, means consonance. And consonance is only 'consonance' as correspondence with that which announces itself as 'at one' or 'alike' in the identity." Heidegger complicates this by noting that "as the possible 'subject' of a predicative definition, being must already be manifest both *prior to* and *for* our predications. . . . *The disclosedness of Being alone makes possible the manifestness of being.* As the truth about Being, this disclosedness is called *ontological truth*" (1969, 19, 23).

The contrapuntal relation of the unredeemed voices of fallenness and unorganized innocence suggests that Jerusalem, a "created" form, is a product of fallen mythmaking. Criticism has tended to regard the providential figures in the poem in the same terms as the redemptive vision of Night the Ninth. This tendency becomes problematic when such criticism tries to account for the Beulah vision in this complexly transitional Night: "By the time Night VIII was written, Blake was certainly suggesting a positive attitude toward both the 'shadowy Vortex' and its descent into 'Eternal Death'. . . . Night VIII is a war Night (Blake still had not disentangled the idea of apocalypse from the imagery of war)" (Wagenknecht 1973, 236–37). Yet Blake consciously upholds the distinction between nostalgia and redemptive vision, "re-vision" as opposed to memory. In Night the Eighth, divinity is still beheld as external:

> Then sang the Sons of Eden round the Lamb of God & said
> Glory Glory Glory to the holy Lamb of God
> Who now beginneth to put off the dark Satanic body
> Now we behold redemption Now we know that life Eternal
> Depends alone upon the Universal hand & not in us
> Is aught but death In individual weakness sorrow & pain
>
> (E. 376, 104:5–10)

This must be distinguished from the epiphany of Night the Ninth in which Vala recognizes that the Lord she had sought as Luvah is the echo of her own voice. The difference, of course, is that here in Night the Eighth, the Sons of Eden, blind to inner vision, regard all within them as evil. In spite of his "subversive" reading, Ault equates the narrator with Blake's perspective, thereby claiming that Blake succumbs to orthodoxy in Night the Eighth:

> Blake disturbingly acknowledges our need for a relief from the nearly unbearable tension of increasing complexity in the poem by incorporating into the narrator's intrusive judgments a version of our yearning to behold a redemption in a fiction external to ourselves (and to the text) and by projecting *in the characters* a need for and belief in a form of salvation that displaces responsibility away from themselves. (1987, 243)

When one allows for the interplay of fallen and redeemed moments as a means of deriving the authorial voice, however, one sees that the characters are far from personae for Blake.

This song of the Sons of Eden in Night the Eight gives the most direct reference to the synecdoche of the divine hand. One realizes it is the product of fallen vision through the orientation of Night the Ninth. Redeeming this moment, Vala's own voice in Night the Ninth transforms the call and response of the sons of Eden into the echo of a single voice:

> Follow me O my flocks & hear me sing my rapturous Song . . .
> I will call & who shall answer me I will sing who shall reply
> For from my pleasant hills behold the living living springs . . .
> I sing & you reply to my Song I rejoice & you are glad
>
> (E. 397, 128:9–15)

The "living living" echo intimates that, when Vala expects the answering voice to be separate from her self, it is her own voice that answers. Her gentle flocks are the positive counterimage of Ahania's fear of Urizen's "flocks of Wolves," an innocence underscored by the image of Vala leaning on a ram as she sleeps. Vala's sinless voice echoes and redeems as well the rejoicing "Glory, Glory, Glory" of the Sons of Eden in Night the Eighth.[7]

It is not surprising, then, that it is Vala who completes the transfiguration of Ouroboros into mandala. She, more than any of the other figures, embodies the saving epiphany of the human divine. This transformation is perhaps the most critical reason why a purely Jungian reading of Vala impoverishes Blake's representation by casting her in

> the role of the uroboric Great Mother who threateningly holds her son in the grip of the unconscious. Jung would call her a "Devouring Mother." Throughout the poem, Luvah is encompassed in the fiery round of the "Furnaces of affliction & sealed" as the embryo is in the womb. (Gallant 1978, 60)

Vala's newfound "sinless soul" transcends the nostalgia for the mythical golden world because it recognizes the simultaneity of fallenness and redemption. This dissolution of difference is figured in the vocalization of inner divinity. First, however, Vala must desire this union:

Her garments rejoice in the vocal wind & her hair glistens with dew
She answerd thus Whose voice is this in the voice of the nourishing
    air . . .
O thou creating voice that callest & who shall answer thee
Where dost thou flee O fair one where doest thou seek thy happy place
                                        (E. 395–96, 126:35–127:1)

At this point, Vala still thinks the voice is outside of and separate from herself. It is significant that the reader knows no more than Vala, perceiving only that the wind carries the "creating voice." Vala longs for the presence of that voice, imagining the *locus amenus* it synecdochally represents to her. One might contrast this "creating voice" to what Irving Massey calls Pope's "uncreating word," a wholly antithetical version of apocalypse and language. Massey discusses Pope's antithetical portrayal of apocalypse in *The Dunciad* as

> the word that undoes creation; it is the word that rolls the film of experience back off the reel of time. It is the answer to God's word, and it restores the silence before the beginning. It is also the word of aphasia, the word that allows us to sink back into the golden age before meaning had been invented. (1970, 87–88)

Vala, by contrast, embodies the Blakean epiphany. Raine, suggesting that Vala's source in Greek mythology is Psyche, compares Vala to Thel through Psyche:

> [She] makes the descent Thel refused; and her figure is enriched by attributes of Psyche. She too comes to the Northern Gate, and the porter admits her; but she does not enter the world alone: she is accompanied by a divine lover who has prepared a garden for her. . . . Like Psyche, Vala is attended, in her bodily house, by invisible servants. These are the spiritual agents of all natural appearances; "for," so Blake believed, "every Natural Effect has a Spiritual Cause." But it is not only her servants who are invisible to her; it is the divine lover himself. As Psyche could hear the voice of Cupid though she could not see him, so Vala hears the voice of Luvah. . . . All follows as in the old legend. (1963, 24, 27)

Yet Vala departs from the myth through her turn inward, which she achieves through the inner link to divinity. The crucial turn toward epiphany thus occurs in the assimilation of call and response. Vala, projecting divinity as external, seeks a response that, in turn, becomes the paradoxical harbinger of epiphany. The synecdochal "creating voice" eludes her as she imagines it belonging to her truant lover, her own fiction of the sun:

> Alas am I but as a flower then will I sit me down
> Then will I weep then Ill complain & sigh for immortality
> And chide my maker thee O Sun that raisedst me to fall
> So saying she sat down & wept beneath the apple trees
> O be thou blotted out thou Sun that raisedst me to trouble
> That gavest me a heart to crave & raisedst me thy phantom
> To feel thy heat & see thy light & wander here alone
> Hopeless if I am like the grass & so shall pass away
>   (E. 396, 127:16–23)

This fiction is curious in light of the fictions other characters create regarding her seduction of Albion, the composite story that defines fallen consciousness in the earlier Nights. Vala here transposes the lover from the poem's mythology to the archetypal Sun as the center and creator of the universe. The authorial voice further complicates the multiple layering of representation by locating her under the apple trees, an image resonating with the Garden of Eden and suggestive of Vala's enslavement to the Tree of Mystery in Night the Seventh.

What are we to make of this dense interweaving of allusions? The question is best addressed by reading further, which not only complicates but also completes the effect. The turn from Vala's darkness to light comes at the moment when she speaks to her Self:

> Rise sluggish Soul why sitst thou here why dost thou sit & weep
> Yon Sun shall wax old & decay but thou shalt ever flourish
> The fruit shall ripen & fall down & the flowers consume away
> But thou shalt still survive arise O dry thy dewy tears
>   (E. 396, 127:24–27)

Vala recognizes the soul's immortality as opposed to the natural world, whose center, the Sun, she had ironically sought for rescue from the labyrinth of her natural existence. The form of address is reminiscent of the conventional stance of the Petrarchan lover toward his unattainable love. Vala, however, reverses the traditional *carpe diem* seduction. Reappropriating the lover as the Self, Vala celebrates the recognition that the bliss she seeks is not confined to the perception of the lover, not merely "another" in the unpredictable world of nature to which even the Sun is subject.

This freedom from duality can be seen as the key to the multiple layers of representation. At this moment of apocalypse, the veil is torn off by Vala, whose name suggests that she represents the phenomenal world as a veil to fallen consciousness. Criticism has acknowledged that Vala "is both the veiled and the veiler, and the seductive valley transforming, like a womb, those spirits that enter," but it has disregarded that she is also a crucial figure in the tearing off of the veil (Hilton 1983, 137). The critical tendency to divide the Blakean universe into mutually exclusive innocent and fallen realms, leaving no room for organized innocence, has had, among all the figures in the poem, the direst consequences for interpreting Vala's character: "In the last analysis, Beulah and Babylon, vastly different and yet mutually reminiscent, can best be thought of together: Babylon is a hideous perversion of Beulah. The coverings, counterpanes, sheets, and blankets of Beulah become Vala's veil in Babylon" (Hagstrum 1983, 106). Vala, now reliteralizing the sun, recognizes the eternal in the fallen, the essential Self behind its veil. Such a revelation illustrates most clearly that Blake's is an apocalypse that destroys not literal nature but rather the dualism of fallen consciousness that projects the universe outside the Self. Thus, a new joy emerges as Vala accommodates her love of nature to the newfound vision:

> Hah! Shall I still survive whence came that sweet & comforting voice
> And whence that voice of sorrow O sun thou are nothing now to me
> Go on thy course rejoicing & let us both rejoice together. . . .
> Can you converse with a pure Soul that seeketh for her maker
> You answer not then am I set your mistress in this garden
> Ill watch you & attend your footsteps you are not like the birds
>
> That sing & fly in the bright air
>
> (E. 396, 127:28–36)

The simplicity of this state of innocence has often been mistaken for nostalgia on Blake's part. Instead, though, the epic here reaches its climactic nostos: actual rather than wished-for homecoming.

This nostos derives from the multiple perspectives of the poem, all of which are brought into alignment at the apocalypse of Night the Ninth. The apocalypse reveals that surrendering the desire for an irretrievable past brings the awareness of the eternal present. Returning to Night the Seventh, for instance, one can see that Los's nostalgic lamentation following the corruption of Orc by Urizen suggests that Los cannot understand the sourness that has tainted his own vision of Enitharmon:

> He spoke not he was Silent till he felt the cold disease
> Then Los mournd on the dismal wind in his jealous
>   lamentation
> Why can I not Enjoy thy beauty Lovely Enitharmon
>   (E. 357, 81:21–23)

The hint was provided six lines earlier: "Her Shadow went forth & returnd Now she was pale as Snow." This is the Urizenic covering that freezes nature. Los is nostalgic for the days when he controlled animals rather than warred with monsters. Nostalgia here as elsewhere lies in idealizing past ignorance. The point can be expanded to the perspective that *The Four Zoas* offers many versions of the golden world, evidence of the compulsive need of the fallen figures to reread and regret the loss of innocence. Just as there are many versions of the irretrievable past, so too do the fallen characters revise the story of a historical fall. Each story gives a different account of a historical moment of the fall that supposedly caused the contemporary chaos; they are fictions never authenticated by the authorial voice.

Vision as redeemed retrospect thus stands in dynamic contrast to these distortions, functions of the fallen faculty of memory that the figures in the fallen state regard as historical truth. In Night the Ninth, Vala embodies the redeemed retrospect of vision. Her epiphany takes her beyond the veil of unorganized innocence:

> For in my bosom a new song arises to my Lord
> Rise up O Sun most glorious minister & light of day
> Flow on ye gentle airs & bear the voice of my rejoicing
> Wave freshly clear waters flowing around the tender grass
> And thou sweet smelling ground put forth thy life in fruits & flowers
> Follow me O my flocks & hear me sing my rapturous Song

> I will cause my voice to be heard on the clouds that glitter in the sun
> I will call & who shall answer me   I will sing   who shall reply
> For from my pleasant hills behold the living living springs
>   (E. 396–97, 128:3–11)

Crucial in this passage is Vala's direct reference to causality. Her rhapsody consists of a sequence of imperatives directed at natural beings. Vala states that she "will cause" her voice to be heard by any being in the outer world, now with the understanding that it is but an extension of her self.

As mentioned earlier, the echo "living living" reaffirms that "who shall answer me" is always an outward manifestation of the Self. The significance of echoing comes to the surface in the climactic moment when

> Vala lifted up her hands to heaven to call on Enion
> She calld but none could answer her & the Eccho of her voice returnd
> Where is the voice of God that calld me from the silent dew
> Where is the Lord of Vala dost thou hide in clefts of the rock
>   (E. 398, 129:31–34)

In her fallen state, Vala asks Urizen where he has hidden Luvah, whom she refers to as "god of my delight." In eternity, however, she does not direct her question to Urizen, and more important, she does not confound fallen Luvah with God. The answer that the echo of her own voice points to, in fact, is that the voice of God is her own.

In her analysis of the metamorphosis of the butterfly soul in Blake, Irene Chayes adds a crucial element to Raine's suggestion that Psyche is the source for Vala. According to Chayes, the heart of this allusion is

> the descent of the love god into unequal union with a mortal woman. . . . Like Cupid, Luvah is invisible, except in Vala's dream, but he visits her in daylight, and Vala does not yield to the temptation of either curiosity or lust. (1970, 237–38)

Chayes, retaining Raine's application of the myth of Cupid and Psyche in Vala's seeking Luvah, cannot account for Vala's recognition of the Self as the lover-god she has been seeking. Nevertheless, Chayes's reading suggests the connection of a later moment in Night the Ninth with the myth:

"Folding the pure wings of his mind" would mean preparing to return to
the first stage after having reached the last; hence, the males are being
warned against trying to undergo in their own persons the sleep of the
chrysalis that precedes the awakening. (238)

It is not until this moment of epiphany that Vala can address her formless
Soul, personifying it though she does. Yet this is the first reference to the
Soul without mythological naming. Thus when Vala sings, "I will cause my
voice to be heard . . . / I will call & who shall answer me I will sing who
shall reply" (E. 397, 128:9–10), the indefinite "who" is striking: all the
living are infused with the projected Self, "who" are thus the "living living"
(E. 397, 128:11). This apocalypse razes nature perceived as wholly external, and externally holy: "O how delicious are the grapes flourishing in the
Sun / How clear the spring of the rock running among the golden sand" (E.
397, 128:17–18). Recognizing that all she beholds is part of the Self, Vala
represents the achievement of organized innocence, the human
reappropriation of the divine.

    A final point in showing why the attainment of this golden world is the
epic's nostos rather than nostalgia emerges in the feast at the end of the
poem. Rather than being a mere wish for an irretrievable past, this is the
epic return of the wandering hero:

> While the flail of Urizen sounded loud & the winnowing wind of
>   Tharmas
> So loud so clear in the wide heavens & the song that they sung was this
> Composed by an African Black from the little Earth of Sotha
> Aha Aha how came I here so soon in my sweet native land
> How came I here Methinks I am as I was in my youth
>
> When in my fathers house I sat & heard his chearing voice
> Methinks I see his flocks & herds & feel my limbs renewd
>   (E. 403, 134:32–135:2)

This literal homecoming revises the traditional epic nostos, since the return to innocence is the center rather than the end of the myth. Throughout the poem, further, Blake decomposes the figure of the epic hero who,
in wholeness, is shared by a composite consciousness. Blake appropriately
gives the role of the returning quester to a freed slave of Mystery: "They

look behind at every step & believe it is a dream / Are these the Slaves that groand along the streets of Mystery" (E. 402, 134:24–25).

The end of Mystery means that concepts and systems that are in themselves neither good nor bad burn in the fire. The apocalypse is therefore not the destruction of the world at the end of time, but the continuous annihilation and inevitable rebuilding of the dualistic world and its infinite variations, and the return to pure consciousness. In the dream that human experience knows as waking life, such a return is available continuously though held in precarious balance.

Prophetic Disclosure and Mediated Vision:
Blake in the Context of the
English Romantic Sublime

BLAKE EMBLEMATIZES THE EPIC NOSTOS, the homecoming as a return to wholeness, when Luvah rises from the feast just before the final conflagration: "His crown of thorns fell from his head he hung his living Lyre / Behind the seat of the Eternal Man" (E. 403, 135:23–24). These appear to be gestures of closure: the end of human history that completes the work of the Messiah, and the end of the epic that lays the lyre to rest. Yet the question arises: How can Blake proceed from a scene of completion to bring to "dreadful Non existence" nature, the human as well as the "furious lions and "ramping tygers" that "play / In the jingling traces"? What does it mean, in other words, for the two gestures of apparent resolution and stillness to precede a scene of raucousness and suffering, in which the lyre and other instruments are picked up by creatures about to be ground out of existence?

Blake, it appears, is pushing consciousness across the "limen" up to which it has stopped until now (hence, the "sublime" literally as "up to the lintel"). Consciousness as quester undergoes its initiation when it emerges whole, past differentiation, through the ring of fire. This movement is more difficult for the figures in the poem than all the horrors of fallenness, because it requires the surrender of the limited self's illusion of autonomy. Until this point they, the decomposed elements of consciousness, have asserted their primacy over each other.

This stage of the epic is as difficult for the reader as it is for the characters. Prior to it, many gestures of completion precede their undoing; this moment promises to complete history and storytelling in the largest terms. Though this sense of ultimate narrative betrayal seems to deny the promise of salvation at the end of time, it is *in eternity* that Luvah hangs up the *living* lyre behind Albion: the rest from action and its representation is the abode of the eternal. This glimpse of stillness does not preclude history or art. It is rather a state of silence—songless and imageless—available at the heart of each moment.

In *The Four Zoas,* the freedom with which form or closure yields to revelation, or the opening out of vision, is precisely the point of tension on which the self-consciousness of English romanticism is founded. Implied in the phrase "romantic sublime" is the conflict between the yearning *past* the sublime and the fear of undifferentiated consciousness that stands as the central obstacle toward fulfilling the quest. This is the inability, for Blake, of the dualistic mind to move past the final threshold, the ring of fire surrounding the sacred center. Keats's phrase "the egotistical sublime" suggests a state of compromise achieved when the poet protects his identification with his limited self by creating distance from the immortality that has nevertheless been the goal of the journey.[1]

Thomas Weiskel discusses how absolutely Blake's sublime differs from that of high romanticism: "Blake uses the word *sublime* as a general honorific and obviously had no use for the distinction, fashionable after Burke (1757), between the sublime and the beautiful. His sublime is not the Romantic sublime" (1986, 67). In his annotations to Reynolds's *Discourses,* Blake writes unequivocally that "Burke's Treatise on the Sublime & Beautiful is founded on the Opinion of Newton & Locke on this Treatise Reynolds has grounded many of his assertions. . . . They mock Inspiration and Vision" (E. 660). The statement encapsulates the difference between Blake's notion of the sublime and the high romantic sublime that evolves out of Burke's definition, whose fundamental rule is that the subject maintain a safe distance from the sublime object. According to Frances Ferguson, Burke "connects the sublime with death in order to attest to the genuineness of sublime emotions," adding what Ferguson calls a "safety net—the condition that danger and pain must not 'press too nearly.'" As Ferguson points out, this "safety net" "threatens to render the sublime into something of a shell game" (1992, 46).[2] Thus, the poets of the romantic sublime inherit the eighteenth-century legacy of projected anxiety. As this study has explored, *The Four Zoas* ironizes this projection as the distortion of the fallen mind.

In terms of the quest motif, Blake breaks Burke's rule of safe distance by turning the journey inside out so that the goal is no different from the quester or the labyrinth.[3] He achieves this by decomposing consciousness so that even as the various figures, acting alone against a notion of otherness, fail to attain the goal of nondualism, the whole remains untouched by the failure of the parts. Thus the romantic sublime, by which is indicated the etymological "up to the threshold," is not an issue for Blake's poetry even though it is very much the issue for his decomposed figures of fallen consciousness. These characters set up boundaries for self-protection by which they then imagine themselves bound.

Whereas Blake's mythos redescribes the epic journey as one of consciousness moving paradoxically beyond time and space to freedom from subject-objection duality, poets from the 1740s into the high romantic period tend to journey into a landscape of projected self-consciousness. Though this process may suggest nonduality, it actually reinforces the dominance of the ego rather than the dissolution of the limited self into undifferentiated consciousness.

By contrast with Blake's mythos, the question of success or failure on a prophetic journey into the landscape of self-consciousness is founded on the means by which the poet mediates his identification with the sublime. This is the high romantic variation on what Eliade identifies as "the supreme rite of initiation," namely to enter a labyrinth and return from it (1958, 382). The temple, the archetypal sacred home of Truth, becomes a de-familiarized reflection of the Self. "Is it a mirror—or the Nether Sphere?" Wordsworth asks in "Composed by the Side of Grasmere Lake." The double force of the language in that poem suggests an answer. The genius loci echoes the poet's prophetic exclamation, "Lo!": "Great Pan . . . low-whispering." Identification with the genius loci brings the archetypal parodic transformation of the prophetic quest into dangerous proximity to the apocalyptic vision. "Lo" is an exclamation of both delight and pain: the sublime is mirror and Nether Sphere.

For William Collins, the sublime derives from the *unheimlich*, de-familiarizing landscape. He is the emphatic exception to Schiller's rhetorical question in "On the Sublime": "Who does not prefer to tarry among the spiritual disorder of a natural landscape rather than in the spiritless regularity of a French garden?" (1966, 204). The question truly is a question for Collins. Reading further in Schiller's essay, one discovers the loophole through which Collins has slipped: "We are led much further by nature viewed as terrible and destructive than as sensuously infinite, provided we remain merely free observers of her" (208). Collins cannot merely be a free observer, but neither can he, as Blake does, plunge into the *jenerseit*. When Collins confronts the genius loci, he has only the choice of retreating to his Augustan society or, as in the "Ode on the Popular Superstitions of the Scottish Highlands," drowning with the "drowning banks."

For Collins more than for his poetic successors, then, the impulse to "tarry among the spiritual disorder of a natural landscape" is synonymous with cultural self-exile. When he casts himself out of London society, literally and allegorically, he denies himself the security of a patron as well as the "spiritless regularity of a garden."

Collins's anxiety is elaborately played out in "Ode on the Popular Superstitions of the Scottish Highlands," a poem that allegorizes the need of the poet to secure a position in society by wedding him to its "stock vocabulary," images and ideology.[4] The supernatural represents anxiety projected onto the landscape, suggesting that anxiety is responsible for the poet's failure to achieve the prophetic vision he seeks. The quest after the *genius loci* finds Collins fleeing back to the protective confines of neoclassicism after a terrifying confrontation with the unmediated sublime.

Both Blake and Collins locate themselves in the waning (but, to both, still very oppressive) Augustan age. Contrasting Blake's use of the prophetic quest with that of Collins is, in this respect, more complicated than comparing Blake with Wordsworth or Shelley. Blake, by contrast to Collins, is able to break through the barriers of the Augustan world in his poetry. This is witnessed by the fact that Blake worked on *The Four Zoas* by night while working by day on the commissions of his patron, Hayley.

In "The Popular Superstitions," Collins addresses his friend Home, a playwright whose tragic drama had recently been rejected in London. Collins's poem is a letter to Home, urging him to leave London for the more "congenial" themes of the Scottish Highlands: "H——— Thou return'st from Thames, whose Naiads long / Have seen thee ling'ring with a fond delay" (Collins 1979, 56, lines 1–2).[5] His stay in London has been pleasant. In such a description of "Thames" one hears "themes" peopled by Augustan

figures such as Naiads, Schiller's "spiritless" conventions. But Collins himself employs such figures, thus identifying him with Home. His lingering
with "fond delay" suggests his own avoidance of the "Genial." It is the land
of the genius that will prove to be the threatening "Nether Sphere." Thus,
ambivalence is introduced through the very hesitation by which the poet
identifies with his subject. As Hartman writes, "The dread of a threat lies in
its deferred fulfillment: the threat hangs over us, and unless strictly delim-
ited . . . it is hard to see what could purge it from the now conscious ear"
(1981, 156–57).

More specifically, the poet introduces the figure of the "cordial Youth,"
a name he will play on later, when the linguistic "fond delay" is over and
cordial comes to mean "of the heart." But here, the "cordial Youth" is Home's
foil. "Cordial" simply means "decorous," for it has not moved beyond the
social context. He urges him to find a fitter audience:

> To Thee thy copious Subjects ne'er shall fail
> Thou need'st but take the Pencil to thy Hand
> And paint what all believe who own thy Genial Land.
>
> (lines 15–17)

Those who "own" this spirit-filled wilderness, as opposed to the patrons of
London, can acknowledge (implied in "own") the poet's prophetic vision,
for they themselves exist within the labyrinth.

As though the poet foresees the problems of such an identification as
Home enters the labyrinth, he emphasizes the double meaning of his friend's
name: "Nor Thou, tho learn'd, his homelier thoughts neglect / Let thy sweet
Muse the rural faith sustain" (lines 31–32). "Homelier" is "like *you*," and
thus the de-familiarized "homeland" is established as the place of the heart:
"fill with double force [thy sweet Muse's] heart commanding strain" (line
35).

The "superstitions" themselves derive from the "Gifted Wizzard Seer"
whose "framing hideous Spells" resembles the framer in Blake's "Tyger":
He too frames a spell—the Tyger—out of "forests of the night." Collins's
Wizzard Seer, "Lodg'd in the Wintry cave . . . / Or in the Depth of Ust's
dark forrests" appears a prototype for Blake's shaper of darkness (lines 53,
56).

It is at this point in "The Popular Superstitions" that the crucial turn

toward the parodic comes and the quester fails. Attention is shifted to the
"fated Youth" to be devoured by the Kelpie:

> They know what Spirit brews the storm full day
>   And heartless oft like moody Madness stare
>   To see the Phantom train their secret work prepare!
>
> (lines 67–69)

This unfortunate swain seems a victim to the Wizzard Seer more than he is
to the monster of the story.

The inversion of "heart commanding strains" into "heartless spirit"
announces the parodic transformation of the prophetic quest, as described
in archetypal terms by Fletcher:

> The ambivalence of the labyrinth is a prominent case of mythological
> "parody" whereby, for example, a demonic image provides a travesty of
> an apocalyptic image. The wasteland is the demonic parody of the de-
> lightful maze. (1971, 34–35)

Blake does not privilege a surface text over the parodic in *The Four Zoas*,
thus complicating the structural relationship between the archetypal parody
and the apocalypse. In Wordsworth and Shelley, by contrast, the parodic is
the subtext of the poem from the outset. For Collins, the "fond delay"
introduces the ambivalence with which he himself approaches the allegorical level of his text. Yet when the parodic element comes to the surface here,
it is evident that the archetypal "test" is operative: "The key to the direction
of parodic change will be the hero's freedom to continue the quest" (Fletcher
1971, 36).

Even in Blake's "Tyger" one can see the contrast with Collins's failure
to continue. Blake's framer and the Tyger are essentially the same; out of
the narrator's separation of created and creator evolves the myth of a distant
and fearful God. This self-fulfilling "framing" is the same impulse seen in
the contraction that arises from casting out divinity in *The Four Zoas*.
Collins's "untutor'd swain," by contrast, becomes the "luckless swain" when
he wanders, unprotected, to the genius loci: "late bewilder'd in the dank
dark Fen / Far from his flocks and smoaking Hamlet. . . . / To that sad spot"
(lines 105–7). He leaves the protection of "home," a mediated concept of

the Genial Land, to confront the archetypal parodic temple. His "moody Madness" is thus represented by the "Grim and Griesly Shape" that appears in the "drown'd Banks."

"The cordial Youth" himself returns at the end of the poem (line 126), no longer an ironically "cordial" other but Home himself. With this conflation of the two figures comes the final collapse of the possibility of language to restore the genius of poetic representation. The false closure is literalized in the "unclosing gate" at which the errant swain's Bairns had lingered (line 124). It is still open, and the swain reduced to a "blue swoln face," though Collins has sought to latch the gate of language closed behind him.

Though in one sense Collins fails, the risk he has taken can be seen to break ground in the romantic genial land. Geoffrey Hartman's analysis of closure applies significantly to Collins:

> Closure is a sealing with healing effect. Yet Freud showed in his analysis of mourning that there is psychic "work" to be done before the healing closure can take effect. . . . A convergence of Freud's special theory of mourning with a general theory of literature suggests that the affective power of the word itself is what is enclosed by the literary work. . . . Closure formally seals that brooding. (1981, 150)

Blake, in contrast to his contemporaries, does not appear to need this sort of closure because his poetry does not "brood," though there is much brooding among the figures of *The Four Zoas*. Blake's quest is not one of self-consciousness, but of consciousness as the Self.

From Collins's failure to find a poetics of mediation, one can turn to Wordsworth to see how the poet of self-consciousness achieves a compromise between vision and closure. As opposed to Collins, Wordsworth succeeds in distancing the poet figure from the object of his contemplation, such as the leech gatherer in "Resolution and Independence." Collins peoples his poems with figures that suggest each other and ultimately himself.[6] Wordsworth, by contrast, uses a persona for the poet-as-quester to face the relation of nature and the imagination. Whereas Blake represents vision as the paradoxical movement past movement, the crossing of thresholds into eternity that has no thresholds, Wordsworth carefully positions himself at the brink of vision. Hence, Wordsworth embodies the high romantic sublime

because his poetry discovers the tension at the edge between the autono-
mous self, the creating poet of imagination, and the eternal that threatens
to erase him as such.

The contrast between Blake and Wordsworth can be seen, for instance,
by turning back to *The Four Zoas* and contrasting Vala at the moment of
epiphany to Wordsworth's description in *The Prelude* of viewing the water
and "bottom deeps" from a carefully positioned perspective in a "slow-
moving boat":

> As one who hangs down-bending from the side
> Of a slow-moving boat upon the breast
> Of a still water, solacing himself
> With such discoveries as his eye can make
> Beneath him in the bottom of the deeps,
> Sees many beauteous sights—weeds, fishes, flowers,
> Grots, pebbles, roots of trees—and fancies more,
> Yet often is perplexed, and cannot part
> The shadow from the substance, rocks and sky,
> Mountains and clouds, from that which is indeed
> The region, and the things which there abide
> In their true dwelling; now is crossed by gleam
> Of his own image, by a sunbeam now,
> And motions that are sent he knows not whence,
> Impediments that make his task more sweet
>   (Wordsworth 1979, 136–38, bk. 4, 247–61 [1805 version])

Wordsworth uses the image of seeing in and through the watery world to
describe his relation to the phenomenal world, seeking a balance between
his own image and the vast world of nature reflected in and beneath the
water's surface.

The notion of the "true dwelling" of each object in nature is signified
in Blake's mythos by the house that Luvah makes for Vala just before the
moment in Night the Ninth when Vala sings, "I will cause my voice to be
heard . . . / I will call & who shall answer me I will sing who shall reply" (E.
397, 128:9–10). The echoing of the indefinite "who" suggests the permeation of all the living with the projected Self, "who," as the "living living"
return the auditory image of the Self (E. 397, 128:11).

Vala can fully represent this newfound nature infused with vision without the contracted tendency to see with the eyes rather than through them (to paraphrase Blake's objection at E. 566 to the idolatry of nature). As opposed to Wordsworth, Blake's redeemed nature can see itself without fear of annihilating the limited self:

> She called to her flocks saying follow me o my flocks
>
> They followd her to the silent vall[e]y beneath the spreading trees
> And on the rivers margin she ungirded her golden girdle
> She stood in the river & viewd herself within the watry glass . . .
> And as she rose her Eyes were opend to the world of waters
>
> (E. 398, 129:11–16)

This double vision of reflection and the opening of the "watry world" stands in direct contrast to the moment in *The Prelude* discussed above. Vala, Blake's figure for the aspect of human consciousness that perceives and hence is the phenomenal world, must find its true home, rather than Wordsworth's viewer seeking a stable dwelling for each object in nature.

The effect of Vala at the margin, then magically in the river, is caused by her unbinding of the golden girdle, the romantic image of bounded nature that the viewer seeks to transcend. One can see the more dramatic contrast in Collins, who in "Ode on the Poetical Character" makes the cest the central image of poetical power:

> The band, as Fairy Legends say,
> Was wove on that creating Day,
> When He, who call'd with Thought to Birth
> Yon tented Sky, this laughing Earth,
> And drest with Springs, and Forests tall,
> And pour'd the Main engirting all
>
> (lines 23–28)

While for Blake, boundaries like the green girdle and "tented sky" are arbitrary markers that alter their image depending on one's "stance in eternity," for Collins the girdle is what Jung might describe as the protective circle. Wordsworth's contest, by contrast to that of Collins, is not to win the symbolic girdle but to create it against the creating day.

In this way, Wordsworth shares Blake's power to hold imagination as

the home of the sublime. However, the central difference between
Wordsworth and Blake is that Blake does not hold imagination as the home
of the sublime unless it is connected to vision, as seen in Golgonooza's
collapse after Night the Seventh.

By contrast, Wordsworth's sonnet "Composed by the Side of Grasmere
Lake" illustrates the heart of Wordsworth's ambivalence toward giving up
the autonomy of imagination:

> Clouds, lingering yet, extend in solid bars
> Through the grey west; and lo! these waters, steeled
> By breezeless air to smoothest polish, yield
> A vivid repetition of the stars;
> Jove, Venus, and the ruddy crest of Mars
> Amid his fellows beauteously revealed
> At happy distance from earth's groaning field,
> Where ruthless mortals wage incessant wars.
> Is it a mirror?—or the nether Sphere
> Opening to view the abyss in which she feeds
> Her own calm fires?—But list! a voice is near;
> Great Pan himself low-whispering through the reeds,
> "Be thankful, thou; for if unholy deeds
> Ravage the world, tranquility is here!"
>
> (Wordsworth 1932, 348)

There are here many striking differences from Blake. For Wordsworth, the
sonnet form itself creates a protective distance from the controlled epiphany
that occurs exactly at the center of the sonnet. As the speaker looks into the
water the abyss opens. He wonders whether what he sees is a reflection or
the nether sphere, a moment like the one in *The Prelude* discussed earlier, in
which the speaker looks into the water and attempts to separate his own
reflection from the reflections of both the outer world and the underwater
world. Wordsworth chooses the figuration of mythological personification,
returning to the familiar pastoral world of Grasmere through the classical
figure of Pan. The "low-whispering" Pan echoes the earlier "and lo!" of the
poet, the classical harbinger of the epiphanic moment. The echo suggests
that the speaker's need for the familiar, distanced perspective has succeeded
in rescuing him from the nether sphere.[7]

For Blake, human conflict transpires within consciousness. The outer form of *The Four Zoas* denies the reader a safe retreat from vision, since the poem remains within the subsuming dream, never quaintly sporting with a consciously allegorical Pan. Wordsworth's protective circle is the circumference, the center as the horrifying abyss. The outer circle is defined in the first line: "Clouds, lingering yet, extend in solid bars." The breaking of this protective circle is the poem's interest, though, for the caesura in the second line is a compression of the rupture at the center of the poem: "Through the grey west; and lo! these waters steeled / By breezeless air." The epiphany is at first a solid reflection of the cosmos by the waters, for they "yield / A vivid repetition of the stars."

The speaker assures himself that "Jove, Venus, and the ruddy crest of Mars / Amid his fellows [is] beauteously revealed." Weiskel's application of the Burkean relation of the beautiful and the sublime is relevant here, for the speaker attempts to remove himself from the image of bloody Mars at a "happy distance from earth's groaning field." The speaker realizes that violence is an aspect of consciousness. Immediately following this, he asks whether the waters are a mirror or the nether sphere. The painful answer seems to be that it is not an either-or question, that all the horrors of the underworld are reflected in and by the viewer. The speaker thus removes himself before this perception can rise to the surface, distracting himself by the physical noise near him. He thus precludes vision with the reimagined voice of Nature: "Be thankful thou; for, if unholy deeds / ravage the world, tranquillity is here!" It is significant that the sonnet ends with the emphatic "here!" for it redirects epiphany from the terror of the sublime to the familiar beauty of the lakeside. The title thus takes on a certain irony: "Composed by the Side of Grasmere Lake" can be understood as the speaker composing himself—or finding composure—by the *side* of the lake as opposed to the horror he experiences when he finds himself at its center.

In its claim to a courageously uncompromising quest after the absolute, Percy Shelley's apocalypse is closer to Blake than to Wordsworth, for Shelley tends to plummet to the depths of the nether sphere rather than to retreat from it. Nevertheless, though he too disdains Wordsworth's "composure," or the compromising of vision for mortality, he cannot ultimately face the annihilation of the limited self that such vision entails. "Mont Blanc" is one of Shelley's strongest revisions of the high romantic quest, revealing his paradoxical kinship to both Blake and Wordsworth.

From the beginning of "Mont Blanc," Shelley revises the relationship between subject and object, implicit in the deep structure of the poem's first sentence: "The everlasting universe of things / Flows through the mind" (Shelley 1977, 89, lines 1–2). Grammatically, the subject is the universe, yet the prepositional phrase "through the mind," placed before the caesura in line 2, throws the weight on the implicit subject, the mind. Thus, "through" itself suggests its etymological root in Old English, so that the universe of things flows "by reason of" the mind (OED). If the phenomenal world is represented by the Arve, "flowing through the mind," then the channel that directs its course, the mind, is represented by the Ravine.[8]

The suggestion of the mind as a ravine comes implicitly from the last words of the first verse paragraph: "a vast river / Over its rocks ceaselessly bursts and raves" (lines 10–11). "Raves" suggests Ravine: "Thus thou, Ravine of Arve-dark, deep Ravine" is the odic apostrophe recalling, for instance, Collins's address to Home. Yet Shelley's immediate apprehension of the danger of inundation (a mind that "raves" as it receives and attempts to direct phenomena) indicates the subtextual presence of the parodic element, already yoking prophetic exhilaration with the terror of annihilation.

Thus, Shelley's quester pursues a path through the labyrinth by keeping his ear to the ground of the Genial Land. The association between raving and Ravine brings him to the point of Collins's luckless swain, maddened by the spell of the Wizzard Seer. Shelley is able to maintain both roles through this stage of the journey: It is the "Dizzy Ravine" which evokes in him "a trance sublime and strange" (lines 35–36). The ode's epiphanic "Thou art there!" at the end of the second verse paragraph has been undermined by the growing ambivalence in the poem's sub-text: "Thou art" echoes the preceding "Thou art pervaded with that ceaseless motion, / Thou art the path of that unresting sound— / Dizzy ravine!" (lines 32–34). Arve becomes art—existence through representation—by means of the raving mind. Though the epiphany rings with the Wordsworthian desire for autonomy ("To muse on my own separate phantasy, / My own, my human mind" [lines 36–37]), the presence of the parodic demon throws the weight of "Thou art there!" on "there!"

Parody in Wordsworth and Shelley stands in striking contrast to that in Blake, then, whose project is never to distance himself from the threat of nondualism. In this way, one speaks of the parodic "subtext" in Wordsworth, Collins, or Shelley undermining the ostensible project because the will of the persona is often at odds with the thinking the poem does. Blake, by contrast, lays open the ambivalence of his figures so that the poem itself remains free. De Man, when interviewed by Mitchell, explained why he himself would not use deconstruction as a critical tool for analyzing Blake:

> I asked de Man if he had ever noticed that Blake, unlike the other Romantics, did not consistently privilege voice over writing. De Man replied that of course he had noticed this. Well then, I asked, doesn't this make his work of peculiar interest for deconstruction, particularly its "science of writing" or "grammmatology"? De Man's reply: Not at all. Blake's privileging of writing makes him less interesting to deconstruction, because it makes his work less resistant to its strategies. (Mitchell 1986, 91)

This observation underscores why so many readers become frustrated that there is no surface in Blake's text by which to orient themselves. Implicit in the common complaint is the need for a means to describe Blake's disorientation.

Unlike Blake's perpetual removal of landmarks, Shelley in "Mont Blanc" attempts to overcome the distance he himself creates between identity and desire, or the Self and otherness, by metaphorically encompassing the phenomenal world with the imagination:

> Thine earthly rainbows stretched across the sweep
> Of the etherial waterfall, whose veil
> Robes some unsculptured image
>
> (lines 25–27)

The rainbow closes the circle begun by the ravine. This image would draw a happy closure if the quester did not perceive a new element in his cosmography: the temple of prophetic vision remains veiled by nature.

This "unsculptured image" eludes his art in contrast to the subjectivity of his vision of nature (Arve as art). The subtextual epiphany thus undermines the traditional odic epiphany. Even in a landscape crowded with vegetation, "thy giant brood of pines around thee clinging," comes a dread of an impoverished vision through "the strange sleep / Which when the voices of the desert fail / Wraps all in its own deep eternity" (lines 20, 27–29).

The parodic transformation surfaces in the third verse paragraph. The

earlier affirmative sense of "I seem as in a trance sublime" now throws the
weight on the doubtful verb "seem":

> Has some unknown omnipotence unfurled
> The veil of life and death? or do I lie
> In dream, and does the mightier world of sleep
> Spread far around and inaccessibly
> Its circles? For the very spirit fails
>
> (lines 53–57)

The "lie" in line 54 sets the passivity of the mind that "now renders and
receives fast influencings" against the fear of false prophecy (line 37). For
Shelley's prophet, "the very spirit fails" in the moment of doubt and silence.
Not until the end of the poem can Shelley reconcile himself to the
silence he will associate with Mont Blanc. Significantly, at this earlier moment of doubt, Mont Blanc appears for the first time, "Far far above, pierc-
ing the infinite sky" (line 60). This stands in contrast to Blake's Snowdon,
which, because it is contained by undifferentiated consciousness, is unlike
Mont Blanc, already beyond reach for Shelley's quester and appearing to
move further from his grasp.[9]
A still more specific difference between Shelley's Mont Blanc and Blake's
Snowdon is the difference between the superhuman beings that inhabit
them. Blake's Council of God lodged on top of the mountain is the projection of divinity that ensues when Albion turns his eyes outward, whereas
Shelley's Mont Blanc is home of the "old Earthquake-daemon" (line 73), a
genius loci that is closer to Collins's Wizzard Seer. The volatile nature of the
mountain's potential to "teach awful doubt" qualifies the "faith so mild"
that attempts to close the gate on "the mysterious tongue" of the wilderness
(lines 76–77). This suggests yet another contrast to Blake's externalized
divinity: the Daughters of Beulah, attempting to arrest the fall, close the
Gate of the Tongue in *The Four Zoas*.
Out of his anxiety at the distance between himself and the mountain
temple comes the means of recovery for Shelley's quester. Paradoxically,
this is only possible through the surfacing of the parodic, for it is the explo-
sive Earthquake-Daemon who can repeal "Large codes of fraud and woe."
In so stating the potential power to redress worldly evils, the quester comes
to recognize his closeness to the Truth itself:

[Daedalus] invents wings . . . and he invents the maze. It seems important that Daedalus is thus the inventor of the original prison, which he could redeem or transform by his parodic invention of the means of freedom. (Fletcher 1971, 37)

Shelley's quester transcends the "daedal earth" by the "wandering wings" of his own making, namely, the "legion of wild thoughts." The revelation itself is a parodic creeping toward self-assertion. The mountain's voice is "not understood / By all, but which the wise, and great, and good / Interpret, or make felt, or deeply feel" (lines 81–83).

The quester reconciles himself to the parodic "Earthquake-Daemon." Though he can now reestablish his earlier power of subjectivity, the mind-nature dichotomy is clearly no longer appropriate, and so the metaphor of Ravine-Arve is dropped. He de-forms the earlier landscape so that the once clinging pines are now transformed by "a flood of ruin . . . ; / vast pines are strewing / Its destined path, or in the mangled soil / Branchless and shattered stand" (lines 107–10).

So too is the earlier and premature "Thou art there!" transformed. Shelley no longer addresses the Ravine, his own mind, but beholds Mont Blanc, the "higher order": "Mont Blanc yet gleams on high: the power is there" (line 127). He discovers the mediating distance not in the false closure of convention, but in the reconciliation between identity and desire. This comes through a reinterpretation of the mountain's law. No longer the threatening and parodic "Earthquake-Daemon," the rule is one of suggestion. Such a "measure" allows the poet to approach an understanding of the invisible and silent:

> The secret strength of things
> Which governs thought, and to the infinite dome
> Of heaven is as a law, inhabits thee!
>
> (lines 139-41)

He has reached the archetypal temple through suggestion: the vision of the mountain suggests "the dome of heaven." In this way, the "unsculptured image" is paradoxically realized through the mountain. In the spirit of the redeemed Urizen's epiphanic question, revelation emerges at the end of "Mont Blanc":

And what were thou, and earth, and stars, and sea,
If to the human mind's imaginings
Silence and solitude were vacancy?

(lines 142–44)

The hidden contents of the "temple" are, paradoxically, silence and solitude. Through his parodic eruption of the "universe of things," the poet
learns that nature itself is not the source of the mind's ravings. This is the
pivotal moment at which Collins had given up the quest.

Shelley's "primaeval mountains / Teach the adverting mind" about a
moment that precedes and lives beyond even their own long lives (lines
99–100). By moving beyond the "everlasting universe of things" to a self-
mediating identification with the "unsculptured image," Shelley, in "Mont
Blanc," succeeds in providing a vehicle for both traveling in and escaping
the "daedal labyrinth" to the "dome of heaven." However, his ambivalence
is complex, especially as it evolves in later poems. A brief look at "The Two
Spirits—An Allegory" shows how Shelley challenges not only the
Wordsworthian in him, but even his own earlier persona. He complicates
the Daedalus allusion by adding not only Icarus but an implicit third voice.

Perhaps on a first reading of "The Two Spirits," the two-part debate
between the precursor spirit and the defiant pupil seems to be won by the
latter. Yet on closer inspection, in the coda of two conflicting legends Shelley
reveals a third, objectified voice; this is as close as Shelley gets to the Blakean
equipoise. The third voice challenges not only his precursor but his earlier
voice with a startling ability to remove himself through the legend framework
and further to question the power of "the torch of love" over darkness.

The first spirit is Daedalus, warning Shelley's Icarus persona of the
dangers of aspiring beyond his earthly limitations: "O Thou who plumed
with strong desire / Would float above the Earth—beware!" (lines 1–2).
The Daedalus poet does not warn that the second's plumes will be melted
by the sun or that he will be drowned by the sea, however, but that his path
will be veiled by darkness. The threat imaged is the erasure of the path of a
shooting star, for its glory is not in its own body, but the trail it leaves
behind. Here again is a crucial difference between the poets of self-consciousness and the Blakean mythos that breaks down the artist figure into
characters that ultimately transcend any one persona.

In "The Two Spirits," the Icarus poet declares,

> If I should cross the shade of night
> Within my heart is the torch of love
>   And that is day—
>
>   (lines 10–12)

Since the torch of love is his own light, the Daedalian warning of the first spirit does not disturb him. His "golden plumes" form the vehicle for his journey to the center. This torch of love makes natural light dim by contrast, so that "the moon will smile with gentle light" (line 13). Indeed, the trajectory of the comet is transformed into an orbit revolving in slow motion around the "torch of love," his sun, in an intensified version of the egocentricity of the romantic sublime.

The Daedalus figure, however, urges the second spirit to observe the natural world and thereby make the phenomenological projection that he hopes will teach his pupil: "The red swift clouds of thee hurricane / Yon declining sun have overtaken" (lines 21–22). If the second spirit's inner "sun" can tame meteors, he implies, what of the flash of lightning that cannot be slowed or dimmed, or the clouds that overtake the setting sun? The second spirit defies the first's phenomenology. He does not deny his own perception of the storm: "I see the glare and I hear the sound," yet he will not equate nature's declining sun with his eternal torch of love (line 25). He says that he can use the force of the storm to propel him inward.

The question "The Two Spirits" raises is not whether the vision ever existed, but how it can be maintained and kept distinct from darkness. Thus, if this is the triumphant voice of the second spirit, his claim can only be made through the paradox of "night day." At this point, one does not hear the later Shelley's despair, which de Man identifies in "The Triumph of Life": "Not just because it is an unbearable condition of indetermination which has to be repressed, but because the condition itself, regardless of how it affects us, necessarily hovers between a state of knowing and not knowing" (1979, 51). By the end of "The Two Spirits," "night day" provides a temporary resolution that seems on the brink of the Blakean brinkless nondualism: For the new voice, accepting his human form means straddling the threshold; the traveler can internalize the second spirit in his visionary dream and surrender it when he wakes to "the fragrant grass."

One might respond to Shelley through Luvah who, in eternity, sees that "Attempting to be more than Man we become less" (E. 403, 135:21).

What he recognizes is perhaps too simple for the mind bound by dualism to grasp, namely, that being whole necessitates equanimity rather than striving for something that one is not already. As soon as one thinks in terms of the more-than-human, one is already outside the Self and since this is impossible, one thus becomes less: the contracted self.

For Blake, the center is deeper than Jerusalem, in whose bosom is the divine lamb, in whose incarnation is God—a Chinese box of infinite centers, the redeemed vortex. At the same time, the dream of such a romance is greater than Albion's sleep because it is frameless. The narrator of "The Tyger," the bewildered voice of experience, cannot conceive of a creature or creator beyond measure and, typical of voices of experience, cannot conceive of eternity as answerless.

The figures of *The Four Zoas* discover the dissolution of questions and answers in an apocalypse that is the source and goal of all form and action; glimpses of this apocalypse appear in the sparks of Los's prophetic head, the ring of fire surrounding Orc, the furnaces imprisoning Luvah and the harrowing of a separate natural order that brings renewed wholeness to the created and creating consciousness.

Notes

Chapter 1. Blake's Mythos

1. Among the philosophers challenging the Lockean hierarchy were Shaftes-
bury and Hutchinson, who valorized "moral sense" and "sympathy," and Hartley
and Hume, who claimed that the intuitive operation of association was necessary
to an understanding of logic. The poets of "sensibility," including Thomson, Gray,
Cowper, and Collins, emphasized feeling over reason.

2. Beer likewise divides the terms "pathos" and "sublimity" into dualistic camps,
problematic for Blake; as many critics, such as Thomas Weiskel, have shown, Blake's
sublime is radically different from the high romantic sublime, vexing the issue of
these traditional oppositions from the start.

3. To avoid the spatial or linear implication of the phrase "higher innocence,"
as it has often been called, this study links organized innocence with nondualism
or undifferentiated consciousness.

4. Nostalgia, homesickness as a disease, according to the O.E.D., derives from
the Greek *nostos,* return home.

5. Some readers might see the tracing of this impulse from early to late works
as reverting to the formalism of Northrop Frye and other systematizers of Blake's
corpus. More recent scholarship, however, has reexamined Blake's evolving mythos.
Robert Essick, in spite of his challenge to Frye's "structuralist dynamic" that ex-
trapolates missing elements from the system he derives (1989, 197), acknowledges
that "like the city of Golgonooza, Blake's later poetry encompasses within its wide
embrace all that has come before in his earlier works" (195). Tracing this continuity

through the corpus of Blake's works, rather than being equated with a rigid formulation of fixed symbols, should underscore Blake's lifelong commitment to exploring the nondual relationship of innocence and experience.

6. See Erdman (1954, 271) as well as C. M. Bowra, who claims "Blake followed his own maxim that 'without Contraries is no progression'" by arranging his poems into the two groups (1970, 139). Although Damrosch, for another example, rightly warns against applying a dialecticism to the prophecies, he implies its presence in the earlier works (1980, 176).

7. Harold Bloom hierarchizes innocence and experience in Bloom 1971, 33ff. Beer aptly qualifies the criticism of linear readings, speaking to Blake's deepening vision during his writing the *Songs of Innocence*. He argues shrewdly against the claim that Blake moved from naïveté to bitterness in the transition from *Innocence* to *Experience*. Blake's visionary writing begins after 1787, which Beer associates with the death of Blake's brother Robert: "Up till now he had cultivated an amused and defensive detachment, allowing the imaginative element in his verse to appear more and more in subjection to that detachment. Now he was to place the visionary experience at the very centre of life as its true controlling and interpretative reality" (1969, 60).

8. This manifests as Golgonooza in the prophetic books, the City of Art whose completion depends on the reunion of Los and Urthona.

9. Describing Blakean innocence as vital and nondual offers an alternative to readings that categorize the poems of Innocence and those of Experience, respectively, as nostalgic and ironic. Rajan, for instance, sees the irony of Experience as a corrective to the self-deception of Innocence: "The poems of Experience function ironically to alert the reader to 'gaps' in the poems of Innocence that call into question the sentimental fiction of a transcendental or original innocence" (1980, 264). While this is true of several pairs of poems, such as "Holy Thursday," it cannot account for the counterbalances to experience often provided by innocence, including those that appear within the poems of Experience.

10. This is reminiscent of "Mad Song," whose speaker is trapped in a materialist universe of his own making:

> Lo! to the vault
>   Of paved heaven
> With sorrow fraught
>   My notes are driven
>   (E. 415)

11. The incongruity of the design of the smiling, innocuously cartoonlike tyger challenges Shaviro's reading. Even if one sees the smile as that of a beast sated after devouring its prey, the image remains an ironic comment on that depicted in the

poem. In light of the tendency toward separation and fragmentation as a characteristic of experience, the speaker appears to have created the terrifying beast he describes.

12. For an alternative interpretation of the Bard, see I. A. Richards, who sees the Bard as embracing the ethical ideals of "giving, receiving and forgiving each other's trespasses." Richards 1974, 200–201.

13. Along with the narrator of "The Tyger," this echoes the entrapment of the speaker of "Mad Song" in his self-made prison of materialism.

14. Kierkegaard's *Repetition* has interesting implications for fallen and redeemed echoing in Blake. Howard and Edna Hong, discussing Kierkegaard's "double-movement of resignation and faith," note that "[i]n the paradox of faith, possibility is affirmed where there is manifestly only impossibility, because with God all things are possible" (Hong and Hong 1983, xviii–xix).

15. See Frye on "the covering cherub" (1947, 37-39).

16. These four lines encapsulate one of the central dramatic interests of *The Four Zoas,* in which the tendencies of Zoas and Emanations in their fallen state to forget their oneness perpetuates and intensifies their ruptures, whereas their reintegration at the apocalypse emerges out of the freedom from jealousy that comes from the recognition that there is no Other.

17. That Blake had originally included this pair of poems in *Songs of Innocence* suggests, as does his switching of many other of the Songs between the two collections, that each, to varying degrees, contains the interplay of both states.

18. Blake describes the apocalyptic work of the visionary engraver in *The Marriage of Heaven and Hell* as "printing in the infernal method, by corrosives, which in Hell are salutary and medicinal, melting apparent surfaces away, and displaying the infinite which was hid" (E. 39, pl. 14).

19. Though Ault correctly points out that similarities between the bindings of Urizen and Orc exemplify Blake's antilinear strategy, Ault's ultimately linear treatment of the poem does not fully account for Blake's revolt against traditional structure (Ault 1987, 197).

20. Lincoln's acknowledgment of Blake's irony toward traditional history points toward this reading (1995, 9). However, Lincoln's procedure of peeling away layers of text to arrive at a development of Blake's myth leads to a fundamentally different interpretation. The most significant example of this difference is in Lincoln's suggestion that Blake ran into trouble making the transition from satirizing the biblical relationship between the divine and the human and offering "an alternative view of divine providence" (25). The final section of Lincoln's book is devoted to what he argues is the last stage of composition: Nights VIIb through IX as "A Christian Vision." This study, by contrast, argues that the revisions do not reveal that Blake ever doubted the nondual relationship between the human and divine that replaces the traditional Christian one.

21. See, for example, the passages from *Jerusalem* cited at the beginning of this chapter.

22. See Northrop Frye and Harold Bloom, who both describe Blake's career culminating in *Jerusalem*.

23. See chapter 5.

24. A recent reading of *The Four Zoas* concludes that "by Night IX of *The Four Zoas*, Blake is demanding a transformation of society and culture so total that it constitutes a critique even of those revolutions which have gone before" (Di Salvo 1983, 240). See also Philip Cox, who argues that Blake "deconstructs" the commercial myth that "masks the vicissitudes of nascent capitalism" (1994, 102). Though these points are well taken as an aspect of Blake's apocalypse, they are limited by their linearity. Acknowledging the nonlinear relationship of Night the Ninth to the previous Nights without eschewing such insights about Blake's sociopolitical vision allows for a fuller understanding of the way each element of Blake's mythos, including the structure of the poem, serves to superimpose these historical concerns onto the eternal.

25. This takes its most surprising turn in the transformation of Urizen in Night the Ninth, the fear-filled creator of physicality and temporality, who comes to recognizes that "futurity is in this moment."

26. See Damrosch 1980, chaps. 5 and 6, in which he proceeds from the treatment of dualism to the relationship of God and man. Damrosch concludes that although Blake rejects the Trinity he must reinvent it because man needs an external godhead for salvation, a position which this study strongly opposes.

27. This externalized divinity, especially in its manifestation as the Council of God, is the projection of fallen consciousness that is yet subsumed by expanded vision. As David Punter states, "[S]cience must start from the apprehension of man as a being with a single yet double life" (1982, 207). Chapter 5 explores the externalization of divinity that Damrosch cites as evidence for Blake's concession to orthodoxy.

28. For other anti-apocalyptic readings, see Essick 1989 and Goldsmith 1993.

29. As noted earlier, Lincoln's is the fullest and most recent reconstructive study (1995).

30. Contrast Rajan's discussion of labor in Blake's poetry, in which the "figure of labor can be set against the image of mental fight. . . . Labor suggests an attempt to produce something, a belief in the value of what one is doing as an activity if not as something that continuously corresponds to the truth" (1990, 214). While the observation is useful regarding Blake's representation of labor in his poetry, it is complicated by his own sense of artistic labor as play, which enters the poetry in the form of Golgonooza. Golgonooza cannot be created until labor is redeemed, at which point it becomes play.

31. See part 2 of Lincoln 1995 for a more fully developed reconstruction of

the stages in which Blake composed Nights III through VIII. Otto's argument nevertheless remains: a later version does not necessarily supplant an earlier version if one maintains that Blake's interest from the inception is finding a means of representing the dynamic between the dual and nondual.

32. For another reading of the designs, see Chayes 1991.

33. Steven Vine provides a useful critique of the methodologies of Diana Hume George and Christine Gallant, Freudian and Jungian readers of Blake, respectively (1993, 14–15). Of the psychological approaches to Blake's myth, the Jungian comes closest to Blake through its use of archetypes that lead to self-healing. Nevertheless, this approach also has limitations: Jung does not allow for the dissolution of ego, essential in overcoming duality. Perhaps the psychological reading of *The Four Zoas* that is freest from reductiveness is Martin Bidney's *Blake and Goethe,* a study that explores the problems of "psychological negation" by describing the oscillation between selving and unselving (1988, 51).

34. Damrosch regards Plotinus and Boehme as significant influences on Blake though often, he claims, the influence takes the form of reaction against them (see, for instance, 1980, 6). Though Damrosch is correct, the de-emphasis of Blake's sources allows what is essentially Blakean—that which is perpetually drawn to these sources—to emerge.

35. Bernard Blackstone notes the translations of Sanskrit texts by Wilkins as well as Sir William Jones as probable influences on Blake (1949, 77). Singh notes further that it is likely that Blake met both Charles Wilkins and Sir William Jones through his teacher James Basire, official engraver to the Society of Antiquity and to the Royal Society, to which Wilkins and Jones were elected in 1772 and 1788 (1988, 28). Kathleen Raine gives detailed textual support for suggesting that specific images in Blake's poetry, such as the inverted tree, derive directly from the *Bhagavad Gita* and other Eastern texts (1968, 2:34-35). Although there are significant differences among Eastern philosophies, the various views on such issues as transmigration of the soul and reincarnation are not the subject of this study. See Thomas Altizer on the Buddhist analogue (1967, 180).

Chapter 2. *"Pangs of an Eternal Birth"*

1. Emerson attributes this to Augustine in "Circles." *Selections from Ralph Waldo Emerson,* ed. Stephen E. Whicher (Boston: Houghton Mifflin, 1957) 168.

2. This study refers to ego as the limited or contracted self because it is closer to Blake's terminology.

3. Huizinga's notion that play is more than a symbolic identification has important applications in challenging Damrosch's assessment of Blake's symbolism. See chapter 4 for the fuller argument.

4. See chapter 1 for the full discussion of the various methodologies that have been applied to readings of the poem.

5. Though Arnheim disowns this description in his introduction to the 1988 edition, claiming that "Cartesian grid" was too specialized a term to apply to an antithetical force to centricity (viii), it provides a useful analogue for the purposes of looking at Blake's structural representation of the interplay of linear and centric forces.

6. See Pierce 1988–89 for a detailed study of Blake's textual revisions involving Tharmas as well as a compelling suggestion for Blake's changing attitude toward Tharmas's role: "Blake saw him as an increasingly important figure or quality to be tapped in the process of undoing the effects of the fall" (97).

7. While Philip Cox notes that the pastoral beginning is here "deprived of its original innocence," the poem is structured in such a way that innocence, the reader learns by Night the Ninth, is never taken away as such, but forgotten (90). Cox's essay is perceptive in its treatment of the first Eight Nights, but typical of most criticism on the poem, it ignores Night the Ninth. The most significant revision this would entail involves Tharmas's return to innocence in Night the Ninth. See also Frye's interpretation that "[t]he Fall begins in Beulah" with the fall of Tharmas, and that "[t]he fall of Beulah is primarily a loss of innocence" (1947, 278–79).

8. Pierce offers an alternative reading of the change: "Although his latest revisions were not thoroughly consistent, Blake eventually replaced 'Enitharmon' with "Jerusalem" in Tharmas' opening speech. It seems probable that Blake made this change around the time he added the ideas of language of Sin and Repentance to his text" (1988–89, 97).

9. Donald Ault plays on the word "re-vision" with a contrary interpretation: "In the poem Blake experiments with creating a text that cannot sustain its authentic existence independent of and prior to the narrative world in the process of being constituted through sequential acts of reading" (1986, 109). Ault's reading differs from the one presented here in that he does not allow for a redeemed voice of "re-vision" through the apocalypse of Night the Ninth; instead he holds that the reader maintains "a state of failed imaginative judgment" (128).

10. Ault notes that Jerusalem is "an external projection of the hiding process itself while being a product of division" (1987, 46). This has significant implications for the fallen tendency to project divinity outward as well as for the fallen tendency to hide as a result of the illusion of separation. Ault, however, suggests that "Jerusalem disappears from the poem's surface until Night VIII when she reappears suddenly, surprisingly, as the product of the fabrication of bodies for the spectres of the dead," thus taking the characters' misperceptions as authorial(282). Albion's recognition that Jerusalem has never been absent reorients the reader's perspective of the events of the first eight Nights.

11. See Margoliouth's speculations about the order of composition (1956, xxiii).

12. For an interesting discussion of this section of the poem, see Nelson Hilton's "Sweet Science of Atmosphere in *The Four Zoas.*" *BIQ* 46 (Fall 78): 80-86.

13. See chapter 4 for a more detailed discussion of this motif.

Chapter 3. Prophecies, Visions, and Memories

1. Other readers have discussed the technique of embedded narratives in the *Zoas*, including Donald Ault (1987, 19, 58) and Vincent De Luca (1991, 116).

2. Otto raises the interesting suggestion that the narrator is "an 'effect' of the story that he recounts" (1987a, 144).

3. White notes that the etymology of "narrative" links the Latin *gnarus* (knowing) and *narro* (relate, tell) with the Sanskrit root *gna* (know). This provides a fascinating key to Blake's ironic linking of claimed knowledge and the storytelling that perpetuates distorted perception through the first eight Nights of the poem.

4. See the discussion in chapter 5 of Vala's revelation in Night the Ninth. Having sought the voice of the Lord, she says, "Whose voice is this in the voice of the nourishing air" (E. 396, 126:36), giving rise to the revelation: "I will cause my voice to be heard on the clouds that glitter in the sun . . . / I will call and who shall answer me I will sing who shall reply" (E. 397, 128:9–10). Vala's revelation that the voice she hears as God is actually her own leads to the reinternalization of divinity at the apocalypse.

5. "The Sleep of Albion." See Chapter Two for the fuller discussion of Raine's point.

6. Blake's poem "The Smile" suggests that even such a malignant smile contains the seed of divinity: "There is a Smile of Love/and there is a Smile of Deceit/And there is a Smile of Smiles/In which these two Smiles meet" which is yet another instance of the potential state of redemption even in the most fallen gestures (E. 482).

7. For alternative readings of Tharmas's role, particularly in Night the Fourth, see Pierce's essay, "Changing Mythic Structure," in which he comments that the "appearance of Tharmas in Night 1, although sequentially earlier in the narrative, seems chronologically later in the development of the poem" (1989, 490), and Ault's section of *Narrative Unbound* entitled "Telescopic Reduction in Night the Fourth" (1987, 162–84).

8. This image is a focal point of chapter 3.

9. Magno and Erdman trace the lightly penciled detail on manuscript page 9 (Night I). They refer to this as "Saviour in globe," which illustrates not only the contemporaneity of divinity and the fallen state, but the redeemed circle with

divinity at the center, which chapter 4 discusses in further detail (Magno and Erdman 1987, 30, 123). See figure 8.

10. See chapter 5 for the fuller discussion of the building of Golgonooza.

Chapter 4. Centricity and the Vortex

1. The differences between Blake and the "high romantic" writers regarding symbolism is the subject of the excursus.

2. See chapter 5, which takes up the culmination of this contrast in Night the Seventh [a] and [b]. The two versions focus respectively on the struggle to build Golgonooza before wholeness has been achieved and on allegory as the extreme form of dualistic representation.

3. Raine notes that Blake may have derived the mandala symbolism from Swedenborg (1968, 266).

4. The observation of the modern-day mystic mentioned in the chapter 1—that the only difference between the Buddhist void and the existential abyss is fear—can be applied to Blake's representation of the vortex. There is no fear because, from the nondual perspective, one is no different from the empty center, the goal of the spiritual quest.

5. See DeGroot 1969 on the archetypal signification used in Renaissance symbolism, discussed later in this chapter.

6. Blake's use of Dante's epic is crucial here, since he re-spatializes Dante's relation of inferno and paradise, a point that is developed later in this chapter.

7. Complicating the interpretation of these images (figures 5 and 6) is the fact that they were originally illustrations for Young's *Night Thoughts*. As Grant Scott's intriguing paper has suggested, the relationship of *The Four Zoas* text and design with the *Night Thoughts* proofsheets is deserving of further exploration.

8. Blake's representation of punishment for a figure's role in the formation of the fallen world has interesting connections to Dante's *Inferno*, since Blake has the figure immediately experience the effects of his action, as has been discussed in chapter 3 in terms of the punishment of Luvah in Night the Second. However, Blake's rejection of the merciless punishment of Dante's suffering sinners is clear from the fact that Blake has the same figures experience paradise who experience the worst torments of their created hell.

9. See other representations of madness in Blake, such as the narrator of "The Tyger" and the singer of the "Mad Song." Both project material universes that then threaten them.

10. See, for example, Penelope's dream in *The Odyssey*, bk. 19.

11. See chapter 5 for the fuller discussion of the apocalypse.

12. See figure 7. Blake's illustration, from Young's *Night Thoughts,* represents the snake as Ouroboros. It is a critical clue about the movement of figuration at this point, in which the vortex and snake merge in the Ouroboros.

13. See Magno and Erdman's tracing of the image (1987, 30).

Chapter 5. City of Art, Temple of Mystery

1. These are the editorial decisions of Erdman and Keynes, respectively. Paul Cantor suggests that version [b] is the earlier because it contains material from the earlier minor prophecies that is not present in version [a] (1984, 59).

2. For alternative critical approaches, see *BIQ* 46 (fall 1978): essays on Night the Seventh by Johnson and Wilkie (100–106); John Kilgore (107–14); Andrew Lincoln, (115–33); Mark Lefebvre (134); and Erdman (135–39). See also Ault (1987, 327–33).

3. To draw the reader's state into this—as Luvah does, in Night the Second— is to suggest that signification eludes a single constrictive reading, but rather engages the reader in a dynamic relationship with the elements of the text.

4. Urizen's parodic empty center stands in contrast to the effect of Asia's revelation at the heart of Demogorgon's cave, in Shelley's *Prometheus Unbound,* that "the deep truth is imageless" (116). Immediately upon apprehending this, Asia is liberated and so able to participate in the liberation of Prometheus.

5. Shelley's horror at the apparent instability of signifiers, in spite of his quest after the Absolute in *Prometheus Unbound,* differs significantly from Blake's portrayal of the potential for liberation in such a discovery. See the discussion of this difference in the excursus, below.

6. This is another situation in which critics project Blake onto the fallen characters. Webster, for example, suggests that it is Blake rather than the fallen male characters who is misogynistic in his representation of the Emanations.

7. Vala's epiphany is a haunting prolepsis of Maria Jane Jewsbury's 1829 poem "To My Own Heart":

Spirit within me, speak; and through the veil
That hides thee from my vision, tell thy tale;
That so the present and the past may be
Guardians and prophets to futurity.
Spirit by which I live, thou art not dumb,
I hear thy voice; I called and thou art come.

186 NOTES TO THE EXCURSUS

Excursus. Prophetic Disclosure and Mediated Vision

1. The male pronoun is consciously chosen here since the questers into the egotistical sublime are typically male personae. A significant exception to this is Asia's crucial role in *Prometheus Unbound*, the most Blakean of Shelley's poetry. Asia's quest to Demogorgon's cave is the vital stage of the epic, since Prometheus cannot be unbound without the knowledge that she attains from her journey.

2. See also *Johns Hopkins Guide to Literary Theory and Criticism*, s.v. "Edmund Burke."

3. See De Luca 1991 for an elaborate study of Blake's sublime in the context of the Burkean sublime. De Luca aptly points to Blake's critique of romantic questers through his depiction of Urizen, though he does not suggest, as this study does, a redeemed representation of quest in the poem.

4. For a useful discussion of the code language of Augustan poetry, see Arthos 1949.

5. It should be noted that, although the name may have been pronounced "Hume," orthographically the effect of seeing "Home" creates the effect of the pun.

6. Though this is suggestive of Blake, who decomposes the quester so that any figure at any moment takes up the role of moving consciousness toward eternity, it lacks the freedom of Blake's authorial voice from being invested in a single figure as persona at the expense of the whole. See the discussion of Ernest Jones's term in chapter 3.

7. See de Man 1984, 126–33, for a discussion of the indeterminacy of mimetic and symbolic language in this sonnet.

8. It is well known that these lines are Shelley's revision of Wordsworth's ambivalent lines in "Tintern Abbey," whose reference is to "a presence"

> . . . that impels
> All thinking things, all objects of all thought,
> And rolls through all things.
>   (lines 100–103)

Shelley reverses the relationship so that the mind contains the universe of things.

9. Blake's Snowdon also contrasts with Wordsworth's at the end of *The Prelude*. Lost in his "private thoughts," Wordsworth divides inner and outer realms: "[B]y myself / Was nothing either seen or heard that checked / Those musings or diverted" (1979, 459, bk. 14, lines 18–21 [1850 version]). Thus, when Snowdon appears in its sublimity, it is to Wordsworth "the emblem of a mind / That feeds upon infinity, that broods / Over the dark abyss," a projection of his own state (lines 70–72).

Bibliography

Works of Blake

Erdman, David, ed. 1982. *The Complete Poetry and Prose of William Blake.* Garden City, N.Y.: Anchor Books.

Erdman, David, et al, eds. 1980. *William Blake's Designs for Edward Young's "Night Thoughts": A Complete Edition.* 2 vols. Oxford: Clarendon Press.

Essick, Robert, and Jenijoy LaBelle. 1975. *Night Thoughts, Or the Complaint and the Consolation, Illustrated by William Blake, Text by Edward Young.* New York: Dover.

Keynes, Geoffrey, ed. 1970. *Blake: Complete Writings.* New York: Oxford University Press.

Magno, Cettina, and David Erdman, eds. 1987. *"The Four Zoas" by William Blake.* Lewisburg, Pa.: Bucknell University Press.

Margoliouth, H. M., ed. 1956. *William Blake's "Vala."* London: Oxford University Press.

Other Works

Abhinavagupta. 1938–43. *The Isvarapratyabhijna Vivritivimarsini.* Edited by Madhusudan Kaul. 3 vols. Kashmir Series of Texts and Studies, nos. 60, 62, 65. Srinagar: Research Department, Jammu and Kashmir State. Quoted in

Paul E. Müller-Ortega, *The Triadic Heart of Shiva: Kaula Tantricism of Abhinavagupta in the Non-Dual Shaivism of Kashmir* (Albany: State University of New York Press, 1989).

Abrams, M. H. 1984. "Apocalypse: Theme and Variations." In *The Apocalypse in English Renaissance Thought and Literature*, edited by C. A. Patrides and Joseph Wittreich, 342–68. Ithaca: Cornell University Press.

Adams, Hazard. 1955. *Blake and Yeats*. Ithaca: Cornell University Press.

———. 1983. *The Philosophy of the Literary Symbolic*. Tallahassee: Florida State University Press.

———. 1987. "Synecdoche and Method." In *Critical Paths: Blake and the Argument of Method*, edited by Dan Miller, Mark Bracher, and Donald Ault, 41–71. Durham, N.C.: Duke University Press.

Altizer, Thomas J. 1967. *The New Apocalypse: The Radical Christian Vision of William Blake*. East Lansing: Michigan State University Press.

Arnheim, Rudolf. 1982. *The Power of the Center*. Berkeley: University of California Press.

———. 1988. *The Power of the Center*. Rev. ed. Berkeley: University of California Press.

Arthos, John. 1949. *The Language of Natural Description in Eighteenth-Century Poetry*. Ann Arbor: University of Michigan Press.

Ashfield, Andrew, ed. 1995. *Romantic Women Poets, 1770–1838*. New York: Manchester University Press.

Aubrey, Bryan. 1986. *Watchmen of Eternity: Blake's Debt to Jacob Boehme*. New York: University Press of America.

Ault, Donald. 1986. "Re-visioning *The Four Zoas*." In *Unnam'd Forms: Blake and Textuality*, edited by Nelson Hilton and Thomas Vogler, 105–39. Berkeley: University of California Press.

———. 1987. *Narrative Unbound: Re-Visioning "The Four Zoas."* Barrytown, N.Y.: Station Hill Press.

Barfield, Owen. 1964. *Poetic Diction: A Study in Meaning*. New York: McGraw-Hill. Quoted in Angus Fletcher, *Allegory* (Ithaca: Cornell University Press, 1964), 75–76.

Beer, John. 1969. *Blake's Visionary Universe*. New York: Barnes & Noble.

Bentley, G. E. 1958. "The Failure of Blake's *Four Zoas*." *TSIE* 37:102–13.

Bidney, Martin. 1988. *Blake and Goethe: Psychology, Ontology, Imagination*. Columbia: University of Missouri Press.

Billingheimer, Rachel V. 1986. "The Eighth Eye: Prophetic Vision in Blake's Poetry and Design." *Colby Library Quarterly* 32:93–110.

Blackstone, Bernard. 1949. *English Blake*. Cambridge: Cambridge University Press.

Bloom, Harold. 1963. *Blake's Apocalypse*. Garden City, N.Y.: Anchor Books.

————. 1971. *The Visionary Company*. Ithaca: Cornell University Press.

Bowra, C. M. 1970. "Songs of Innocence and Experience." In *William Blake: Songs of Innocence and Experience*, edited by Margaret Bottrall, 135–59. New York: Macmillan.

Bracher, Mark. 1987. "Rouzing the Faculties: Lacanian Psychology and *The Marriage of Heaven and Hell* in the Reader." In *Critical Paths: Blake and the Argument of Method*, edited by Dan Miller, Mark Bracher, and Donald Ault. Durham, N.C.: Duke University Press.

Brisman, Leslie. 1978. "Re: Generation in Blake." In *Romantic Origins*, 224–75. Ithaca: Cornell University Press.

Britton, Bruce K., and A. D. Pellegrini, eds. 1990. *Narrative Thought and Narrative Language*. Hillsdale, N.J.: Lawrence Erlbaum.

Brooks, Peter. 1984. *Reading for the Plot: Design and Intention in Narrative*. New York: Knopf.

Cantor, Paul A. 1984. "The Myth Unbound." In *Creature and Creator*, 55–74. New York: Cambridge University Press, 1984.

Cassirer, Ernst. 1955. *Mythical Thought*. Vol. 2 of *Philosophy of Symbolic Forms*. Translated by R. Manheim. New Haven: Yale University Press.

Chayes, Irene. 1970. "The Presence of Cupid and Psyche." In *Blake's Visionary Forms Divine*, edited by David Erdman and John E. Grant, 214–43. Princeton: Princeton University Press.

————. 1991. "Picture and Page, Reader and Viewer in Blake's *Night Thoughts* Illustrations." *Studies in Romanticism* 30 (fall): 439–71.

Clark, Lorraine. 1991. *Blake, Kierkegaard, and the Spectre of Dialectic*. New York: Cambridge University Press.

Coleridge, Samuel Taylor. 1983. *Biographia Literaria*. Edited by James Engell and W. Jackson Bate. Princeton: Princeton University Press. Originally published in 1873.

Collins, William. 1979. *Works*. Edited by Richard Wendorf and Charles Ryskamp. Oxford: Clarendon Press.

Cooke, Michael G. 1979. *Acts of Inclusion*. New Haven: Yale University Press.

————. 1984. "Romanticism and the Paradox of Wholeness." *Studies in Romanticism* 23, no. 4 (winter): 435–53.

Cox, Philip. 1994. "'Among the Flocks of Tharmas': *The Four Zoas* and the Pastoral of Commerce." In *Historicizing Blake*, edited by Steve Clark and David Worrall, 86–104. New York: St. Martin's Press.

Cox, Stephen. 1992. *Love and Logic: The Evolution of Blake's Thought*. Ann Arbor: University of Michigan Press.

Curran, Stuart, and J. A. Wittreich, eds. 1973. *Blake's Sublime Allegory*. Madison: University of Wisconsin Press.

Daghistany, Ann, and J. J. Johnson. 1981. "Romantic Irony, Spatial Form and Joyce's *Ulysses.*" In *Spatial Form in Narrative*, edited by J. R. Smitten and A. Daghistany, 48–60. Ithaca: Cornell University Press.

Damon, S. Foster. 1947. *William Blake: His Philosophy and Symbols*. New York: Peter Smith.

Damrosch, Leopold, Jr. 1980. *Symbol and Truth in Blake's Myth*. Princeton: Princeton University Press.

Dawson, P. M. S. 1987. "Blake and Providence: The Theodicy of *The Four Zoas.*" *Blake: An Illustrated Quarterly* 20 (spring): 134–43.

DeGroot, H. B. 1969. "The Ouroboros and Romantic Poets." *English Studies* 50:553–64.

De Luca, Vincent. 1991. *Words of Eternity: Blake and the Poetics of the Sublime*. Princeton: Princeton University Press.

de Man, Paul. 1979. "Shelley Disfigured." In *Deconstruction and Criticism*, edited by Harold Bloom et al. New York: Continuum.

———. 1984. *The Rhetoric of Romanticism*. New York: Columbia University Press.

DiSalvo, Jackie. 1983. *War of the Titans: Blake's Critique of Milton and the Politics of Religion*. Pittsburgh, Pa.: University of Pittsburgh Press.

Eliade, Mircea. 1958. *Patterns in Comparative Religion*. Translated by Rosemary Sheed. New York: World Publishing.

———. 1969. *Images and Symbols*. Translated by P. Mairet. New York: Sheed & Ward.

Emerson, Ralph Waldo. 1957. *Selections from Ralph Waldo Emerson*. Edited by Stephen E. Whicher. Boston: Houghton Mifflin.

Erdman, David. 1954. *Blake: Prophet Against the Empire*. Princeton: Princeton University Press.

Erdman, David, and John E. Grant, eds. 1970. *Blake's Visionary Forms Divine*. Princeton: Princeton University Press.

Essick, Robert. 1989. *William Blake and the Language of Adam*. Oxford: Clarendon Press.

Farrer, Austin. 1949. *A Rebirth of Images: The Making of St. John's Apocalypse*. London: Dacre Press.

Ferber, Michael. 1985. *The Social Vision of William Blake*. Princeton: Princeton University Press.

———. 1991. *The Poetry of William Blake*. New York: Penguin.

Ferguson, Frances. 1992. *Solitude and the Sublime: Romanticism and the Aesthetics of Individuation*. New York: Routledge.

Finch, G. J. 1991. "Blake and Civilization." *English* 40 (autumn): 193–203.

Fletcher, Angus. 1964. *Allegory*. Ithaca: Cornell University Press.

———. 1971. *The Prophetic Moment*. Chicago: University of Chicago Press.

Fox, Susan. 1977. "The Female as Metaphor in William Blake's Poetry." *Crit* 1, no. 3:507–19.

Frye, Northrop. 1947. *Fearful Symmetry*. Princeton: Princeton University Press.

———. 1987. "Blake's Introduction to Experience." In *William Blake's "Songs of Innocence and Experience*," edited by Harold Bloom. New York: Chelsea House.

Gadamer, Hans-Georg. 1993. *Truth and Method*. Translated by Joel Weinsheimer and Donald Marshall. New York: Continuum.

Gallant, Christine. 1978. *Blake and the Assimilation of Chaos*. Princeton: Princeton University Press.

Glausser, Wayne. 1985. "The Gates of Memory in Night VIIa of *The Four Zoas*." *Blake: An Illustrated Quarterly* 18 (spring): 196–203.

Goldsmith, Steven. 1993. "Apocalypse and Representation: Blake, Paine and the Logic of Democracy." Chapter 3 in *Unbuilding Jerusalem: Apocalypse and Romantic Representation*: Ithaca: Cornell University Press.

Hagstrum, Jean H. 1973. "Babylon Revisited, or the Story of Luvah and Vala." In *Blake's Sublime Allegory*, edited by Stuart Curran and Joseph A. Wittreich, 101–18. Madison: University of Wisconsin Press.

Halmi, Nicholas. 1993. "An Anthropological Approach to the Romantic Symbol." *European Romantic Review* 4, no. 1 (summer): 13–33.

Harper, George M. 1965. "Apocalyptic Vision and Pastoral Dream in Blake's *The Four Zoas*." *SAQ* 64:110–24.

Hartman, Geoffrey. 1981. *Saving the Text*. Baltimore: Johns Hopkins University Press.

Heidegger, Martin. 1969. *The Essence of Reasons*. Translated by Terrence Malich. Evanston, Ill.: Northwestern University Press.

Heschel, Abraham J. 1962. *The Prophets*. Vols. 1 and 2. New York: Harper.

Hilton, Nelson. 1978. :Sweet Science of Atmosphere in *The Four Zoas."Blake: An Illustrated Quarterly* 46 (fall): 80–86.

———. 1983. *The Literal Imagination: Blake's Vision of Words*. Berkeley: University of California Press.

Hong, Edna, and Howard Hong. 1983. Introduction to *Fear and Trembling/Repetition*, by Søren Kierkegaard. Princeton: Princeton University Press.

Howard, John. 1984. *Infernal Poetic Structure in Blake's Lambeth Prophecies*. Cranbury, N.J.: Associated University Presses.

Hughes, Daniel. 1969. "Blake and Shelley: Beyond the Uroboros." In *William Blake: Essays for S. Foster Damon*, edited by Alvin Rosenfeld, 78–83. Providence, R.I.: Brown University Press.

Huizinga, Johan. 1950. *Homo Ludens: A Study of the Play-Element in Culture*. Translated by R. F. C. Hull. New York: Roy Publishers.

Husserl, Edmund. 1962. *Ideas*. Translated by W. R. Boyce Gibbon. New York: Macmillan.

Jones, Ernest. 1949. *Hamlet and Oedipus*. New York: Norton.

Jung, Carl. 1953. "The Symbolism of the Mandala." In *Psychology and Alchemy*, translated by R. F. C. Hull. New York: Pantheon.

———. 1969. *The Archetypes and the Collective Unconscious*. Translated by R. F. C. Hull. Princeton: Princeton University Press.

Kilgore, John. 1978. "The Order of Nights VIIa and VIIb in Blake's *The Four Zoas*." *Blake: An Illustrated Quarterly* 12 (fall): 107–13.

Lacan, Jacques. 1968. *The Language of the Self*. Translated by Anthony Wilden. New York: Delta.

Leader, Zachary. 1981. *Reading Blake's Songs*. Boston: Routledge and Kegan Paul.

Lee, Judith. 1983. "Ways of Their Own: The Emanations of Blake's *Vala, or The Four Zoas*." *ELH* 50:131–53.

Lincoln, Andrew. 1978. "The Revision of the Seventh and Eighth Nights of *The Four Zoas*." *Blake: An Illustrated Quarterly* 46:115–33.

———. 1995. *Spiritual History: A Reading of William Blake's "Vala or the Four Zoas."* Oxford: Clarendon Press.

Lovejoy, Arthur O. 1930. *The Revolt Against Dualism*. New York: Norton.

Massey, Irving. 1970. *The Uncreating Word*. Bloomington: Indiana University Press.

McNeil, Helen. 1970. "The Formal Art of *The Four Zoas*." In *Blake's Visionary Forms Divine*, edited by David Erdman and John E. Grant, 373–90. Princeton: Princeton University Press.

Mee, Jon. 1992. *Dangerous Enthusiasm: William Blake and the Culture of Radicalism in the 1790s*. Oxford: Clarendon Press.

Mellor, Anne K. 1974. *Blake's Human Form Divine*. Berkeley: University of California Press.

———. 1982/83. "Blake's Portrayal of Women." *Blake: An Illustrated Quarterly* 16 (winter): 148–55.

Merleau-Ponty, Maurice. 1964. *The Primacy of Perception*. Translated by James M. Edie. Evanston, Ill.: Northwestern University Press.

Mitchell, W. J. T. 1983. "Metamorphoses of the Vortex: Hogarth, Turner and Blake." In *Articulate Images*, edited by Richard Wendorf, 125–68. Minneapolis: University of Minnesota Press. .

———. 1986. "Visible Language: Blake's Wond'rous Art of Writing." In *Romanticism and Contemporary Criticism*, edited by Morris Eaves and Michael Fischer, 46–95. Ithaca: Cornell University Press.

Moskal, Jeanne. 1994. *Blake, Ethics, and Forgiveness*. Tuscaloosa: University of Alabama Press.

Müller-Ortega, Paul E. 1989. *The Triadic Heart of Shiva: Kaula Tantricism of Abhinavagupta in the Non-Dual Shaivism of Kashmir*. Albany: State University of New York Press.

Ostriker, Alicia. 1982/83. "Desire Gratified and Ungratified: William Blake and Sexuality." *Blake: An Illustrated Quarterly* 16 (winter): 156–65.

Otto, Peter.1987a. "Final States, Finished Forms, and *The Four Zoas*." *Blake: An Illustrated Quarterly* 20:144–46.

———. 1987b. "The Spectrous Embrace, the Moment of Regeneration, and Those Two Seventh Nights." *Colby Library Quarterly* 23:135–43.

———. 1991a. *Constructive Vision and Visionary Deconstruction.* Oxford: Clarendon Press.

———. 1991b. "The Multiple Births of Los in *The Four Zoas*." *SEL* 31, no. 4 (autumn): 631–53.

Paley, Morton. 1970. *Energy and Imagination: A Study of the Development of Blake's Thought.* London: Oxford University Press.

———. 1973. "The Figure of the Garment in *The Four Zoas, Milton* and *Jerusalem*." In *Blake's Sublime Allegory,* edited by Stuart Curran and Joseph A. Wittreich, 119–39. Madison: University of Wisconsin Press.

Pierce, John B. 1988/89. "The Shifting Characterization of Tharmas and Enion in Pages 3–7 of Blake's *Vala or The Four Zoas*." *Blake: An Illustrated Quarterly* 22 (winter): 93–102.

———. 1989. "The Changing Mythic Structure of Blake's *Vala or The Four Zoas:* A Study of Manuscript Pages 43–84." *Philological Quarterly* 8:485–508.

Punter, David. 1982. *Blake, Hegel, and Dialectic.* Amsterdam: Rodopi.

Raine, Kathleen. 1963. *Blake and Antiquity.* Princeton: Princeton University Press.

———. 1968. *Blake and Tradition.* Vols. 1 and 2. Princeton: Princeton University Press.

———. 1983. "Blake and Maya." *Indian Horizons* 32, no. 3:5–24.

———. 1986. "The Sleep of Albion." *Michigan Quarterly Review* 25 (fall): 684–98.

Rajan, Tilottama. 1980. *Dark Interpreter: The Discourse of Romanticism.* Ithaca: Cornell University Press.

———. 1990. *The Supplement of Reading: Figures of Understanding in Romantic Theory and Practice.* Ithaca: Cornell University Press.

Rosenfeld, Alvin, ed. 1969. *William Blake: Essays for S. Foster Damon.* Providence, R.I.: Brown University Press.

Rosso, George, Jr. 1993. *Blake's Prophetic Workshop: A Study of "The Four Zoas."* Lewisburg, Pa.: Bucknell University Press, 1993.

Rothenberg, Molly Anne. 1993. *Rethinking Blake's Textuality.* Columbia: University of Missouri Press.

Rudd, Margaret. 1956. *Organiz'd Innocence.* London: Routledge & Kegan Paul.

Said, Edward. 1975. *Beginnings.* New York: Basic Books.

Schiller, Friedrich von. 1966. *On the Sublime.* Translated by Julius Elias. New York: Ungar.

Schwab, Raymond. 1984. *The Oriental Renaissance*. New York: Columbia University Press.

Scott, Grant. 1994. "Aesthetic Education in Blake's Illustrations to Young's *Night Thoughts*." Paper delivered at NASSR Conference, Duke University, 11 November.

Shaviro, Steven. 1982. "Striving with Systems: Blake and the Politics of Difference." *boundary 2* 10, no. 3:229–50.

Shelley, Percy. 1977. *Poetry and Prose*. Edited by Donald Reiman and Sharon Powers. New York: Norton.

Singh, Charu Sheel. 1988. "*Bhagavadgita,* Typology and William Blake." In *The Influence of the "Bhagavadgita" on Literature Written in English*, edited by T. R. Sharma, 23–36. Meerut, India: Shalabh Prakashan.

Snell, Bruno. 1960. *Discovery of the Mind*. Translated by T. G. Rosenmeyer. New York: Harper.

Tayler, Irene. 1973. "The Woman Scaly." *Midwestern Modern Language Association Bulletin* 6:74–87.

Thompson, E. P. 1993. *Witness Against the Beast: William Blake and the Moral Law*. New York: The New Press.

Vine, Steven. 1993. *Blake's Poetry: Spectral Visions*. New York: St. Martin's Press.

Wacker, Norman. 1990. "Epic and the Modern Long Poem: Virgil, Blake and Pound." *Comparative Literature* 42 (spring): 126–43.

Wagenknecht, David. 1973. *Blake's Night: William Blake and the Idea of Pastoral*. Cambridge: Harvard University Press.

Webster, Brenda. 1983. *Blake's Prophetic Psychology*. Athens: University of Georgia Press.

Weiskel, Thomas. 1986. *The Romantic Sublime*. Baltimore: Johns Hopkins University Press.

White, Hayden. 1987. *The Content of the Form: Narrative Discourse and Historical Representation*. Baltimore: Johns Hopkins University Press.

Wilkie, Brian, and Mary Lynn Johnson. 1973. "On Reading *The Four Zoas*: Inscape and Analogy." In *Blake's Sublime Allegory*, edited by Stuart Curran and Joseph A. Wittreich, 203–32. Madison: University of Wisconsin Press.

———. 1978. *Blake's "Four Zoas": Design of a Dream*. Cambridge: Harvard University Press.

Wordsworth, William. 1932. *The Complete Poetical Works*. Edited by Andrew J. George. Boston: Houghton Mifflin.

———. 1979. *The Prelude: 1799, 1805, 1850*. Edited by Jonathan Wordsworth et al. New York: Norton.

Youngquist, Paul. 1989. *Madness and Blake's Myth*. University Park: Pennsylvania State University Press.

Index

wholeness, 69, 140, 147, 159
  narrative, contrasted with fragmented
    narratives, 70
  as nondual, 61, 90, 148, 176
  and redemption, 50, 60, 116, 133
  See also fragmentation, and whole-
    ness; synecdoche, and wholeness
Wilkie, Brian, 19, 21, 35–36, 185 n. 2
Wilkins, Sir Charles, 31, 181 n. 35
Wordsworth, William, 19, 162, 164,
  170, 174
  "Composed by the Side of Grasmere
    Lake," 161, 168–69

Prelude, The, 166–68
"Resolution and Independence,"
  165
World of Death,
  created by Los, 100
worship, 61
wrapping, 89, 114, 116, 137

Young, Edward
  Night Thoughts, 27, 29, 184 n. 7, 185
  n. 12
Youngquist, Paul, 29